ORDERS AND MINISTRY

THEOLOGY IN GLOBAL PERSPECTIVE SERIES

Peter C. Phan, General Editor
Ignacio Ellacuría Professor of Catholic Social Thought,
Georgetown University

At the beginning of a new millennium, the *Theology in Global Perspective* series responds to the challenge to reexamine the foundational and doctrinal themes of Christianity in light of the new global reality. While traditional Catholic theology has assumed an essentially European or Western point of view, *Theology in Global Perspective* takes account of insights and experiences of churches in Africa, Asia, Latin America, Oceania, as well as from Europe and North America. Noting the pervasiveness of changes brought about by science and technologies, and growing concerns about the sustainability of Earth, it seeks to embody insights from studies in these areas as well.

Though rooted in the Catholic tradition, volumes in the series are written with an eye to the ecumenical implications of Protestant, Orthodox, and Pentecostal theologies for Catholicism, and vice versa. In addition, authors will explore insights from other religious traditions with the potential to enrich Christian theology and self-understanding.

Books in this series will provide reliable introductions to the major theological topics, tracing their roots in Scripture and their development in later tradition, exploring when possible the implications of new thinking on gender and sociocultural identities. And they will relate these themes to the challenges confronting the peoples of the world in the wake of globalization, particularly the implications of Christian faith for justice, peace, and the integrity of creation.

Other Books Published in the Series

Trinity: Nexus of the Mysteries of Christian Faith, Anne Hunt

THEOLOGY IN GLOBAL PERSPECTIVE
Peter C. Phan, General Editor

ORDERS AND MINISTRY

Leadership in the World Church

KENAN B. OSBORNE, O.F.M.

Richard Williams
P.O. Box 1136
Port Orford, OR 97465

ORBIS BOOKS

Maryknoll, New York 10545

Founded in 1970, Orbis Books endeavors to publish works that enlighten the mind, nourish the spirit, and challenge the conscience. The publishing arm of the Maryknoll Fathers and Brothers, Orbis seeks to explore the global dimensions of the Christian faith and mission, to invite dialogue with diverse cultures and religious traditions, and to serve the cause of reconciliation and peace. The books published reflect the opinions of their authors and are not meant to represent the official position of the Maryknoll Society. To obtain more information about Maryknoll and Orbis Books, please visit our website at www.maryknoll.org.

Library of Congress Cataloging-in-Publication Data

Osborne, Kenan B.
   Orders and ministry : leadership in the world church / Kenan B.
Osborne.
       p. cm. — (Theology in global perspective)
   Includes bibliographical references (p.   ) and index.
   ISBN-13: 978-1-57075-628-3 (pbk.)
1. Priesthood—Catholic Church. 2. Christian leadership—Catholic
Church. 3. Pastoral theology—Catholic Church. I. Title. II. Series.
   BX1913.O79 2005
   262'.142—dc22
                           2005020334

Contents

Foreword

by Peter C. Phan

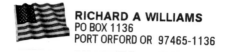
On any reckoning, the Roman Catholic conversation about the theology and practice of ministry, in particular ordained ministry, begun after the Second Vatican Council has become something less than a dialogue. Ordained ministry, and even the term "ministry" itself, is controverted. The hierarchy prefers to limit the term to the activities of deacons, priests, and bishops, and the latter two are reserved to celibate males. Meanwhile, the retirement, death, and departure of so many priests and bishops, combined with the downturn in men presenting themselves to have their "vocations" tested, are causing a precipitous depletion in the ranks of the clergy, particularly in the West, with no realistic hope of a reversal in sight. Although the West still has the highest ratio of priests to laypersons, the aging structure of the clergy means that the number of priestless parishes will continue to increase. Furthermore, the recent scandal of sexual abuse by both bishops and priests, compounded by a cover-up on the part of many bishops, has ripped the credibility of the hierarchy to shreds. To compound the problem, the number of Catholics in the so-called third world has increased dramatically, making overpowering demands on the church's ministry, especially in its sacramental dimension. More fundamentally, ordained ministry in the Catholic Church, still tethered to its Western cultural and theological roots, is outstripped by the changes in a world that has become increasingly global. Thus, for a healthy and vibrant life of the church, a theology of ministry and orders from a global perspective is more urgent than ever.

Perhaps no theologian in the American Catholic Church is more qualified to develop such a theology than Kenan Osborne, OFM, who has written extensively on the sacraments and ministry. His colleagues have recognized his contribution to theology by electing him President of the Catholic Theological Society of America and by granting him the John Courtney Murray Award for Achievement in Theology. Though himself an Anglo, Professor Osborne, who has taught on many different continents, is keenly sensitive to the challenges that globalization presents to the church. While fully acknowledging that the Christic and Pneumatic dynamics of Christian ministry are perennial, he draws attention in this book to its mutable elements "in order that the perennially valid elements may give the life of God's Spirit to followers of Jesus in whatever culture." To highlight the capacity of all cultures

ix

to embody the Gospel adequately, he coins the word "equicultural" to replace the more common "multicultural." He warns us of the dangers of what is called today "white privilege," all the more pernicious as it is not always consciously acknowledged.

Professor Osborne begins his global theology of orders and ministry by reflecting on the meanings and implications of globalization, and within this context he traces the long and varied trajectory of the church's inculturation of its ministry into the Hellenistic, Latin, Germanic, and contemporary Western cultures. He then presents a detailed history of the development of the threefold church ministry of *episkopos*, *presbyteros*, and *diakonos*, from the New Testament to Vatican II. He highlights three major issues confronting this traditional understanding of ministry in the global context, namely, the manifold impact of globalization on church life, the tendency toward micromanagement, and the racial, gender, and cultural discrimination in the church. To provide a benchmark for judging the validity of certain ways of exercising ministry, Osborne examines the way Jesus exercised his ministry, since the ministry of Jesus is "the icon and foundation of every theology of order."

Against this background Professor Osborne develops a global theology of ministry and priestly order (i.e., bishop and priest—leaving the treatment of the diaconate to another volume). After a historical review of how these two ministries have been exercised, Osborne broaches the delicate issues of honest dialogue on church order, Sunday without eucharist, ordination policies, and ordination of women. Another vital theme in the theology of ministry is the role of the laity, to which Osborne devotes a lengthy study.

Finally, since church order and ministry are at bottom questions of church leadership, Osborne invites us to imagine and to dream of new styles of Christian leadership on the basis of new cultural styles of leadership that demonstrate genuine communication and sincere respect for local autonomy. As he eloquently concludes, "We need, in all of this, not simply to be multicultural, but equicultural. A global perspective of order and ministry is the only possible way in which the church's present order and ministry will, today, survive. This is the dream for the future." Whatever validity and appeal Osborne's theological dream for the church's ministry may have, it is beyond doubt that he has begun a conversation—honest and at times painful and disturbing—that no one deeply concerned about the future of the church's ministry and of theology in global perspective can ignore.

Abbreviations Used in This Work

In citing official Roman Catholic documents, the common abbreviation for that document will be found in parentheses followed by a number. The number is the article or paragraph number referred to or quoted from that document. Thus "(AG 12)" means *Ad gentes*, article 12. All quotations of documents of Vatican II are taken from the version edited by Austin Flannery, O.P., *Vatican Council II*, 2 volumes (Northport, N.Y.: Costello Publishing Company, 1996-98).

AA   *Apostolicam Actuositatem*, Vatican II Decree on the Apostolate of the Laity (November 18, 1965).

AG   *Ad Gentes*, Vatican II Decree on the Church's Missionary Activity (December 7, 1965).

CCC   *Catechism of the Catholic Church*, 2nd ed. (English translations by various publishers). The 2nd Latin edition was promulgated on August 15, 1997, by Pope John Paul II in the apostolic letter *Laetamur magnopere* (first ed., promulgated October 11, 1992).

CIC   *Codex Iuris Canonici* ("Code of Canon Law of the Roman Catholic Church"), promulgated by Pope John Paul II, January 25, 1983. English translation under the auspices of the Canon Law Society of America, *Code of Canon Law: Latin-English Edition* (Washington, D.C.: Canon Law Society of America, 1983).

DS   Denzinger, H., and A. Schönmetzer, eds. *Enchiridion Symbolorum: Definitionum et Declarationum de Rebus Fidei et Morum*, 36th ed. Freiburg: Herder, 1976.

DN   Dupuis, J., and J. Neuner, eds. *The Christian Faith in the Doctrinal Documents of the Catholic Church*. Staten Island, N.Y.: Alba House, 2001.

EN   *Evangelii Nuntiandi*, On Evangelization in the Modern World, Apostolic Exhortation of Pope Paul VI, December 8, 1975.

FABC *For All the Peoples of Asia*, 3 vols. (Quezon City: Claretian Publishers, 1986-2003).

GS   *Gaudium et Spes*, Vatican II Pastoral Constitution on the Church in the Modern World (December 7, 1965).

LG   *Lumen Gentium*, Vatican II Dogmatic Constitution on the Church (November 21, 1964).

PO   *Presbyterorum Ordinis,* Vatican II Decree on the Ministry and Life of Priests (December 7, 1965).

RH   *Redemptor Hominis,* "The Redeemer of Humankind," encyclical letter of Pope John Paul II, 1979.

RM   *Redemptoris Missio,* encyclical letter of Pope John Paul II on evangelization, March 25, 1987.

SC   *Sacrosanctum Concilium,* Vatican II Constitution on the Sacred Liturgy (December 4, 1963).

UR   *Unitatis Redintegratio,* Vatican II Decree on Ecumenism (November 21, 1964).

Introduction

The Challenge of Globalization
to Order and Ministry in the Church

Enlightenment is like rain that falls on the mountain and gathers into rivulets, that runs into brooks, and then into rivers which finally flow into the ocean.

—*The Sayings of the Buddha*

The synthesis between culture and faith is not just a demand of culture, but of faith. A faith which does not become culture is a faith which has not been fully received, not thoroughly thought through, not fully lived out.

—Pope John Paul II

IN TODAY'S CATHOLIC CHURCH a renewal of order and ministry has been urged and encouraged by the bishops at Vatican II, by Popes Paul VI and John Paul II, and by many conferences of bishops throughout the world. Individual diocesan bishops have added their voices, calling for a renewal of both ordained and nonordained ministry in their own dioceses and nations. All these official statements have occasioned a major effort to rethink and to reimagine what church ministers at all levels might do in new ways. This includes the ministries of bishops, priests, religious, laymen and laywomen. Key theologians and pastoral leaders have written books and articles, directives and analyses on the renewal of ministry in the Catholic Church today, and the contemporary Catholic Church has been blessed with a large amount of written material on ministry and enthusiasm for new developments in pastoral service.

One of the most amazing characteristics of the current interest in and enthusiasm for the reform of ministry is the globalized scope of the situation facing the church. The series in which this volume is published, Theology in Global Perspective, under the leadership of Peter C. Phan, intends to focus directly on the *worldwide dimensions* of theological issues involving the

1

Roman Catholic Church. This particular volume deals with the global dimension of a theology of Christian order and ministry.

Globalization, of course, includes much more than the reality of culture. Economic issues, political concerns, and revisions of systems of education to provide workers for the emerging global economy and interdependent political life have all faced calls that they take account of globalization. These calls have also been contested, because globalization is an intensely ambiguous phenomenon. Its many good effects are accompanied by negative effects. Its negative aspects often are accompanied by positive developments. No matter what view one takes on such matters, it is impossible to deny that a given person or a given people may live in a small part of the physical planet earth, but with the Internet, TV, wire services, and the like, we also live in a virtual community with neighbors who are separated physically from us by oceans and mountains. We are still village people, for the most part, but the village now extends far beyond our next-door neighbor and it is affected by developments in places we were scarcely conscious of a generation ago.

Globalization brings together many people of differing cultures and differing ethnic backgrounds. As the seas and cultural fences that long kept us apart from our neighbors begin disappearing, we meet people who neither think as we do, nor look like us. We become aware of different languages and different views of the world. A decision on dropping tariffs on cloth and clothing brought to Europe and the United States is made with good intentions at one level to encourage world trade, but in our globalized world, textile mills in El Salvador and South Africa may discover that they cannot compete with the Chinese. A chimpanzee bites a man in Central Africa and a decade later an autoimmune system disease becomes a worldwide epidemic. Cultural artifacts such as action movies may be protected by freedom of expression laws in one part of the world, while in another they are seen as products of an evil empire attempting to erode local morals and traditional ways of life.

Viewed from a sociological perspective, Catholics are members of the world's largest religious body. But even they are not a majority worldwide, and even when all the world's Christian families are totaled, they represent only about one-third of the world's peoples. Even within the Catholic communion, the economic interests of Catholics in one land may clash with those in another. From a North American Catholic perspective, the "others" may not be fellow Catholics or even Christians. And so, from the perspective of international Catholic leadership, the question arises, Whose culture is to provide the norms for shaping Catholic communities in this worldwide church? And then, How does one balance local values and ways of exercising leadership with the need to promote unity? The list of questions goes on and on.

Until recently, and unfortunately in the attitudes of too many, the *we* that provided the cultural standards was Western and its norms were European and North American. That *we*, for the most part, was white and gained much prestige by being the world's leaders in developing modern technology. The *we* had a relative abundance of money, and if the *we* you identify most closely with is that made up of citizens of the United States of America, you are a citizen of the only military superpower in the world. All of this is true, and all of this easily moves us into a way of thinking that we are "better." Even if the word "better" was often not part of the mind-set of Westerners, they were beneficiaries of what we are increasingly calling "white privilege." By that we mean that whether the attitudes of whites to Australian native peoples, Africans, Asians, Pacific Islanders, and Indians in both North and South America were, in the strictest sense of the word, "racist," whites in the world of actual life acted to set up privileged enclaves for themselves.

Whether they were fully conscious of it or not, people from white, Western cultures presumed they had the right to go abroad and interfere in the lives of other peoples. Nevertheless, the Western domination of world Catholicism has, at least statistically, ended. Has our cultural domination been revamped? Is the era of white privilege ended? Should it be? We long considered that our ways of organizing the church were better, that our languages were the best for theological discussion. Asking a question does not mean that *we* might not be "better" in some ways, but those ways are incidental to what Paul in Galatians termed the transcendent value of our unity in Christ: "There is no longer Jew or Greek, there is no longer slave or free, there is no longer male and female; for all of you are one in Christ Jesus" (Gal. 3:28).

This book revolves around an attempt to understand what leadership means in a church that is forced by globalization to think about both the dynamics of Christian ministry that are *perennial*—linked to the essence of Christian life—and the elements that *need to change as culture changes* in order that the perennially valid elements may give the life of God's Spirit to followers of Jesus in whatever culture.

The Roman Catholic Church is part of our globalized world. To the extent that globalization is dominated by Western money, cultural models, and political power, however, Catholicism's lingering Western cultural style is at least ambiguous, and in many ways profoundly problematic. Some suspect that the ordained leadership of the church does not realize that it may be mistakenly considering its own culture to be one of the perennial elements, when in fact it may merely be an example of a bygone era's ways of exercising leadership. Such attitudes can be extended also to belief that Western languages are better ways to express what the church believes and to downplay other vernaculars. We know Latin, English, German, Italian, Spanish, Portuguese, and French. Do we really need to formulate Christian identity in languages such as Thai or Swahili? Do we need to change liturgical rules that ensure that even if Mass is celebrated in Japanese or Chimbu, the liturgical ceremonies are more or less uniform across the whole world. Some Catholics are very proud that there is such a strong affinity and similarity that our church rituals and church activities have with the Vatican itself. These Catholics argue that since Roman Catholics alone constitute the only one, holy, catholic, and apostolic church, therefore the "only real" form of church life is our Euro-American form of church life. Yet asking such questions does not prejudge the answer. External uniformity may promote internal unity in the Spirit. Uniformity may, however, also promote attitudes at odds with deeper communion. (The real issue in thinking about order and ministry in a global context is that we endeavor to open ourselves up to the radicality of the challenges that confront us.)

The Euro-American form of church we have described above is, of course, a cultural church, whether this is openly admitted or not. Euro-American church life has been expressed and continues to be expressed in and through the culture of Euro-America.[1]

Nonetheless, contemporary church leadership, from the Vatican curia itself to local dioceses, has urged Catholics to be sensitive to the multicultural dimensions within our church life. In the last few years, many theologians have written extensively on the current multicultural church. Ecclesiastical documents on a multicultural church are, today, abundant. We Catholics do not lack literature, analyses, and studies on the issue of the church in a multicultural world. There has appeared, however, a form of multiculturalism that, in subtle ways and even at times in not so subtle ways, has caused great concern. In some of these theological and official church statements, formulated either in a direct or in a presumed way, there are some major presuppositions. These presuppositions indicate that Euro-Anglo-American culture is the benchmark for all other cultures, and that Euro-Anglo-American ways of

---

1. The term "Euro-American," sometimes written "EurAmerican," can mislead. The difficulty in using it is that there is no single term that clearly includes the cultures of Europe, the British Isles, Ireland, and North America. One could possibly use the adjective "first-world," but this too has problems. My use of the term is meant to include a way of thinking and acting that is dominated by a variety of cultural elements found primarily throughout Europe and North America. The contemporary Roman Catholic Church, particularly in its central leadership, is dominated by this Euro-American way of thinking.

being Roman Catholic are the benchmarks for all other multicultural Roman Catholic theologies and practices. In the following pages, we will unravel the implications of these major concerns and presuppositions. We will also see why many contemporary Roman Catholic leaders and scholars have developed serious misgivings about this benchmark approach to the multicultural aspects of today's Roman Catholic Church.

The Roman Catholic Church is not alone in this Euro-American approach as the global benchmark. The governments of most Western nations presume the validity of the same benchmark pattern. We find this standard operating in the directives of the World Trade Organization and the World Bank. Numerous free-trade agreements contain provisos which indicate that the economic and political patterns of the West are the standard for all international treaties and international aid institutions. Follow Western standards, these protocols seem to say, and only if you follow them may you trade globally. Follow them and you will get a loan. In many of these major global protocols, the demand that the Western approach be the benchmark for the second world and the third world is patently obvious.[2]

I believe that the term "multicultural" should be retired. My personal preference is the term *equicultural,* since this term indicates that all the cultures represented in a particular field of discourse should be equally reverenced and honored. One single culture amid all the various cultures cannot be considered *the* benchmark, since each culture has unique qualities that can deeply enrich all other cultures. No single culture is totally perfect or totally ideal. In this volume on the challenges to the church's theology of order and ministries in our new global context, I will frame my material, as best I can, on the basis of an equicultural structure rather than a multicultural structure. In doing this, I do not want to say that the term "equicultural" is *the answer.* The term has problems of its own. It does not imply that there are no gradations among cultures. Its primary emphasis is simply this: all cultures should be equally honored and treated with reverence. Equicultural does not intend to imply that all cultures, in their respective details, are of equal value. "Equiculture," as a term, however, will serve in this volume to indicate that there is no theological benchmark that one culturally expressed theology of order and ministry can claim to be normative over the culturally expressed theologies of

---

2. See Franz-Josef Eilers, ed., *For All the Peoples of Asia,* vol. 3 (Quezon City: Claretian Publications, 2002). The Federation of Asian Bishops' Conferences openly criticizes Western economic structures by name; cf. p. 7: "Governments are forced to adopt policies and practices such as the Structural Adjustment Policies (SAP) dictated by the IMF, the WB and the WTO. These policies are devoid of a human face and social concern. The model of economic development promoted by the transnational corporations in Asia is not acceptable." Hereafter, the volumes in this series will be referred to as *FABC.*

order and ministry that other cultures either already have or are currently developing.

A study of the issues of both order and ministry in the Roman Catholic Church is a study of church leadership itself. "Order" in the Catholic Church's historical use of the term in the phrase *sacramentum ordinis* ("the sacrament of [holy] order[s]") refers to the "ordained" clerical order (used here as meaning a social class), and it is the clerical order that dominates the leadership of the contemporary Catholic Church. In Latin, "order" is singular. In English, however, it has become common practice to speak of the sacrament of holy "orders." One advantage of using the singular is that it can more easily connote one of the essential aspects of office. Those in the college of officeholders, the ordained, have as one of their main tasks shepherding the community so that the "order" of a concrete church corresponds to the ideal of "apostolic order." By this is meant helping a community be a communion that really manifests the "order" or shape of the earliest churches. The term "ministry," by contrast, includes both clerical and nonclerical ministries, and when these ministries are officially sanctioned by the clerical leadership, these ministries also involve to some degree a role in church leadership. The consequences of this interconnection are obvious. Any discussion of church order and ministry must also include a connection to church leadership. In this volume, the interconnection will focus more on local and regional leadership needs than on the central leadership of the church.

The structure of this volume is fairly straightforward. There are five chapters, which can be outlined as follows:

In chapter 1, on the meanings and implications of globalization, we will consider the meaning of globalization. Since the major theme of this volume, the two issues of order and ministry, is to be studied in and through a global perspective, a clear initial presentation of the meaning of global perspective is needed. In today's world, the use of the phrase "in global perspective" raises the issue of globalization, which is a reality of major consequence at this precise moment of time. Second, a global perspective involves the issue of culture. Consequently, both an initial discussion of culture and a brief review of current cultural studies need explicit expression. On the basis of this twofold introductory material, a reader will have a well-focused global perspective, by and through which she or he will understand the specific material on order and ministry in today's church.

In chapter 2, "The Ministry of Jesus: The Foundational Model for All Ministries," I will present a detailed description of the theological meaning of the terms "order" and "ministry." These pages attempt to define how the two words are understood in the current theological and official positions of the Catholic Church. In the third part of the chapter, I will focus on three major issues that characterize both the current global world and the current global Roman Catholic Church. I will indicate how these three issues seriously impact the meaning of ecclesial order and ministry, and therefore church leadership as well. In the fourth part of the chapter, I will examine the so-called *tria munera* ("three tasks") by which the bishops at Vatican Council II characterized ministry and mission in the Roman Catholic Church. In the conciliar documents, the *tria munera* apply to Jesus' mission and ministry, to the mission and ministry of every baptized and confirmed Christian, and to the specific missions and ministries of those Christians who have a special role because of an official order or because of an official ministerial appointment. In the final section, I will indicate the key characteristics of the mission and ministry of Jesus himself. The characteristics of Jesus' own mission and ministry provide the foundation for all mission and ministry in the entire church, Anglican, Orthodox, Protestant, and Roman Catholic. Jesus' own ministry is the primary criterion for understanding and judging all Christian order and ministry. Jesus' own ministry is the foundational point of departure for every discussion of Christian order and ministry. Since the theology of church leadership is linked intrinsically to Jesus himself, this section of the volume on the mission and ministry of Jesus also presents the fundamental criterion for evaluating church leadership. Jesus, and Jesus alone, is the primary basis for the meaning of all church leadership, of which orders and ministry are two key aspects.

In chapter 3, "Priestly Order and Ministry: Their History and Meaning Today," I will describe the current meaning of the titles "bishop" and "priest." The focus is on what these two titles mean in today's actual world. Out of this analysis the question arises: Have the terms "bishop" and "priest" always meant the same thing as they do today? To answer this question, we will trace the many historical developments in the meaning, function, and shape of episcopal and priestly orders over the years. We will see that in the course of church history there have been several major changes in the role and function of both bishops and priests. This historical summary has implications for today and raises another important question: In light of the changes in the functioning of both bishops and priests, is there a basis for not considering the possibility of allowing changes in those offices today? This leads to the final section of the chapter, in which I will indicate some serious reasons why structural changes in both order and ministry need to be made in our contemporary situation.

Readers will note that I have not included the diaconate in this chapter but have focused exclusively on bishop and priest. Although I initially attempted to include the diaconate, the complex history of the diaconate in the Western Roman Catholic Church created a problem for a book of this size and nature. In some ages of church history, it is easy to speak of bishop, priest, and deacon. Then, in a subsequent age the deacon becomes almost nonexistent and, ministerially speaking, minimally important. After Vatican II there has been a resurgence of the diaconate, but this involves another complex history, since the renewal of the diaconate in the postconciliar church is internationally uneven and unclear. Thus, I admit that there is a lacuna in my presentation. Given the nature of this particular series, I opted for treating these issues in a revision of my book *The Diaconate in the Christian Church: Its History and Theology* (Chicago: National Association of Diaconate Directors [NADD], 1996). In the revised edition, I include a section on the diaconal ministry in a global perspective.

The importance of chapter 3 for theology in a global perspective is underlined by the fact that—in the present globalized context—unless we develop a theological understanding of episcopal and priestly order and ministry in which change is possible, discussion of the episcopal and priestly order and ministry is fruitless. In light of the multicultural and globalized situation of church life today, serious problems call for a variety of changes in regard to church leadership. This is necessary for the credibility of the global Roman Catholic Church in the majority, non–Euro-American areas of the world. This entails a serious rethinking of the standard and operative theological understanding of both a Roman Catholic bishop and a Roman Catholic priest.

Culture is not an accidental issue that affects our theology only in an accidental way. Culture is a radical part of human nature. Cultures are not merely accidental but integral elements in all spheres of human endeavor. The radicality of this insight into cultures applies to theological expression as much as it does to all other areas of human life. The importance of rethinking order and ministry in the context of the vortex of forces benign and malignant operating today in our globalized world cannot be bracketed and set aside for discussion at some later moment. If order and ministry are not restudied and restructured to meet the needs of a global church and a global world, the vitality of the Roman Catholic Church will be seriously weakened. The current Roman Catholic Church leadership must be able to speak to a multi- or equicultural world in a credible way. If the church leadership is unable to do this, its message will simply be disregarded.

In chapter 4, "Lay Ministry: Its History and Meaning Today," I trace out two major and different forms of all leadership, namely, the *structural or institutional* form of leadership and the *charismatic* form of leadership. On the basis of this general foundation, we will consider the meaning of leadership in the Roman Catholic Church, as expressed in Vatican II and in the post-conciliar period. This section deals with the several, current, rather diverse interpretations of lay involvement in ministries of leadership. It is obvious that there is a struggle going on today over how to implement some of the directions that Vatican II endorsed and how to adopt and implement the conciliar orientation for lay leadership. Postconciliar lay leadership in the church is based on the matrix of all ministerial leadership—that is to say, on the call and commission of *all* Christians to share in the threefold mission and ministry of Jesus. This matrix is part and parcel of the sacraments of initiation. Only on this basis is lay ministry meaningful. To provide a framework to address the current issues of lay leadership in the church, it is necessary to review the history of the involvement of lay men and women in the church. This is the fourth focus of chapter 4. This history is complex, and I can only provide a brief summary of the most salient points in this historical review. The principal thing to keep in mind is that in the course of Western church history, the role of the layman and laywoman carrying out ministerial roles has varied. Finally, the chapter will consider some basic needs for lay leadership in today's church from a global perspective. Changes in regard to lay involvement in church ministry that Vatican Council II initiated have profound repercussions for a globalized theology of Christian ministry. The standard, pre–Vatican II understanding of lay ministry is no longer viable. Nor is a Euro-American perspective on lay ministry viable. Today, the standard for lay ministry must be appreciated from a global perspective, far beyond the limiting dimensions of either a European or a North American interpretation.

In chapter 5, "Dreams for the Future," I will offer—I hope—well-grounded judgments on the ways in which an equicultural order and ministry can continue to develop during the first part of the third millennium. In doing so, I do not want to paint a picture that is only a pipedream. Rather, I want to offer a portrait that is a well-founded dream. Only a well-founded dream gives hope to the new and younger generation that, in a global perspective, the Roman Catholic Church will indeed have a powerful and exciting future.

I want to thank the general editor of this series, Peter Phan, for his help and encouragement throughout the process of writing this text. Peter Phan has had his own encouraging dream: to acknowledge, in an open and frank way, both the global and the equicultural world and the global and equicultural church in which we live today. His dream includes a means of realizing these goals, especially through this present series, Theology in Global

Perspective. This series is a positive help for all Catholics today. The goal of
this series is to encourage the formation of healthy and deeply spiritual relationships between our Catholic theology and practice, on the one hand, and
a complicated global and equicultural world and church, on the other hand.
I want to thank William R. Burrows, Managing Editor of Orbis Books, for
his assistance in this endeavor. I am grateful for his help in writing and
rewriting this volume. His suggestions on the many dimensions of globalization throughout the world and introducing me to the term "glocalization," as
it applies to church structure, ministry, and leadership, were especially important. Without his guidance this volume would not have the depth that the
revised text has profoundly gained.

1

Globalization

What Does It Mean?
What Does It Imply?

THE FOCUS AND PERSPECTIVE OF THIS VOLUME

THE FOCUS OF THIS BOOK is a consideration of the theologies of church order and of church ministry from a global perspective. Order and ministry in the Roman Catholic Church are, without doubt, two major realities of the church itself, and church leadership is found, in large measure, in the people who belong to a specific church order or to a specific church ministry. Whenever the realities of church leadership become the topic of discussion, there is a clear sense that we are focusing on a central, complicated, and very delicate issue of the church. In this series of books, a number of theological themes will be considered by various authors from the standpoint of a global perspective. The particular theme of this volume, order and ministry, is in many ways not simply another theological theme. Since church leadership is at the center of both order and ministry, this volume examines a fundamental church theme, not something peripheral or secondary in church life.

The centrality of leadership in both order and ministry indicates that whatever a global perspective brings to the discussion will have major implications for today's church. These major implications can be enormously enriching, and, at the same time, they can be enormously challenging. Changes in leadership never occur in an easy fashion; in the church, even slight changes are often seen as disturbing, alarming, or even threatening. On the other hand, changes in leadership have been seen as helpful, necessary, and even life-giving. In the contemporary Roman Catholic Church, one must honestly admit that there exists a leadership struggle—put simplistically, it is a struggle between those for a liberal Roman Catholic Church and those for a traditional Roman Catholic Church. Everyone, however, is liberal in some issues and traditional in other issues. No one is totally liberal, and no one is totally traditional. Thus, the designation of liberal versus traditional is simplistic. Nonetheless, there exists today, as we shall see, some sort of struggle, a tug-of-war, between groups in the Roman Catholic Church who are vying for actual leadership. We find this at the parish level, the diocesan level, the national church level, and the Vatican curial level. This struggle over leadership today is simply a fact that we have to acknowledge and live with. The goal of the present volume is not to settle the issues behind today's struggles within the church's competing leadership groups. Rather, the goal is simply to lay the cards on the table, with the hope that an openness regarding this discussion on order and ministry will indeed offer some abatement to today's highly sensitive leadership debates.

In the course of these pages, then, the connection of the terms "order" and "ministry" with the New Testament will be noted. Then the ways in which order and ministry have been used in the history of the Roman Catholic Church will be presented in detail. Finally, the role of both order and ministry from the standpoint of the Second Vatican Council to the first years of the third millennium will indicate how in today's church they are both operative and valued.

Such a focus on order and ministry is important, for in the Roman Catholic Church a major share of church leadership is found precisely in those who are in a given church order and who service in a special and defined ministry. A study of ecclesial order and ministry is, as mentioned above, a study of church leadership, and leadership in any society indicates the health and strength of a given society.

This volume, however, is meant to focus on church leadership from a very defined perspective, namely, from a global perspective. Such a perspective has a contemporary ring about it, since today, the word "globalization" is an "in" word.[1] It is used with abandon in business, in banking and trade, and in politics. In 1943, the word "globalism" began to appear regularly in the political field. Slowly but surely, this word was accepted into the Webster dictionary system. In dictionaries today, "globalism" has received a definition. It denotes "a national policy of treating the whole world as a proper sphere for political influence." Some dictionaries offer a cross-reference so that the reader can flesh out the meaning of the term, and in the case of globalism, the cross-references are to "imperialism" and "internationalism."

---

1. Highly recommended books for the current understanding of globalization include Malcolm Waters, *Globalization* (New York: Routledge, 1995); Mike Featherstone, ed., *Global Culture: Nationalism, Globalization and Modernity* (London: Sage, 1990); Roland Robertson, *Globalization: Social Theory and Global Culture* (London: Sage, 1992); and Jonathan Friedman, *Cultural Identity and Global Process* (London and Thousand Oaks, Calif.: Sage, 1994). More recently, there is the four-volume series, *God and Globalization*, ed. Max Stackhouse et al. (Harrisburg, Pa.: Trinity Press International, 2000, 2001, 2002, 2004).

The University of Pittsburgh sociologist Roland Robertson has become interested in the total picture of globalization and its effects, including its effects on religion. Globalization itself, he notes, is not so much a new phenomenon as it is

> the compression of the world and the intensification of consciousness of the world as a whole. The processes and the actions to which the concept of globalization now refers have been proceeding, with some interruptions, for many centuries, but the main focus of the discussion of globalization is on relatively recent times.[2]

Robertson goes on to observe something that is extremely important for our own consideration, the link of globalization with modernity. Almost all discussion of globalization has become, in effect, a discussion of modernity and its positive and negative effects. Nations and regions that have led and undergone the process of modernization associated with industrialization and the European Enlightenment—which can be roughly thought of as movements beginning in the eighteenth century—tend to have one set of reactions to globalization in its current phase. Nations and regions of the global South, which are undergoing modernization with all the countervailing social change it entails at the same time as they are facing global economic pressures, tend to view it another way. Traditional societies are, for instance, being confronted in the span of a generation or two with pop culture and its violence and blatantly open portrayal of sex. At the same time, they become aware that their housing and treatment of women are looked down upon with disdain by the sorts of people who create the exciting, sexually titillating movies that, because of DVD players and portable generators, can now be viewed in isolated jungle villages. Young people look at traditional values in one place as unenlightened and something to be fled. Huge slums have grown up around Nairobi, Karachi, and Lima. Thousands of Muslims migrate to London and Amsterdam for jobs and find themselves on the lowest rung of society. And in twenty years a second generation looks at the parents who moved for better economic opportunities and accuses them of abandoning true Islam.

Modernization, as it is linked with globalization and portrayed as a process that necessitates the abandonment of traditional cultural and religious elements, has become highly controverted. And as globalization moves ahead with little visible benefit for sub-Saharan Africa or the Altiplano of Peru, it

---

2. Robertson, *Globalization*, 8.

becomes controverted, the symbol of yearning and desire, on the one hand, and the abandonment of everything good and holy, on the other. Thus, globalization is a highly ambiguous phenomenon.

In terms of the Catholic Church, we need to realize that globalization and modernization appear to be viewed by the late Pope John Paul II and the new elected Pope Benedict XVI as bearers of secularization and the lessening of moral sensitivities. A call for the ordination of women or married men, for instance, can be interpreted as a call to embrace a feminism that such leaders believe is hostile to the church and to abandon a tradition that has produced men who give their entire lives to the church and are loyal to that tradition. A call to change church structures to embrace traditional culture in, say, Kenya gets caught up in the question whether this would be embracing a past that many Kenyans are abandoning, despite idealistic attempts to preserve it. The issues we are discussing in terms of the church and globalization are, it must be said, not easy.

A second set of issues must be at least briefly touched upon. They revolve around "glocalization," a term that was apparently invented in Japan to describe local reactions to attempts

> to bring the global, in the sense of the macroscopic aspect of contemporary life, into conjunction with the local, in the sense of the microscopic side of life in the late twentieth century . . . Glocalize is a term which was developed in particular reference to marketing issues, as Japan became more concerned with and successful in the global economy.[3]

A global trend, product, force, idea, or ideal, in other words, needs to be adapted to the culture and outlook of the people to whom it is being sold, proposed, or explained. If this is not done, marketers discovered, it will not be successful. Becoming successful is the result of "glocalizing," adapting marketing and making changes to a product. A glocalized product that answers needs better than traditional products makes more money for its seller. By successfully glocalizing, Toyota became one of the most trusted and admired autos in the United States. A second generation of American Buddhists following Tibetan or Burmese Buddhist traditions makes subtle adaptations and finds its study and meditation centers crowded with men and women who found life as Lutherans, Jews, and Catholics meaningless. A form of glocalized Buddhism attracts adherents.

In addition, attempts to glocalize trends, products, and ideas may meet

---

3. Robertson, *Globalization*, 173.

hostility among many instead of acceptance. Following a different dynamic, the United Nations may separate warring factions and then attempt to institute democracy with one vote for one person, only to have its peacekeeping operation in an area like the Balkans or the lake district of Africa collide with the entrenched interests of traditional leaders. Setting up a video store in a Saudi neighborhood makes the local mullah realize over time that his young people are adopting attitudes that he thinks are godless and destructive. Both democracy and the video store become identified with globalization and globalization becomes a catchall phrase useful to condemn any outside influences.

The phrase "from a global perspective in today's milieu" includes the connotation that we are considering not merely something universal or all over the world. Rather, we are considering something that has an international impact with great varieties of local reactions, including reactions that result in social splits as one group embraces globalization and another feels threatened and opposes it. Economic globalization today without doubt carries an implication of influence from the global North, which is also judged dangerous and even imperial. All of this makes it necessary to begin our study with a few pages not on order and ministry as such but on the perspective from which these volumes are written. Our initial inquiry, then, is this: When applied to the two church terms, order and ministry, what does the phrase "global perspective" mean?

As we move through the pages on order and ministry from this contemporary global perspective, the reader cannot help but notice that two terms keep recurring, namely, "global" and "culture." Each of these terms requires a detailed explanation.

Global is an adjective meaning worldwide. In current media of magazines, books, radio, and TV, "global" is used with frequency, but even more frequently we encounter the abstract noun "globalization." Globalization has assumed, today, a multidimensional reference. First of all, it designates a world-encompassing process and thus has dynamic overtones. This dynamism reaches out to and deeply affects the economic, political, social, military, and religious dimensions of the entire globe. In many ways, the word "globalization" also includes today's neocolonialism, called economic or cultural neocolonialism. This latter interpretation of globalization is felt more acutely in the global South than in Euro-American cultures. Euro-American and Japanese people, governments, and businesses do not, for example, usually include neocolonialism in their understanding of what happens when they build a plant in Guatemala. For them, the kind of globalization that goes with building a new plant is good for the Nike shoe company and for Central America. The emphasis is different, however, in the places that experience the changes that occur when they are "globalized." Neocolonialism is almost always one accusation that traditionalists use as part of their understanding of globalization. Globalization will be the keyword throughout the pages of this volume, and the second part of this chapter will return to it.

Culture is a term that carries with it a series of interrelated words: multi-cultural, acculturation, and inculturation. In the last hundred years, cultural anthropology and cultural sociology have developed in geometric propor-tions. Almost all the major human sciences have been strongly affected by this current interest in culture. A similar appearance of culture can be found in the fine arts. In the Western Christian churches, the presence of followers from many different cultures within the parish community has made the issue of a multicultural church one of the most intense issues of current Christian life. "Culture" is the second keyword used in the succeeding pages. The third section of this chapter provides a detailed interpretation of the term "culture."

GLOBALIZATION

The term "globalization" is used by economists, religious leaders, and politi-cians. Not only is it used with frequency, but it is used in different, even con-tradictory ways. Max L. Stackhouse, in a lecture at the University of Santa Clara, described it as a complex reality calling for a "covenant" among the peoples of the world.

> The current form of globalization is new, in part because of its magnitude and in part because of its character. It is not only expanding our sense of the public world, it is creating a material infrastructure on a scale that could eventuate in a world civilization with a common virtual world of images and information that is, in principle, accessible to all. To be sure, some people still think of the "public" only as having to do with politics, but globalization is not a government project, and no political regime can comprehend the public it engenders. Indeed, the emerging global institu-tions of regulation and development, such as the IMF, World Bank, and WTO, etc., transcend any government's program. In fact it is a frequent accusation against them that they are unregulated by any political order and are too much influenced by the interests of multinational economic interests.[4]

---

4. Max L. Stackhouse, *Globalization, Public Theology, and New Means of Grace* (Santa Clara, Calif.: Santa Clara University, 2003).

Stackhouse then moves beyond a mere economic portrait of globalization and calls for some form of worldwide ethical covenant. This, he states, is needed so that the forces of human destruction in today's economic and transnational globalization might be countered by forces of justice and compassion.

Kim Yong-Bock, in an essay he wrote in 2003, presents a much more stark approach to globalization.

> In the 21st century, the peoples of Asia are facing a grim reality, brought about by the age of globalization. In this age, not only people but all life on earth is groaning and suffering under death and destruction. Life is an interconnected reality, as we can understand from the perspectives of rural communities: people suffer from poverty and hunger, from destruction of their communities, and from the chemicals that are injected into agricultural production in massive doses. At the same time, lands and forests are being destroyed and turned into commodities, and the earth is violated in terms of its integrity and sustainability.
>
> The life of plants and the genes of seeds, as well as human genes, are being destroyed and manipulated. Indeed, the whole ecological system is under threat of destruction, that is the death of all living things.
>
> The primary agency driving this globalization process is the transnational corporate powers, together with their technocratic powers, which dominate the global regulators of the world economy (WTO, IMF, G-7) and the global market.[5]

In a way similar to Stackhouse, Kim develops in the remainder of his essay a spiritual foundation that, in his view, can come only from religion. For Kim, religion provides today the only viable worldwide institution—in all its different forms—that can offer an adequate stabilizing and just remedy for a globalization process, which today is running headlong into world destruction.

Robert J. Schreiter, in his book *The New Catholicity: Theology between the Global and the Local*, offers a carefully worded description of globalization.

> There is no one accepted definition of globalization, nor is there consensus on its exact description. Nearly all would agree, however, that it is about the increasingly interconnected character of the political, economic and social life of the peoples on this planet. Depending again how one sees this interconnectedness, it is a phenomenon of the latter part of the twen-

---

5. Kim Yong-Bock, "An Asian Proposal for Future Directions of Theological Curricula in the Context of Globalization," *East Asian Pastoral Review* 20, no. 3 (2003): 278-79.

tieth century (the term "globalization" itself first appeared, in English, in 1959), or began with the European voyages of discovery in the late fifteenth century, or dates from the emergence of intercultural trade in the Late Bronze Age. I will be using the term here with the first description in mind—globalization as a phenomenon of the latter part of the twentieth century. Globalization certainly has its antecedent in the European colonizing process, but there are distinct differences in its late twentieth-century manifestation. To understand this, we must first note three processes that have shaped the globalization phenomenon in a special way. The first is political, the second is economic, and the third is technological.[6]

Schreiter then explains these three processes. The political process includes the demise of the bipolar political arrangement in 1989, when the collapse of the Russian state ended a bipolar political division. This collapse of the bipolar structure of superpowers, however, also resulted in the division of the world into first world, second world, and third world. The second world also collapsed, leaving the few rich nations and the majority of poor nations. Such an economic process was driven by market capitalism, which was already on the rise prior to 1989, but after 1989 was able to expand to many sectors across the globe. The spread of market capitalism also meant the diminishment of socialism. With the end of socialism, it became more difficult, if not impossible, to imagine an alternative social and economic form that could coexist with global capitalism. The third process, the technological process, came about with the Internet and computerized mass media. Schreiter notes that the convergence of these three phenomena has created a form of globalization that involves a compression of time and space around the entire world and is currently taking place with what one might call an identical global time.[7]

These are but three descriptions of globalization, but they seem to indicate a certain unity. First of all, we can say that there is, in some degree or another, a positive and affirmative side to globalization. It has provided major benefits to large areas of the world. On the other hand, in the words of the commentators quoted above, we clearly hear that there is also a shadow side of globalization. Globalization in the view of many authors produces serious negative effects, even serious destructive effects. Thus, globalization has a positive or sunny side and a shadow side:

---

6. Robert J. Schreiter, *The New Catholicity: Theology between the Global and the Local* (Maryknoll, N.Y.: Orbis Books, 1997), 4-5.
7. Schreiter, *New Catholicity*, 5-8.

- *Seen from the sunny-side perspective*, globalization unifies, brings disparate groups together, and provides a oneness in human life that historically has never before been so profoundly and extensively international.

- *Seen from the shadow-side perspective*, globalization destroys many individualized and intrinsically positive characteristics of various peoples and countries in the current world. Globalization has destroyed and is destroying valuable aspects of both local and regional cultures.

Unity and diversity are the underlying factors that globalization affects; however, globalization produces unity at the expense of diversity and creates an unbalanced diversity. One entity in the globalization process becomes richer, while other entities become geometrically poorer. When globalization begins to affect the Roman Catholic Church—and it is doing so at this very moment of time—then this double effect of globalization is willy-nilly brought into the structural dimensions of the Roman Catholic Church. When globalization affects the leadership roles of church order and ministry, we find the same reality of a sunny side and a shadow side. The positive effect is the unification of the church throughout the world. Because of globalization, the oneness of the church has begun to take shape throughout the various continents of human life in a unifying way never before experienced by the Roman Catholic Church. Similarly, globalization has given new meaning to catholicity—in the sense of all over the globe—since catholicity in virtue of a globalized society appears more sharply as an internationalized identity, even at times to the point of an internationalized cloning process.

There is, however, a negative effect, a shadow side to the globalization of the church. The globalized oneness and catholicity are diminishing the individuality and distinctness of many areas of church life at the expense of global unity. More often than not, the oneness of an ecclesiastical globalization has become the imposition of a central culture and a centralized cultural expression, which leaves local cultures and local cultural expressions meaningless. Unity and diversity play out both positively and negatively in a globalized church. From the beginnings of the Christian church, leadership has continually shared in this polarity of unity and diversity. When Christian church leadership became more organized and theologically defined, the technical terms "order" and "ministry" became prominent, but within this terminology, the polarity of unity and diversity continued to be operative.

Do church order and ministry need to be as tightly unified as possible? How extensively and intensively can unity and diversity coexist in the ecclesial services of order and ministry? Today these are neither hypothetical questions nor mere subtle academic issues. In the real life of the globalized Roman Catholic Church—that is, in the post–Vatican II and third-millennial Roman Catholic Church—this struggle over unity and diversity in the areas of order and ministry is <u>an actual, ongoing, and pervasive struggle</u>. There are at this very moment respected proponents for both sides as well as respected opponents of the others' positions. This is a struggle that one finds at the local level, the parish level, the diocesan level, the national church level, and the Vatican curial level. In many ways this struggle over church leadership, which focuses heavily on a leadership that includes diversity or a leadership that demands unity, is seriously affecting, both positively and negatively, the contemporary Roman Catholic Church. It is not simply an issue of struggle. It is, rather, an issue that, if not remedied soon, will be <u>corrosive to church integrity</u>. Ultimately, the question we need to face in today's "global milieu" is, What is the proper "glocalization" of local churches needed to create communities that will be able to minimize the negative effects of globalization, while helping both the members of such local churches and the wider church adapt to pressures that are unlikely to diminish?

Thus, the simple phrase "from a global perspective" calls attention to a minimizing of and even a destruction of local and regional cultural treasures. This is apparent in economic globalization, in political globalization, and unfortunately in ecclesiastical globalization. In all of these dimensions of current human life, <u>culture and cultural identities</u>, not simply globalization, <u>are at the center of the struggle</u>. Let us consider, then, the second issue: culture.

CULTURE

In the past one hundred years, there has been an enormous interest on the part of international scholars in the issue of culture. We find this in various academic disciplines: anthropology, which "inquires into the basic questions about who human beings are, how they came to be what they are, how they behave and why they behave."[8] Its method, most often, is a comparative method, relating one anthropological example to a different anthropological one. Anthropology has developed two major subdisciplines: physical anthropology and cultural anthropology. Ethnologists, who constitute a division of

---

8. Louis J. Luzbetak, *The Church and Cultures* (Maryknoll, N.Y.: Orbis Books, 1988), 23. Luzbetak provides a clear overview of this anthropological and cultural interest as it has developed academically during the past one hundred years (see pp. 12-63). Luzbetak also provides a lengthy bibliography on the theme of current anthropology and related subjects (pp. 411-52).

scholars of cultural anthropology, often restrict their focus to the earliest appearances of human societies and their cultural manifestations. Other cultural anthropologists focus on existing human societies and their respective cultural manifestations.

In a similar way, contemporary social scientists have become very interested in cultural issues. Emile Durkheim (1858-1917) is one of the major leaders in this effort. He regarded human groups as fairly independent organisms, and as a consequence his specific interest was in comparative social anthropology. Durkheim has had many followers, including A. R. Radcliffe-Brown (1881-1955) and Bronislaw Malinowski (1884-1942). At first, there seems to have been a strong degree of functionalism in the methodology used by scholars who were influenced by Durkheim. This functionalism tended to interpret different cultural activities in a mechanistic way. Later social anthropologists have attributed far more flexibility and dynamism to cultures themselves.

The academic fields of psychology, political science, philosophy, and history have also included the study of culture in their respective research efforts. Perhaps the studies from applied anthropology are the studies that offer the most significance for our theme of globalization, culture, and church leadership in order and ministry. These applied anthropological studies have helped to indicate how cultural customs arise, develop, and endow human societies with profound values. Today it would be fruitless to study the effects of culture on the Roman Catholic Church without utilizing the contributions of applied anthropology and social anthropology. The abundant scholarly work in such social-cultural studies includes the efforts of many renowned writers, for example, Franz Boas, Alfred Kroeber, Margaret Mead, Ruth Benedict, Clyde Kluckhohn, Robert Park, William Partridge, and Clifford Geertz. Michael Omi and Howard Winant's book *Racial Formation in the United States: From the 1960s to the 1980s* has also been a major guide for understanding the cultural mixture currently present in the American churches.[9] Wang Ling-Chi has built on Omi and Winant's position, developing a paradigm for Chinese-American acculturation.[10] Culture and the issue of religion have to some degree also been factors in the literature of social anthropology, especially after Will Herberg's volume *Protestant,*

---

9. Michael Omi and Howard Winant, *Racial Formation in the United States: From the 1960s to the 1980s* (New York: Routledge, 1986).

10. Wang Ling-Chi, "The Structure of Dual Domination: Toward a Paradigm for the Study of the Chinese Diaspora in the U.S.," *Amerasia Journal* 21 (1955): 149-69.

Catholic, Jew, first published in 1955.[11] Herberg, however, understood the role of religion in this process of acculturation more as a conduit through which recent immigrants could more easily negotiate the process of trans-culturation or interculturation. As a conduit, religion plays only a subsidiary role or at best a private role. Herberg's approach has found a major response throughout Euro-American writings. Religion is generally, in these writings, placed at the sideline of social life. Religion in these studies is not given a public voice, and the dimension of religion is relegated to private and familial life. This has had enormous influence in the United States. The call for a separation of church and state is loudly echoed in the rejection of any religious voice in the public and political arenas. In the United States, decisions on such important issues as economics, environment, and human rights are all made in the political and economic arenas. Until the administration of George W. Bush, religious voices have not been welcome in these arenas, because it was believed that religion is a personal, individual, or family matter and therefore should stay in the arenas of the private individual and the family.

This is important for our current study, since a rejection of religion in the public sphere makes it almost impossible for the voices of church leaders to be heard and to have an effect in the decision-making processes of the United States. If a theology of order and ministry lacks a public aspect, then the leadership of various church groups, found primarily in the areas of church order and ministry, will likewise lack a public voice. On the other hand, if a public voice is theologically part of order and ministry, then the public voice of religious leadership itself cannot be determined by a centralizing and supernational organization. Obviously, the centralizing and supernational headquarters for the Roman Catholic Church would be the pope and the Vatican curia. In the recent efforts to elect a Roman Catholic as president of the United States, the issue of the candidate's loyalty to Rome and his loyalty to the United States has been very divisive. The church voice, whether that of the Vatican or the national episcopate, has been viewed as interference in the democratic processes of the United States. Similarly, in the recent instances of American involvement in war, the voice of the American bishops has been diplomatically heard and then diplomatically discarded by those in political power. The role of religion and culture remains a very sensitive issue, and a current theology of church leadership, including a theology of order and ministry, must take into consideration the current interface between religion, culture, and public life.

---

11. Will Herberg, *Protestant, Catholic, Jew: An Essay in American Religious Sociology* (Garden City, N.Y.: Doubleday, 1960).

Two words have been used in the above paragraphs that need some clarification: *acculturation* and *inculturation*. The word "acculturation" was first used in sociology around 1880. "Acculturation" addresses the modification of a specific group or people of one culture adapting traits from a different culture. Acculturation has also at times been used to describe the ways in which an infant learns how to adapt to the culture in which he/she finds himself/herself. In the first instance, which represents the more frequent application of the term "acculturation," the focus is on a situation involving at least two differing cultures and on the ways in which one culture begins to be affected by the other. Fumitaka Matsuoka has recently revised the theory of this intercultural activity. He stresses that the study should not simply be focused on cultural unit A and cultural unit B. One should not concentrate on the traits, characteristics, and habits that are acculturated. Rather, the focus should be on the interstice between the two cultures. The interstice plays a major role in the process of acculturation. In the word "acculturation," the initial letters *ac* are a grammatically nuanced form of the Latin word *ad*, which means "to" or "toward." There is an "into" process in acculturation, which generally includes a reciprocal "into" process. In other words, there is a dynamic interfacing of two cultural units, and Matsuoka emphasizes that this interfacing or interstice is the dynamic area in which a bipolar acculturation process takes place. The term "acculturation" remains in current literature a strongly sociological technical term.

The word "inculturation" is a theological term, and it is rarely used outside the fields of missiology, theology, and religious studies. It is, moreover, a term of very recent use within the theological-religious field. There seems to have been a strong reluctance on the part of religious scholars to use the sociological term "acculturation." In theological writings, the term "acculturation" is not used as a synonym, even a religious synonym, for "inculturation." In other words, inculturation and acculturation are, in the mind-set of theologians and religious-studies scholars, two distinct words and do not mean the same thing. It is not totally clear why "acculturation" was unacceptable, but it is clear that "inculturation" is the word of choice for those who are in the field of theology and religious studies. In theological and religious discourse, inculturation is seen as the process of bringing a different religious message *into* a culture that up to that time had not been influenced by this particular religious message. Inculturation has become a major part of Christian evangelization, which means an infusion of gospel values into a non-Christian culture or into a culture that once was Christian but is no longer predominantly Christian (for example, much of Western Europe), or into a new-age culture. The word "inculturation" does not imply any reciprocity at all.

In the contemporary period, not all Catholic people see inculturation as a one-way street. The voices of non–Euro-American cultures have claimed the validity of their own cultures, and in no uncertain terms they have emphasized the need to de-accentuate the Euro-American aspects of the Roman Catholic Church, chiefly in areas of the world like Oceania, Latin America, Africa, and Asia, to allow for the expression of Christian faith and Catholic tradition in other cultural idioms. Were this to happen, the new forms of Catholic life would be expressed and lived out in and through the cultural forms, symbols, and celebrations of many different cultures. We will see that many bishops at Vatican II were open to such an interpretation of Catholic faith and life, at least in principle. We shall also see that, since Vatican II, inculturation has had an ambiguous reception—indeed, that those who believe it should be done fairly radically have felt restrained by the central leadership of the church, which has disallowed extensive and intensive inculturation. The two major areas of Roman Catholic Church life where tensions have been felt are in the matter of inculturating the liturgy and church law.

DRAWING CONCLUSIONS FROM THE HISTORY OF INCULTURATION

From the recent studies and research on cultural issues, certain factors regarding culture in general have become more and more evident. These factors must be taken into account when we begin to unite the message of the gospel to the peoples who live and form these cultures. Some of the major conclusions we can draw from this material are the following.

First, all cultures are always in a process of development and change. No existent culture is static and immovable. This applies to both sides of a globalization process. Even the aggressive forces promoting globalization are undergoing change. The imposition of a culture from the outside or the attempt to make a foreign culture the standard for social change is almost never successful. When cultures begin to struggle over which values should prevail, both cultures end up altered.

Second, all cultures have profound areas of impact on human life and they also have certain specific and more surface areas of influence. Not every cultural characteristic of a given society carries the same weight. The more profound the cultural dimension is, the more it affects the self-identity of the social unit, and therefore any compromising or forced change in these profound dimensions of cultural life impinges on the self-identity of the social unity.

Third, in their most profound dimensions, both culture and self-identity of a given society are intrinsically united. The attempted domination or destruction of a culture creates a crisis in the sense of self-identity in the culture being threatened. Consequently, to the extent that missionary activity aims at the destruction of major cultural elements—which in the minds of many missionaries were and are judged to be demonic, satanic, heretical, and pagan—evangelization suffers or is carried on with ambiguous results. It is clear that some Christian missionary practice aimed to destroy basic cultural symbols and practices in many places. Today, though, some of those same basic cultural symbols and practices are recognized as valid by Catholic and many other Christian bodies. For instance, the image of a dragon in Asian cultures, which formerly was disallowed, is now allowed in some churches. The practice of veneration of ancestors (often called "ancestor-worship") has likewise been reinstated in some churches. In other churches, particularly fundamentalist ones, however, this is not the case. Many converts to such churches hurl charges at Catholics that their church does not follow the Bible. Thus, the question of what constitutes proper adaptation is not going away. If anything, it is intensifying. Caution, care, prudence, and dialogue are needed whenever one culture begins to erode another.[12]

Fourth, cultural residue endures in an operative way long after the processes of acculturation have taken place. Historically, there are indeed cultures that no longer exist. Even their languages are no longer considered living languages. A particular form of human social life can indeed come to an end, with the result that these dead cultures are known only from books of historical consideration. For the most part, such cultures no longer effectively guide a current social unit of human life. In actuality, all societies with all of their cultural dimensions can and could be eliminated. This fact indicates that there is no eternal cultural unit of men and women. Nor is there anything eternal about any finite human nature and finite cultural nature.

Many cultures today are reeling from the cultural impact of the process of globalization that began at the dawn of the modern era. First European and later North American cultural, military, and religious power undermined the self-confidence of many peoples. In Asia especially, while enormous amounts of power were applied to bring, for example, Indians and Chinese to accept Western values, silent resistance and outright rejection were common. And

---

12. Two books by Lamin Sanneh are especially important if one wishes to see that the process of evangelization is not a one-way street. In fact, local people creatively interpreted and translated the Gospel, finding in it elements of liberation and truth that they valued greatly. See Lamin Sanneh, *Translating the Message: The Missionary Impact on Culture* (Maryknoll, N.Y.: Orbis Books, 1989) and *Whose Religion Is Christianity? The Gospel beyond the West* (Grand Rapids: Eerdmans, 2003).

cultural resurgence everywhere in the face of globalization is remarkable. While the economic, technical, and military prowess of the West has brought about changes at one level, cultures that were once thought "defeated" are being rejuvenated. Symbols and practices once thought superseded begin to reappear, for example, among the first-nation peoples of Canada and among the Native Americans in the United States. This same reality is even more strongly present among the descendants of Mayan, Incan, and Aztecan peoples in Mexico and in Central and South America. What becomes ever clearer is that peoples in the Americas who became Christian interpreted Christianity in their own cultural and linguistic way and today want to express their experience in liturgy and theology.

Fifth, cultural growth occurs when the people involved continue to have freedom of imagination. Whenever members of a society cannot imagine a future for their society, depression and even atrophy set in. In such situations, cultural identity remains a remembered treasure from the past but loses the dynamism to shape the future. Colonialism, in its darkest moments, stifled the creative cultural imagination of the colonized. Given the fact that the Catholic church is nowhere more vital than it is in the global South, it is clear that Christian mission was not just a chapter in a larger history of Western colonialism. Local peoples found something in both Protestant and Catholic presentations of the message and were quite capable of seeing the gospel pearl even when it was presented by missioners who were often closely allied with colonial governments and foreign economic interests. For the health of the Catholic Church today, however, it is clear that the question of encouraging such cultural imagination is extremely important, since it is primarily in the area of imagination that liturgy expresses the faith of a people and contributes compelling images that enlist the desire of Christians to cooperate with divine grace to make Christ a vital force in daily life. Suppressing cultural imagination in the area of liturgy by insisting that imported laws and rubrics are followed, even when meaningless, defeats the purpose of liturgy and leads to serious disorder and dysfunction.

Sixth, in every vital culture religion is an expression of the sacred dimension at the core of a culture's depth. Paul Tillich memorably coined the phrase, "Religion is the substance of culture and culture the form of religion."[13] Tillich knew well that until a religion takes on forms adequate to mediate the sacred meaningfully and touch the depths of the human heart, religion was going to be superficial. While, in the history of religions, priesthoods have not traditionally been the instigators of new religious move-

---

13. Paul Tillich, *Systematic Theology*, 3 vols. (Chicago: University of Chicago Press, 1951-63), 3:248ff.

ments—that is the role of the so-called charismatic founder—they are the guardians and interpreters of tradition. In the conserving, guardianship role, however, priesthoods are also prone to try to maintain traditions with which they are comfortable even when cultural change makes the outward forms of the tradition seem antiquated and uninspiring. In the case of world Catholicism today, three major forms of cultural challenge present themselves. (1) In "old" churches, particularly in the West, large segments of a nominally Catholic population complain that the ordained leadership has stifled necessary change, holding onto a celibate, male-only ordained leadership model that needs to give way to new societal realties that have changed perceptions of gender roles and sexual identities. Other segments believe that those calling for such changes have been seduced by modernity and the problem is the obscuring of the core of the tradition. (2) In "new" churches, particularly in Africa and Asia, Christianity thrives, but some believe the life of these churches will deepen if inculturation is allowed to use local languages, rituals, and traditions. Still others believe that the radical challenge of Christ will be lost, pointing to the ability of cultures like those of India, Southeast Asia, China, and Japan to adapt creatively to outside influences, such as those brought by Christianity, until their genius is lost. (3) In churches like those in Latin America, an even more complex reality faces Catholics. In five hundred years, both *mestizo* (mixed-race, bicultural) and "white" populations have created a hybrid religious mosaic. That Catholic mosaic is today challenged by evangelicals and Pentecostals who rigorously try to pare away elements that they call "Christo-pagan" and to bring Catholics back to what they call a strictly "biblical" faith. They have had enormous success in many parts of Latin America, to the point that it is likely such churches will count as much as 40 percent, perhaps even 50 percent, of the total population by the year 2025.

What we are getting at, then, is a process of inculturation in which both Christian "conservers" and "innovators" have to be heard. Both sides have real weight behind their arguments. Such issues must be faced in parts of the West where Catholicism seems unable to inspire allegiance any longer. They must be faced in different ways in parts of the world where the gospel has been imported in Western dress. The Euro-American world enjoys no advantage over the rest of the world. As Pope John Paul II has said in *Redemptoris Missio,* his encyclical on mission and evangelization:

Today we face a religious situation which is extremely varied and changing. People are on the move: social and religious realities which were once clear and well-defined are today increasingly complex. We need only think of certain phenomena such as urbanization, mass migration, the flood of

refugees, the dechristianization of countries with ancient Christian traditions, the increasing influence of the Gospel and its values in overwhelmingly non-Christian countries, and the proliferation of messianic cults and
religious sects. Religious and social upheaval makes it difficult to apply in
practice certain ecclesial distinctions and categories to which we have
become accustomed. (RM 32)

Insofar as we are trying to understand how order and ministry need to be
shaped for the contemporary era, then, we are face to face with the reality the
late pope calls the difficulty of applying traditional Catholic distinctions and
categories. Inculturation needs to occur in the North as well as in the global
South. As we shall see below, however, despite statements like the one of
Pope John Paul II quoted above, official documents from Rome often present
the question of inculturation in ways that suggest that the gospel is above all
cultures and therefore can penetrate to the very depths of any culture. In
terms of Stephen Bevans's models of how the gospel–culture relationship is
phrased, the default Catholic approach, as epitomized in the writings of John
Paul II and the curia since the Second Vatican Council, is a "translation
model."[14] Inculturation of the church, in that model, involves relatively minor
adjustments, and the question of orders and ministries can be controlled from
the traditional Roman center.

The adequacy of that translation or "supracultural" model is questioned by
many in the fields of missiology, cultural, and social studies. The challenge
occurs at two levels. First can the gospel message be "above all cultures?" Does
the metaphor of "over" (superior) and "inferior" (lower level) put the matter
in the right categories? Even preaching the gospel involves language that is
intrinsically cultural, and the Gospels were written in one cultural language
(Greek) but are now expressed in other languages, all of which have cultural
nuances that the original language did not have. Second, if religion itself is
cultural to its core, then what does evangelization imply? If evangelization
implies a transculturalization, namely, inserting the gospel into new places
and using it to judge the value of other cultures because it is above all cultures, then evangelization is going to be perceived as a destructive rather than
a constructive force. Given the perception that mission was intimately
involved with and supportive of colonialism, this presents problems in the
South. In Europe, where the church once fought for the role of guiding the
whole of society and enforcing its guidance with the power of the state, such
approaches appear to be trying to roll back the Enlightenment. In the United

---

14. Stephen B. Bevans, *Models of Contextual Theology*, rev. and expanded ed. (Maryknoll, N.Y.:
Orbis Books, 2002), 37-53.

States and many other places, such approaches appear to violate the cultural norm of separating church and state. This delicate but key issue will be touched on in the following chapters.

Such issues as revealed by anthropological, social, and historical studies are necessary to keep in mind as we consider the theological issues of order and ministry from a global perspective. When Gustavo Gutiérrez crystallized the multifaced movement that came to be called "liberation theology," some parts of the leadership of the Roman Catholic Church were seriously concerned over his use of social analysis.[15] In the view of these leaders, the gospel does not need the kind of social analysis provided by the liberationists, seeing their methods marred by Marxist theories of class warfare and economic determinism. We have moved a long way from this late-twentieth-century hesitation. There are, of course, leaders in the Catholic Church who still refuse social analysis as a base for discussing gospel life. Nevertheless, a majority of scholars find such analyses very helpful. Some have even noted that Pope John Paul's own language when he talks about poverty and its alleviation, as well as matters of war and peace, seems to have borrowed from the analysis and language of the Latin Americans. The same is true for cultural-analysis anthropologists and sociologists on the interfacing of Christianity and culture in every part of the world. Not to study seriously the findings of the social-scientific world on the issues of culture would be myopic.

Some final words are needed, regarding another aspect of the Roman Catholic Church, particularly in the West, and its relationship to culture. This aspect is found not in social analysis but in another academic discipline—history. The confrontation of culture and Christianity that is going on today is not the first such confrontation. I will consider historical data on the relationship of the church and Christianity to culture under four headings.

The Semitic Culture of Jesus and His First Followers: The Original Framework of Christian Ministry

The followers of Jesus have had a long history in which various cultures have played major roles. Indeed, from its very beginning the gospel message of Jesus and about Jesus was an inculturated message, spoken first to Palestinian peoples in the time of Jesus' life and after his death. In terms of the message

---

15. The classic text by Gustavo Gutiérrez is *A Theology of Liberation*, trans. Caridad Inda and John Eagleson, 15th anniversary ed. (Maryknoll, N.Y.: Orbis Books, 1988; orig. ed. in Spanish, 1971). The official church response is the document of the Congregation for the Doctrine of the Faith *Libertatis Nuntius,* "Instruction on Certain Aspects of the 'Theology of Liberation'" (August 6, 1984).

of Jesus, he preached and taught in Aramaic within a Semitic culture that was under Roman political rule and had been touched by Hellenistic cultural encroachments. More precisely stated, Jesus' public ministry took place within a Roman-dominated Semitic culture. This meant that the people not only heard Jesus' message from a Semitic cultural standpoint but also factored the Roman standpoint into what they were hearing. The language Jesus used was Aramaic, a spoken form of Hebrew widespread in that period, and, of course, Aramaic, like all languages, was a cultural phenomenon. Jesus could presume that the people understood to some degree the history of the Jewish people and also the many efforts at romanization and hellenization that had been going on in Palestine for two hundred years prior to Jesus' own life. Jesus did not have to explain to his followers the Palestinian culture of his time; the people by and large were well aware of what this culture involved.

After the resurrection of Jesus, the followers of Jesus continued to meet as a "Jesus community." At that time, these followers of Jesus did not have a self-identity as a "Christian," nor did they consider themselves a "church." These men and women were Jewish, and their religion was Judaism. Their first conceptualizations of the message of Jesus took place within Semitic categories. In a similar way, as they began to formulate the message *about* Jesus and his relationship to God, they were bound by these same categories. They went to the temple and to the synagogues for prayer, and they continued to observe the Mosaic Law, the Torah. Although followers of Jesus, they maintained their Jewish self-identity. Today many authors designate these early Jesus communities as one of the many "sects" within the many Judaisms of that time.

The four Gospels give every indication of this Jewishness of the early Jesus communities. Naturally, the Hellenistic world and its culture played a role in the way these early followers of Jesus lived out their daily lives. The New Testament, however, was written in Greek, and this shows that the first records we have of Jesus' message and of the disciples understanding of Jesus were records that were, in effect, an example of translating the message of Jesus the teacher and about Jesus the Christ or Messiah into a new language. Inculturation as the crossing of cultural boundaries, then, is intrinsic to Christian identity from the earliest period. The writers of the New Testament did not use Hebrew, Aramaic, or Latin. They wrote their Letters, Gospels, and other writings in Greek, knowing full well that the members of the Jesus communities for whom they were writing in the Jewish Diaspora around the Mediterranean basin would understand them. Although written in Greek for Greek-speaking communities, the New Testament can only be truly interpreted if its Semitic background is understood, so much so that one of the criteria of modern biblical scholarship for the antiquity of a given idea or doctrine is whether it can be translated from Greek back into Aramaic. If it cannot, then the scholar suspects that the text shows a subsequent generation's thought process. For many scholars, such later interpretations cannot be given the same weight as earlier ones, and around this principle have occurred some of the bitterest fights in biblical studies. The view taken in this book is that the primary lens of interpretation for the New Testament is Semitic— not exclusively Semitic but primarily Semitic.

During the period when the New Testament authors lived, the followers of Jesus were predominantly Jewish. Only little by little did non-Jewish men and women join the Jesus communities, and in their growing numbers they began to influence in a Hellenistic way the cultural interpretation of the Jesus-event.[16]

After the destruction of the Jewish temple in the year 70, there was a stronger process of separation between the leaders of the Jewish communities and the Jesus communities. Expulsion from synagogues had already taken place during the time of Paul's own career, and this continued into the last decade of the first century, 90-100. The separation of the Jewish establishment from the Jesus sect was a mutual decision, taken with such bitterness that it bore with it the seeds of later Christian anti-Jewish attitudes. The separation was not simply an action by the followers of Jesus leaving the Jewish framework. They did this, of course, but the Jewish leadership also acted. They expelled the followers of Jesus. One can clearly and historically say that by 90 C.E., there were two groups: one group followed the Jewish leadership with its new, post-temple base, not in Jerusalem but in Jamnia; the other group comprised the followers of Jesus, who, after 90 C.E. (roughly speaking), began to see themselves as a "different group" from the "Jewish group." The word "Christian" (first used in Acts 11:26) became common around this same time and the term "church" (*ekklēsia*) also became popular. Paul used *ekklēsia* to refer to the Christian "assembly" or community. Only at the end of the first century, then, can one begin to speak of a Jewish religion and a Christian religion. Even this way of speaking, however, has to be done with care, since the separation took place gradually and happened more quickly in some areas of

---

16. Bevans and Roger P. Schroeder represent the views of many missiologists, however, who see the New Testament as an intrinsically missionary document and believe that it was only when events at Antioch (Acts 11:19-26) came to a head that the early church realized fully the meaning of the message of and about Jesus. On this view of the matter, it was the process of missionary inculturation that led to mature Christian self-understanding. It must be admitted that this interpretation is profoundly consonant with Catholicism's view that earliest Christian history needs to be interpreted "as-a-whole" (Greek *kath' holon*, whence "catholic"). See Stephen B. Bevans and Roger P. Schroeder, *Constants in Context: A Theology of Mission for Today*, American Society of Missiology 30 (Maryknoll, N.Y.: Orbis Books, 2004), 1-31.

the world than in others. Too often writers bring into the historical development of the Jesus community the terms "Christian" and "church" at times
when these two words really had no meaning. At best, the two terms are
meaningful at the very end of the first century and at the start of the second
century. Before this, the use of "Christian" and "church" can be and most often
is anachronistic.

When the followers of Jesus began separating themselves from the Jewish
leadership, it was clear that the Christian group did not depart empty-
handed. The followers of Jesus made the following serious claims: Jesus was
the Messiah foretold by the prophets; therefore, the writings of the prophets
belonged to the followers of Jesus. Jesus fulfilled all that the Law of Moses,
the Torah, had demanded; therefore, the Torah, likewise, belonged to the followers of Jesus. Jewish history from its beginnings onward led to Jesus, and
therefore Jesus fulfilled the hopes and dreams of Jewish history. As a result,
the Jewish "writings"—including the many historical Jewish writings—
belonged to the followers of Jesus. The followers of Jesus took on a new identity: the New Covenant, the New Israel, and the new Chosen People. In
many ways, as we find in the Christian literature from the New Testament to
the beginning of the third century, the Christian community thought of itself
as the "true Israel."

Jesus and his followers lived out and understood their message in a cultural
way, namely, in a Jewish or Semitic way. Today, we do not hear the gospel
from and through a Semitic culture. We hear the gospel through our own
culture.

The Move of Christianity
into Hellenistic Culture, 100 to 600

In the period from New Testament times to about the year 600, the first
major inculturation process of the Christian church took place. In spite of the
Jewish roots and foundations that the Christian communities claimed, the
birth culture of Jesus' followers in the West was more and more that of the
Greek culture commonly called Hellenistic. The use of Latin in that Hellenistic world gradually became more frequent. Meanwhile, the separation
from the Jewish cultural world grew ever deeper and more permanent. It is
important to remember, however, that even though our own study centers on
the Hellenistic world in this period, there is growing historical evidence that
the majority of the world's Christians even up to the fourteenth century lived
farther east and south, where a parallel inculturation process was going on. In

this case it was a move from the categories of late Judaism into the liturgical and ecclesial traditions we today call the Syriac, Persian, and Coptic worlds of Eastern (*not* Greek) Orthodoxy.

In the West, though, the new Christians were basically Greek-speaking and Greek-thinking. They rethought the gospel into Hellenistic culture. Parallel with Eastern Orthodoxy, these were the first major inculturations of the gospel message. In the West, the gospel message, which in its origins was spoken, heard, and understood against a Semitic cultural background, became a gospel proclaimed, heard, and understood in Greco-Roman/Hellenistic culture.

Christological dogmas were cast and eventually defined by ecumenical councils in and through the categories of Hellenistic philosophical thought. Meanwhile, farther to the east, the same process was occurring in a different fashion in Syriac and other ancient languages. By the accidents of history, the West (increasingly in Latin) and the Byzantine center (remaining in Greek) at first did not accept these Eastern formulations and later—largely because of the rise of Islam in the seventh century—lost touch with them. In our own day, however, historians have realized that these formulas were orthodox and that these communities had kept faith with the core of gospel tradition. The Latin West and the Greek East are, in other words, not the only major Christian traditions.[17]

In the West, the development of the office of bishop (Greek *episkopos*) is understandable only when the Greek meaning of *episkopos* is taken into account. Why did the early communities use *episkopos* and not a different term? We shall see that the characteristic of service, which lies in the Greek etymology of the term *episkopos*, played a major role in its selection over the other possible terms. The term "priest" (Greek *hiereus*) was rejected, whereas the term "presbyter" (Greek *presbyteros*) was deliberately chosen. Presbyter is often well translated as "elder," and this is indeed its etymological meaning in Greek. The term "elder" also has a rich Semitic history, since in Jewish history as found in the Old Testament, elders often played a major role in Jewish political and social life. Thus, the eventual two main Greek names for leadership in the Christian church, *episkopos* and *presbyteros*, have deep cultural implications, and in their Greek format, deep Hellenic and Hellenistic implications. Etymologically, both terms originally entailed service to the community, not power over the community.

---

17. For more on Eastern Orthodoxy (once called "Nestorian and churches"), see Dale T. Irvin and Scott W. Sunquist, *A History of the World Christian Movement*, vol. 1, *Earliest Christianity to 1453* (Maryknoll, N.Y.: Orbis Books, 2001), 47-153; see also Bevans and Schroeder, *Constants in Context*, 79-136.

The effects of this first major inculturation process of the Christian church remain with us today. Much of Western Christian theology is expressed in terms that have both Hellenic and Hellenistic implications. For example, in our Christian faith we believe that Jesus has two natures, the divine and the human, and that these two natures are united in one person. An understanding of both "nature" and "person" requires some knowledge of the Greek philosophical basis of both terms. Similarly, the Christian belief in the Trinity includes the single nature of God and yet a trinity of persons. The use and interpretation of nature and person in trinitarian expression rely heavily on Greek philosophical thought. The listing could go on, but the inculturation of Greek thought by the Jesus communities of the first six centuries continues to be a major part of the Western and Eastern Christian faith and theology. An original Semitic Christianity was profoundly inculturated into a Greek-based culture.

The Inculturation of Western Catholicism in Germanic Cultures, 600–900

A second major inculturation process of the gospel message took place during the immigration of the Germanic tribes into western Europe. These Germanic tribes have many names: Lombards, Goths, Burgundians, and other tribes. From the seventh century to the tenth century, these groups of people, generally referred to as Germanic cultures, arrived in present-day Europe and brought with them cultural elements. Once again, a process of inculturation began to take place in the Christian community, for the Greco-Roman culture of the Christian people in western Europe had to adapt to the various Germanic cultures that in wave after wave began inundating this European part of the earth. Two areas of the Christian life became the center of this particular process of major inculturation, namely, liturgy and law. Even today, we find example after example of liturgical and canonical issues that stem from this second major inculturation of the gospel message.[18]

The impact of Germanic culture on Christian life in the West remains a strong influence on Christian life and theology today. Contemporary Western Christian liturgy and canon law retain major influences from the Germanic world. In the liturgy, the simple posture of kneeling, which became part of Christian worship through Germanic cultural influences, has in

---

18. For a good treatment of this, see James C. Russell, *The Germanization of Early Medieval Christianity: A Sociohistorical Approach to Religious Transformation* (New York: Oxford University Press, 1992).

today's post–Vatican II world created an issue of immense tension. Some contemporary Roman Catholics demand that people continue to kneel throughout the Eucharistic Prayers and for the reception of Holy Communion. Not to do so is interpreted as disrespect of the sacrament. Even when an explanation is given that kneeling came into Christian liturgical practice only through the influence of Germanic culture, many of these well-intended Roman Catholics dismiss such an interpretation. In their view, kneeling indicates the only true reverence for the Real Presence of Jesus in the eucharist. The fact that during the first eight hundred years of Christian history kneeling was seen—and this was the Greco-Roman view—as unworthy of Christians, since only slaves knelt, makes no impression at all. Other examples of Germanic cultural influence could be adduced, but the point at issue is this: there was a major inculturation process in Western Christianity from the Germanic peoples, and this cultural influence remains profoundly strong even in the ongoing third millennium of Christian life.

After the Germanic immigrations, there were some additional but still very important inculturation processes. In the twelfth and thirteenth centuries, cultural issues arose with the introduction into Western thought of the Latin translations of Aristotle and of the Latin translations of commentaries on Aristotle, written by major Islamic scholars. During this period, the great theologians such as Alexander of Hales, Albert the Great, Thomas Aquinas, Bonaventure, and John Duns Scotus were enriched by the writings of Aristotle and the commentaries of Islamic scholars such as Averroës and Avicenna. Theological thought in the Western Roman Catholic Church was inculturated in no small degree both by the newly discovered Greek philosophical thought of Aristotle and by the Islamic thought of Averroës and Avicenna. As a result, the philosophical theology of the Western church became in large measure Aristotelian from the twelfth century on. It retained its Platonic base, also Greek in origin, however, through the continued influence of Augustine in the Western church. Whether emphasizing Aristotle or Plato, or a combination of both, Western theology was inculturated in a Greek way, and Catholic theology remained this way until the twentieth century. In the twentieth century, modern and postmodern philosophical thinking began to change many areas of Roman Catholic theology. In the thirteenth century, some of the theologians mentioned above were openly referred to as "Islamic." In that century, people of major importance within the church noticed that there was an Islamic cultural influence at work. The condemnation of many theological positions at Paris in 1277 and at Oxford in 1284 was done by church prelates with a deliberate intent to nullify the effects of this Islamic inculturation of Christian thought. These condemnations, however, did not succeed, and Islamic influences from the Middle Ages continue today in the ordinary theology of the Roman Catholic Church.

During the Renaissance period, all of Europe was inundated with the Greco-Roman classical culture. This inculturation is found in literature, art, architecture, and mathematics. When one looks at St. Peter's in Rome, one sees very clearly an architectural and mathematical inculturation in the basilica itself. The basilica of St. Peter by its very existence proclaims a Greco-Roman classical culture. When one considers the great masterpieces of Michelangelo and Da Vinci and realizes the influence these artists have had on Catholic thinking, the Greco-Roman culture is once again seen as highly influential. Consider one instance: the Last Supper. Since Leonardo Da Vinci painted his famous mural of the Last Supper, almost every holy card and major Western portrayal of the Last Supper have reflected what Da Vinci painted. Even in film and stage plays, visual presentations of the Last Supper have reflected the influence of Da Vinci. In many ways, generations of children first visualized the Last Supper from a Da Vinci standpoint: Jesus in the center of a long formal table with the disciples sitting at either side.

When Jesus ate for the last time with his disciples, all of them—if this was a Passover meal—were reclining, not sitting. There was no main table, nor were they all looking in one direction. Rather, they would have been more in a circle than in a U-shaped format. However, most Christians visualize the Last Supper in a Da Vinci framework, not in a Semitic-cultural framework. The Renaissance has also had a strong cultural influence on the ways in which Western Christians build churches, visualize images of Jesus, and even in the ways that liturgy itself is carried out. Both the twelfth-century Aristotelian revival and the later Renaissance revival of Greco-Roman culture were indeed strong cultural influences on the western Roman Catholic Church. In many ways, however, they were not as overarching an inculturation process as the Hellenistic process of the early centuries and the Germanic cultural process of the Middle Ages, nor, as we shall presently see, as intensively and extensively overwhelming as the contemporary process of inculturation.

The Inculturation of Western Catholicism, 1900 to the Present

In the contemporary era, the Christian church is going through a third major inculturation challenge, involving all the countervailing tendencies we noted above in discussing globalization. The modern period includes the revolutions brought about by rise and development of a scientific view of the world and a technological remaking of economic life. It also includes all that the word "postmodern" implies. One needs to realize that today's entire Christian church—Anglican, Orthodox, Protestant, and Roman Catholic—is undergoing a third major process of inculturation. In many ways, this third process of inculturation is far more intensive and extensive than the first major inculturation (the Greco-Roman inculturation) and the second major inculturation (the Germanic-tribes inculturation). It is more intense, first, because the process is global. Second, it is more intense because a new issue for the Christian churches that is presently taking place is the officially sanctioned dialogues between Christian churches and non-Christian major religions. This interfacing of various religions, however, is not merely a matter of official dialogues. There are many local and regional dialogues going on today between Christian people and people of other major world religions. These other major religions are primarily parts of non–Euro-American culture, and thus there is not only a religious dimension to these dialogues but also a cultural dimension.[19]

It is obvious that at this moment we are involved in a transcultural and transreligious process that has never before occurred in the Christian era of history. The complexity of this megacultural process must be taken into account. To expect immediate results is out of the question. The issues are far too complex for any quick fix. The prospects are generous, since in this intricate time of dialogue all religions are searching for a clearer and more universal understanding of the transcendent. For too long, even Christianity has been tempted to remain satisfied with its own domesticated household gods —its own *lares et penates.* Today, dialogue, migration, and study have created an interstice in which the household gods of every religion are coming face to face. It is not a comfortable time for those who are charged with looking out for the identity and integrity of the single religions, because their followers are increasingly put into daily contact with followers of other ways in the dialogue of life. Guardians of orthodoxy in all religions fear syncretism and the weakening of communal boundaries. Viewed from another perspective, however, this new world of religious interchange is one of the most interesting periods in human history. Anyone who presumes to know how things will sort themselves out over the next century is either a genius or a fool. What should be clear for Catholics is that theirs is a church that developed organically within the confines of Western culture from the ninth through the nineteenth century. The process was one in which Hellenic and Roman cul-

---

19. It should be noted that Eastern churches have engaged in cultural exchange far more than the Western Roman Catholic Church. From earliest times, the Eastern churches opened the door to vernacular languages in an extensive way, and, with the introduction of languages other than Greek or Syriac, these churches became deeply multicultural.

tures first shaped it, followed by the encounter with Germanic cultures (though one should not forget that Catholicism also encountered and was influenced by cultures as different as the Slavic and the Celtic). The shape of the church's institutions, styles of worship, and spirituality—its very self-understanding—was heavily influenced by a multitude of cultures, but most importantly by adapting Mediterranean Catholicism to fit within Frankish and Germanic cultures in the north. It is almost as true to say that the Catholic Church is a *German* Catholic Church as it is to call it *Roman*, if one is careful to realize that it is called "Roman" not only for cultural reasons but also because of the growing theological conviction that the see of Rome was the see of Peter and that Rome rightly exercised a unique position over all other churches. The theological *legitimacy* of this claim is a matter of no little controversy, but the *fact* that this claim was generally accepted in the West is not.

Since leadership in any human society plays a major role in the self-identity of such a society, an imposed pattern of leadership can hinder the process of cultural adaptation. It is precisely on raising the question of what forms of leadership are culturally appropriate that this volume focuses itself. The challenge of developing culturally appropriate forms of order and ministry in our globalizing world is significant.

By now the reader understands the complexity of the attempt to understand ministry as a part of doing "theology in global perspective." This global perspective must be kept in mind as we move into the next chapters. Indeed, the entire volume is meant to be a reconsideration of order and ministry in the church from the viewpoint or perspective of globalization.

QUESTIONS FOR REFLECTION

1. What are the main characteristics and issues involved in globalization? Can you offer your own evaluation of the beneficial effects and the harmful effects of globalization?

2. What are the main issues that you associate with the word "culture"? How does culture affect the shape of church order and ministry?

3. What does "inculturation" mean today in theological and religious discussions? Is the process of inculturation good or bad? What are the dangers of implementing inculturation in fast-moving times? What are the dangers of not inculturating in such times?

4. How do globalization and culture affect discussions of church leadership?

SUGGESTIONS FOR FURTHER READING AND STUDY

Bellito, Christopher M. *Renewing Christianity: A History of Church Reform from Day One to Vatican II.* Mahwah, N.J.: Paulist Press, 2001. An accessible overview of church reforms and the crises that occasioned them from the earliest days to our own.

• John Paul II, Pope. *Redemptoris Missio,* Encyclical Letter on the Permanent Validity of the Church's Missionary Mandate. Available in many editions; the one published by Orbis Books includes a commentary on the encyclical by Marcello Zago, O.M.I., one of its drafters, and the text of *Dialogue and Proclamation,* issued by the Pontifical Council for Interreligious Dialogue, and a commentary on that document by Jacques Dupuis, S.J. See William R. Burrows, ed., *Redemption and Dialogue* (Maryknoll, N.Y.: Orbis Books, 1993).

Lee, Jung Young. *Marginality: The Key to Multicultural Theology.* Minneapolis: Fortress, 1995.

Matsuoka, Fumitaka, and Eleazar Fernandez. *Realizing the America of Our Hearts.* St. Louis: Chalice Press, 2003.

• Robertson, Roland. *Globalization: Social Theory and Global Culture.* Thousand Oaks, Calif.: Sage, 1992. The classic work on the various ways in which globalization has an impact on religion and vice versa.

Schreiter, Robert J. *The New Catholicity.* Maryknoll, N.Y.: Orbis Books, 1997.

Stiglitz, Joseph E. *Globalization and Its Discontents.* New York: Norton, 2003. A study that seeks to show how globalization has many negative results and how they can be corrected.

2

The Ministry of Jesus

The Foundational Model for All Ministries

THEME AND GOAL OF THIS CHAPTER

THIS CHAPTER SEEKS TO ESTABLISH the basic issues on which a discussion of order and ministry can be built for grappling with these issues in the context of globalization. In other words, this chapter sets the foundation for the remainder of the volume. There are key issues that directly involve contemporary Roman Catholic theology on church order and ministry that need to be considered as foundational. Foundational elements cannot be set to one side, nor can they be minimized. The second and fourth sections of this chapter focus on these Roman Catholic foundational issues. The third section deals with specific issues that directly involve a contemporary globalization beyond the framework of the church. Within the framework of world history, there have always been social, political, and economic issues that one part of the globe has tried to impose on other parts of the globe. Because both travel and communication were often limited in the past history of our earth, globalization in modern terms was limited.

Still there were limited patterns that resemble the modern period. We see this, for instance, in the history of China. From the Qin dynasty (221-207 B.C.E.) to the end of the Qing dynasty (1644-1911 C.E.), a period of twenty-two hundred years, the influence of China on its neighbors could be called a form of globalization, since almost all of East Asia was influenced in some way by Chinese culture, economics, and social structures. During that same period, China had almost no influence on Europe, much less on Africa or the Americas. Even in the Qing dynasty only a modest amount of cultural influence outside the East Asian world began to take place.[1]

---

1. See Jonathan D. Spence, *The Search for Modern China* (New York: W. W. Norton, 1990), especially part 1, "Conquest and Consolidation" (pp. 1-136).

Today globalization is increasingly a major influence on every part of the world. The Chinese example no longer applies. Globalization has become a worldwide reality. Indeed, globalization today not only affects our planet, but, as technological explorations into outer space continue in intensity, our immediate universe is also pulled into the gravity of contemporary globalization.

Because of this increasing global interrelationship, all of the issues in this chapter are basic and all of them provide the foundation for a serious consideration of a globalized Roman Catholic Church in all of its dimensions. The Catholic Church does not exist apart from the actual world, and therefore if the current world is a globalized one, then the Roman Catholic Church, whether comfortably or uncomfortably, is an institution affected by it, as well as affecting it. Indeed, the modern missionary movement, begun by the church in the late fifteenth century, can arguably be called one of the earliest and most important forces in leading to the world as a global reality. As globalization intensified, the importance of local cultures, paradoxically, has also been increasing, and this raises the question whether there is a foundational reality in church life that needs to be taken into account. The answer to that question is that the foundational basis of and model for all church ministry lie in the person and ministry of Jesus himself.

The goal of this chapter is to acquaint readers with that foundational reality and provide a solid substructure on which readers can develop their ideas on order and ministry in the Roman Catholic Church today.

ETYMOLOGY AND MEANING OF ORDER AND MINISTRY

Introducing the Terminology of Church Order

It is not easy to determine the exact theological meaning of either "order" or "ministry." These terms, however, have been an integral dimension of the Christian community since its beginnings. The term "ministry" was much more common in the earliest phase of church development; the term "order" came into use rather slowly. The term "ministry" was deeply important to the first followers of Jesus. The Greek term for ministry is *dikaiosynē*, and the Greek term for minister is *diakonos*, from which the term "deacon" is derived. If there is one aspect of Jesus that the earliest followers remembered, it was the characteristic of service. In the Gospels one reads that Jesus himself said on several occasions: "I have not come to be served, but to serve." In the writings of the New Testament, all of which were originally written in Greek, the terms "serve," "servant," and "service"—all of which are based on the Greek word *dikaiosynē*—appear again and again. One can say that service is truly the primary word that the earliest followers of Jesus used to describe the relational quality of Jesus' actions and his words. Jesus came to serve.

In the Greek text of the New Testament, the term *dikaiosynē* or one of its cognates such as *diakonein* ("to serve") is used 104 times.[2] All of the New Testament authors include this word in one form or another. Each of the New Testament authors provides an understanding of the early Jesus communities, and in all of the accounts the dominance and frequency of *dikaiosynē* indicate that the issue of "service" was key to the understanding of ministry within the church community. The word "service" was selected because the early Christians remembered how Jesus himself had come to serve and not be served. Service as leadership is a Jesus-word. Service-leadership, therefore, has been and remains the most basic foundation for all ministries in the Christian church.

Among the earliest followers of Jesus, the term "order" presented a very different connotation from that of "ministry." In the many scholarly discussions of order in the early Jesus communities, theologians and historians have presented a complicated and at times a conjectural situation. First of all, there is no single Greek word, such as *dikaiosynē*, that designates order in the first communities. Several Greek and Latin words enter into the discussion, which increases the complexity of the situation. Some of these words are as follows.

Lay/cleric. At an early date, the two terms "lay" and "cleric" (in Greek *laikos* and *klērikos*) began to be connected to the term "order" as used in the Christian community. As a result, this interconnection seriously affected the Christian understanding of order. Is there an order (Latin *ordo*) for both a lay person and a clerical person? Or is there an order only for the *klērikos*?

Order/ordination. After the year 200, the term "order" and its cognate "ordination" gradually became used exclusively for the clerical aspect of early Christian ministry. In Greek, the ritual we call ordination is referred to as the laying on of hands, *cheirothesia*. With the ritual of *cheirothesia*, an early Christian was acknowledged to have a distinct place, *topos* or *taxis*, within a local Christian community. Both ordination (in the Latin-speaking churches) and a ritual of *cheirothesia* (in the Greek-speaking churches) gave a certain distinctive and officially acknowledged role to someone for specific ministries within the local community.

---

2. See Kenan Osborne, *The Diaconate in the Christian Church: Its History and Theology* (Chicago: National Association of Diaconate Directors, 1996), 6-15, for a complete listing of New Testament references to *diakonia*.

Sacred/profane. The discussion of order also raises the question of the sacred and the profane. Once again, the terms "sacred" and "profane" began to affect the way in which the term "order" was understood. Are clerics—therefore, those who have been ordained—in some sort of a sacred place, while those who are lay and nonordained remain in a profane place? In the writings of the early medieval church, we read that those who were ordained received sacred orders. Lay men and women did not receive sacred orders even though they were active in some form of ministry. The sacred/profane issue became a major part of the discussion, but only from about 500 C.E. on.

Social order/institutional structure. The term "ordination" makes sense only if there is a social *ordo* or structure into which one is ordained. Consequently, an understanding of the social nature of *ordo* precedes any understanding of a ritualization called ordination. This involves the social structuring of the church itself, which means the institutional aspect of church life.[3] There was, then, a theology of an institutional church already in place before one was able to use the ritualistic term "ordination."

The scholarly discussion of these interconnected terms and their interrelationship with church ministry continues to this present day, and there is no clear explanation for the use, meaning, and existence of these terms during the first two hundred years of church history. Every interpretation of the meaning and application of these terms is to some degree conjectural. Moreover, no single interpretation of these terms is the unchangeable teaching of the Roman Catholic Church.

In fact, as we shall see later, there is no clear indication in the New Testament or in the first two centuries of church history that any of the ministers of the church were ordained or were even considered to be ordained. The reason why the first Jesus communities rejected the term *ordo* (in Greek, *taxis*, from which our word "taxonomy" is derived) lies in the political and social use of the term "order" as used in the Greco-Roman world at the time of Jesus. What the term "order" meant was counter to the Christian understanding of Jesus' ministry as service. Jesus was a minister not because of some order but because of service. Authoritative order was not the key to Jesus' own ministry; service alone provided the early followers of Jesus with the primary ministerial key to the understanding of their own postresurrection ministries. The *Catechism of the Catholic Church* states this quality of service for all Christian ministries as follows:

---

3. See Kenan Osborne, *Ministry: Lay Ministry in the Roman Catholic Church, Its History and Theology* (Eugene, Ore.: Wipf & Stock, 2003), 18-31.

Intrinsically linked to the sacramental nature of ecclesial ministry is *its character as service.* Entirely dependent on Christ who gives mission and authority, ministers are truly "slaves of Christ" (Rom. 1:1), in the image of him who freely took "the form of a slave" for us (Phil. 2:7). Because the word and grace of which they are ministers are not their own, but are given to them by Christ for the sake of others, they must freely become the slaves of all (1 Cor. 9:19). (CCC 876)

Service is clearly the major characteristic of all church mission and ministry. Thus, service, not order, is the lens through which one interprets the true meaning of order, ministry, and leadership as well as cleric and lay. At times, Roman Catholic writers stress the reality of church order, thereby stressing the role of the cleric. As the *Catechism* clearly indicates, it is service that is the intrinsic character that makes Christian service Christian. If one places service in a secondary role with order in the first role, then order itself has lost its right to be the defining characteristic. The *Catechism*'s further use of such a term as "slave" only intensifies the defining characteristic of service for all orders and all ministries in the church.

In the Greco-Roman political and social world at the time of Jesus, there were indeed well-defined orders. Three such orders were of major importance. First, there was the "order of senators." Men who belonged to the senatorial order were generally, if not always, distinguished, well-educated, and respected men from noble and aristocratic families. A set number of such men were selected by their peers to be the senators of Rome, with the responsibility of aiding the emperor in governing not only Rome but the wide reaches of the Roman empire. People who were not in the aristocratic class were called *plebs*; they were plebeian, regarded simply as the people. In the literature of the Roman world at that time, there are only a few instances in which we find mention of an order of plebeians. The idea of such a plebeian order, however, never caught on. Thus, for the Romans in that period, the term "order" was reserved specifically for special authoritative groups, the first of which was the order of senators.

Second, there was in the same political and social system the "order of decurions." Decurions originally were Roman officers in the cavalry who were in charge of ten men (*deka* is the Greek word for ten). In time, however, the decurions were often placed in charge of various geographical areas, such as a neighborhood, a city, or even a larger area. These social and political administrators were called the order of decurions. In this order, we see again a selection of persons who exercise authority.

Third, there was the order of knights, also known as the equestrian order. Those who belonged to this order were military personnel who were skilled in horsemanship and who, because of their skills, were given command or authority over certain groups of soldiers or even over certain geographical areas.

Terminology and Practice in the New Testament and the Early Church

In both the time of Jesus and the time of the earliest Jesus communities when the Roman empire had spread across today's European world, the three orders were well known, and members in all three orders had administrative and punitive powers. We can say, then, that in Roman society of the first two centuries, the term "order" denoted both power and administrative and legal authority. People who were not in one of the three orders were simply called "the people," in Latin *populus* or *plebs*. Because of this connection to power, the early followers of Jesus were highly apprehensive about the term "order," and they did not use it to describe the leadership in their Christian communities. In their view, the term "order" indicated the exact opposite of service. Order indicated power and prestige; service, however, reflected Jesus himself.

Nonetheless, it would be misleading to think that among the earliest followers of Jesus everyone was considered equal, or that the Christian communities were totally egalitarian and democratic groups of men and women. The New Testament does not give any indication that such a democratic spirit governed the early followers of Jesus. In this respect, there was no golden democratic age, when all the followers of Jesus were equal and no one was in authority. Such a golden-age picture is a chimera or a daydream. Rather, there were actual Christian men and women who were considered, at least within one dimension or another, as servant-leaders. Some were servant-leaders in a ministry to the poor and the needy; others were servant-leaders in preaching; still others were servant-leaders in catechizing and teaching. Christian men and women of deep prayer were servant-leaders in spirituality. In a special way, the Twelve (that is, the twelve apostles) received a great deal of honor and respect from the other disciples and followers of Jesus, for, after all, the Twelve had been close to Jesus and knew him well. In the Acts of the Apostles, the apostles play a major leadership role for the first twelve chapters. After that, the Twelve simply disappear from the text. From chapter 13 to chapter 28, it is Paul alone who becomes the major figure. In these chapters of Acts, it is Paul who is presented as the example of a major leader in the early community. The term "apostles," for example, in chapter 15, appears, but they are referred to only in a secondary way.

We also have to admit candidly that early Christian leadership was not totally harmonious. Again, we do not have a golden age in that early period of Christian life, as if the leaders and the people enjoyed idyllic peace with one another. Paul, a leader in his own right, disagreed seriously with Peter, a deeply respected leader. Paul himself had difficulty with another group who belonged to the Jesus community, the Judaizers, who were intent on making Gentile converts follow the Mosaic Law. In Corinth, there were quarrels about who had baptized whom. When we read in Acts that "the whole body of believers was united in heart and soul" (Acts 4:32), we are reading about an idealized community rather than the actual community. The author of Acts frequently paints an ideal community, since his goal is to move his own community to be at peace with one another. From the very beginnings of the Jesus communities down to today there has never been a totally unified gathering of Christian people. Some centuries of Christian life may be considered better and more peaceful than others, but no century, including the initial century, was a time of total unity. Christian leadership has always had its bright side and its shadow side. This was true at the start and remains true today.

An early Latin Christian theologian, Tertullian (ca. 160–ca. 225), who lived in Carthage (in present-day Tunisia), the main city of Roman Africa, began to apply the term "order" to groups within the Christian community. He may not have been the first Christian to do this, but he certainly was the first Christian who made the term part of ordinary Christian language. His influence in this regard was primarily felt in the Western or Latin churches; his influence in the Eastern or Greek-speaking churches was and remains marginal.[4]

Carthage was devastated by the Roman armies in 146 B.C.E. because it had seriously challenged the leadership of Rome. In fact, Carthage came very close to defeating Rome. The damage from the war, which the Roman armies won, was devastating to the entire area of North Africa, of which Carthage was the key city. The infrastructure of the area was completely destroyed, and the Roman senate made sure that Carthage and its environs would never rise up and challenge Roman authority again. In 123 B.C.E., Gaius Gracchus had tried to reestablish a Roman colony in the Carthage area, but the Roman

---

4. See Tertullian, *De Exhortatione castitatis*, in *Tertulliani Opera*, vol. 2, *Opera Montanistica* (Turnholt: Brepols, 1954), 1024-26; Eng. trans. by William P. LeSaint, *Tertullian* (Westminster, Md.: Newman Press, 1951), 53-54. In this work, Tertullian uses the term "lay" eight times. In four other works, Tertullian uses the term "lay" only twice in each work: *De baptismo*, *De fuga in persecutione*, *De monogamia*, and *De praescriptione hereticorum*. Elsewhere he does not use the term "lay" at all. For a computerized listing of words used in Tertullian, see Gösta Claesson, *Index Tertullianeus A-E* (Paris: Études augustiniennes, 1974). For an excellent background of Carthage, see G. Schölligen, *Ecclesia Sordida? Zur Frage der sozialen Schichtung frühchristlicher Gemeinden am Beispiel Karthagos zur Zeit Tertullians* (Münster: Aschendorf, 1984).

senate prevented any lasting outcome for such an endeavor. Only in 44 B.C.E. did Julius Caesar reestablish a Roman colony in the area of Carthage. This colony grew slowly at first, but in the second and third centuries an economic boom began in North Africa, which coincided with the time in which Tertullian was born, grew up, and eventually wrote his theological material. The expanding regrowth of Carthage required governmental structures, and so the leaders in North Africa developed a mirror of the Roman structure, in a threefold ordering: an order of senators, an order of decurions, and an order of knights. In the local Christian community, Tertullian began to use a version of these political and social orders for the church structures themselves. Tertullian began speaking and writing about an order of bishops, an order of priests, and an order of deacons. In many ways, it was Tertullian who, in the second century of the Christian era, brought about a general acceptance of the term "order" within the Western Christian community. At first, the use of the term "order" for ministerial roles in a Christian community was confined to Carthage and its environs. Only gradually did other Christian communities in different areas of the Roman empire take over the use of the term for their Christian leadership. As we move into the third century, the acceptance of the term "order" by Christian communities had begun to take a firm hold.

As far as we know, the ritual of ordination for bishops, priests, and deacons dates from about the year 200. The rituals are included in a document entitled, in English, *Apostolic Tradition*. This document was originally written in Greek, but unfortunately we have only small fragments of the Greek text.[5] In the *Apostolic Tradition*, the Greek word *cheirothesia* (laying on of hands) is the term that applies to order. Up until the present time, scholars have attributed this book to the theologian and presbyter named Hippolytus. Recently, however, his authorship has been seriously questioned.[6] When one analyzes the texts of these ordination rituals, it is clear that a social structure for the church community was already in place. The *episkopos* was the main leader of the Christian community. Presbyters were in a secondary place of leadership, and deacons were also in a different but secondary leadership role. In other words, in the church at Rome there were several levels of leadership. The three ordination rituals are well crafted, which indicates that they preexisted the text itself and that the author of the *Apostolic Tradition* simply included them in his volume. Because these rituals indicate an established liturgical sophistica-

---

5. See *The Apostolic Tradition of Hippolytus*, trans. B. S. Easton (New York: Macmillan, 1934). For background, see Johannes Quasten, *Patrology* (Westminster, Md.: Newman Press, 1953), 1:180-94.

6. There is considerable scholarly discussion on Hippolytus and his authorship of the *Apostolic Tradition*. See Paul Bradshaw, "Ordination," in *The New Westminster Dictionary of Liturgy and Worship*, ed. Paul Bradshaw (Louisville: Westminster John Knox Press, 2002), 342-43.

tion, it would be correct to say that the ordination rituals antedate the book itself by perhaps ten or twenty years. This would place the earliest forms of these rituals around 180 or 190, but not earlier than this. In spite of all the uncertainties over precise dates, one can say that at the very end of the second century and at the beginning of the third century, an ordination ritual was in place and that the threefold leadership of a Christian community (*episkopos, presbyteros*, and *diakonos*) was also in place. However, this structure applies only to the Christian community in Rome. To go beyond Rome and claim that all other Christian communities did the same thing is not warranted.

The most important information that the *Apostolic Tradition* offers is probably that for the first time in church history we have an ordination ritual. Prior to the appearance of this account of ordination, there is no solid indication that an ordination ever took place in the Christian communities. The way in which a person during the earlier period became a leader of a Christian community cannot be clearly identified. Every suggestion is conjectural.

There is evidence beyond Rome, however, not of ordination itself but of the threefold leadership of *episkopos, presbyteros*, and *diakonos*. For instance, Origen, a Greek-speaking theologian from Alexandria, Egypt (ca. 185-253), describes the threefold structure of a Christian community with the *episkopos* at the top, then *presbyteros* and *diakonos*. Moreover, Origen used a term for these leaders that earlier Christian communities had rejected, namely, *hiereus*, the Greek word for priest.

In the New Testament, *hiereus* was used in only three ways. First, as the technical term for the Jewish priests and high priests, *hiereus* is used frequently throughout the New Testament, since Jewish priests appear in many of the accounts about Jesus. *Hiereus* is the proper Greek translation of the Hebrew word for priest, *kôhēn*. In Jewish literature written in Greek at the time of Jesus, Jewish writers also used *hiereus* for the Aramaic term *kôhēn*. For instance, in the Greek translations of the Old Testament called the Septuagint, which was put together by Jewish scholars, the Jewish priest—*kôhēn*— is referred to in Greek as *hiereus*. As a term for a spiritual leader, *hiereus* carried with it at the time of Jesus all the positive and negative aspects of the Jewish priesthood. The postresurrection Jesus communities did not want their leaders to be thought of in these Jewish categories. They did not want the leadership of their communities to reflect the leadership of the Jewish priests. Naturally, this reluctance of the New Testament to use the Greek term for priest for any Christian leader or minister has many implications and has caused problems. Catholics and the Orthodox today call the ministerial leaders of their communities "priests." How is this to be justified? The New Testament rejected, or at least did not use, such terms for its leadership. Can we legitimately say that the Twelve and other major New Testament leaders were ordained priests, when the New Testament itself does not use such terminology for its leadership?

Second, but only in the Letter to the Hebrews, Jesus himself is called *hiereus.* There are many interesting points to be noted about the way the Letter to the Hebrews includes the office of priest in its designation of Jesus. First, Jesus *becomes* priest when he enters into the holy of holies, which in Hebrews means *after* he rose from the dead, ascended into heaven, and came to sit at the right hand of the Father. In the view of the Letter to the Hebrews, Jesus is a *heavenly* priest; he was not a priest while on earth. The Letter to the Hebrews states that Jesus is a priest in the order of Melchizedek. By this the author of Hebrews indicates that Jesus as *hiereus* was one of a kind, in effect implying that he supplants the Jewish temple priesthood. The followers of Jesus, therefore, no longer need that kind of priest, since Jesus is eternally at the right hand of the Father making intercession for the faithful. In the text of the Letter to the Hebrews, Jesus, the one priest, is totally adequate for his followers and there is no need for any other priest. The nature of the priesthood of Jesus as portrayed in Hebrews, in other words, is quite singular. Minimally, this should make one pause to consider whether later Christian literature speaks of the ordination of the Twelve or other male disciples of Jesus as "priests." On the face of the matter, Hebrews does not seem to favor such an interpretation and may even preclude it.

Third, there are three times in which *hiereus* is applied to *all* the followers of Jesus. In 1 Peter 2:4, all believers are urged to "become a holy priesthood." In 1 Peter 2:9 we read, "You are a chosen race, a royal priesthood, a dedicated nation." Revelation 5:10 says, "You [Jesus, the Lamb of God] purchased for God men and women of every tribe and language, people and nation; you made them a royal house, to serve our God as priests; and they shall reign upon earth."

These New Testament texts in which *hiereus* is used for all the baptized followers of Jesus have engendered enormous discussion by Christian scholars over the centuries. Martin Luther and John Calvin stressed that all believers are priests. In 1563, the Council of Trent (in its canons on the sacrament of order) rejected the Reformers' literal identification of all Christians as priests and maintained that only an ordained member of the church could truly be considered, in the strictest sense, a priest (Latin *sacerdos*). The priesthood of the laity, as it came to be called in Roman Catholic literature, was rejected as "Protestant" and therefore wrong. Catholic theologians went out of their way to explain the three passages mentioned above as poetic, analogous, or derivative. These scholars maintained that *hiereus* in its true meaning was applicable only to an ordained person. From 1521, the year Luther was excommunicated, down to Vatican II, the notion of a priesthood of all believers became an apologetic issue, and interpretations of these three New Testament passages continually reflected either a Protestant or a Catholic bias.

In the 1960s, however, the bishops at Vatican II officially reinstated the New Testament understanding of the priesthood of all believers as a critical part of church ministry and in so doing were acting to recognize the importance of the Reformers' insights. According to the conciliar documents, all baptized and confirmed followers of Jesus are members of the common priesthood (LG 10-13). The theological understanding of the ministerial priesthood that the documents of Vatican II present can be understood only on the basis of the common priesthood of all believers. The ministry of the ordained priest is one of service to the common priesthood of all believers.

Besides these three groups of people, the New Testament does not call anyone else a priest. Nowhere in the entire New Testament is a leader of the Jesus communities ever designated as *hiereus*. In the minds and hearts of the early Jesus communities, the term *hiereus* was rejected as a term for a specific Christian minister, because in the Jewish and the Greco-Roman world of that time, *hiereus* was connected with the exercise of power and was not seen as connected primarily to service.

Only toward the end of the second century did the rejection of *hiereus* by the Christian community begin to be reversed. Slowly the Greek word began to designate the sacred leaders of the early Christian communities. This was a major step for the development of the social structure of the early church. Two sources indicate this hieratic change. The first is the Syriac writing *Didascalia Apostolorum* ("The Teaching of the Apostles"). That document appears to date from the first decades of the third century and was addressed to a Christian community in the northern part of Syria. Although it was written in Greek, only a few passages or fragments of the Greek text remain. The complete work is known only in a Syriac translation.[7] In this work, the *episkopos* is referred to as high priest, *archiereus*. Throughout the work there is a strong anti-lay emphasis. The *episkopos* alone is in charge of the Christian community.

The second source is Origen, who was mentioned above. From Origen on,

---

7. On the *Didascalia Apostolorum*, see Quasten, *Patrology*, vol. 2, 147-52. See also Hans von Campenhausen, *Ecclesiastical Authority and Spiritual Power in the Church of the First Three Centuries*, trans. J. A. Baker (Stanford, Calif.: Stanford University Press, 1969), 239-47; R. Hugh Connolly, *Didascalia Apostolorum* (Oxford: Clarendon Press, 1929).

many Christian writers began to equate the office of the leader of the Christian community with the priesthood of Aaron.[8] Origen himself, however, did not make this connection in a literal way. For Origen, the allegorical understanding of the Old Testament was paramount. The priesthood of Aaron was a faint shadow of what priesthood in Jesus truly means. Nonetheless, in various places Origen does not hesitate to describe the actual situation of *episkopoi* in his own time. For example:

- The most sordid methods of intrigue and demagogy are brought into play as soon as there is a chance of snatching an office, especially the highest and most lucrative office, that of bishop (*Homily on Numbers* 9.1; 22.4).
- Clergy brag about their seniority (*Homily on Genesis* 3.3).
- They try to ensure that their children or relatives will succeed them (*Homily on Numbers* 22.4).
- Such clergy are in fact serving Pharaoh rather than God (*Homily on Genesis* 16.5).
- These tyrants will not take advice even from their equal, much less from a layman or a pagan (*Homily on Exodus* 11.6).

These are indeed harsh judgments on the *episkopoi* of Origen's time. On the other hand, Origen the educator sees the ideal *episkopos* as a spiritual teacher whose life and words reflect the message of Jesus. When he speaks of this ideal picture of an *episkopos*, his words are words of service, care, compassion, wisdom, love, and high standards. What an *episkopos* should be ideally is one thing; what many *episkopoi* are in practice was quite a different thing. In contrast to the *Didascalia Apostolorum*, Origen is not canonical or juridical in outlook. Origen is not reiterating legal issues; rather, his view of *episkopos* is deeply spiritual.[9]

The power of the *episkopos*, *presbyteros*, and *diakonos* is, in his view, not a canonical or juridical power. It is the power of the Logos, the Word of God, and the Spirit of Jesus. Origen's ideal description of church ministers is part of his educational endeavor; he wants to instruct the Christian leadership of his day on the deepest meaning of service-leadership in the church. Origen's writings indicate that a threefold church ministry, *episkopos*, *presbyteros*, and *diakonos*, had developed in Alexandria and its environs. Even when we connect this threefold Alexandrian church leadership to the threefold Roman

---

8. For a comprehensive overview of Jewish priestly leadership as found in the Old Testament, see Günther Bornkamm "πρεσβυς – πρεσβυτερος" [*presbys – presbyteros*], in *Theological Dictionary of the New Testament*, ed. Gerhard Friedrich (Grand Rapids: Eerdmans, 1968), 6:651-83.

9. See von Campenhausen on Origen, *Ecclesiastical Authority*, 248-64. The tone in the *Didascalia* and in Origen's writings may be different, but the overall picture of church authority is very similar.

church leadership, we cannot generalize. We cannot state that by 200 the entire Christian community had a threefold church leadership. The dominance of a threefold church leadership came about through a lengthy process. In the *Apostolic Tradition* and in the texts of Origen we see its earliest attestation. Eventually the triadic form of church leadership did become standard, but throughout the first half of the third century this process appears only in its earliest stages.

During the first decades of the third century, in which the terms *hiereus* and "order" became descriptive of Christian ministry, a third factor began to take place. The combination of *hiereus* and order led, little by little, to the interpretation of the ordained church leadership as a social structure in the church *based on sacred power*. The climax of this development from a *service-oriented* understanding of church leadership to a *power-oriented* understanding of ordained church leadership was reached at the end of the twelfth century, when priesthood was theologically defined as an order that confers the power to consecrate bread and wine into the body and blood of Jesus and the power to forgive sin. In medieval Western theology, the Latin word *potestas* ("power") was deliberately chosen. The process began in the third century, but theologically the power interpretation of priesthood became the acceptable Western definition of priest as a man with spiritual power only at the end of the twelfth century and the beginning of the thirteenth century. The power interpretation of priesthood remained dominant in the Western church until the Second Vatican Council. In a later section of this book, we will see how the bishops at Vatican II officially brought about a major change, in which power was not the central focus of order and priest. The bishops at Vatican II returned to the service-oriented understanding of priesthood.

In summary, we can say that three things took place almost simultaneously. First, in North Africa Tertullian applied the term "order" to a threefold church leadership structure (*episkopos*, *presbyteros*, and *diakonos*). Second, in Rome, Hippolytus presented an ordination ritual to establish church ministerial leadership. Third, we have the author of the *Didascalia Apostolorum* and the theologian Origen, who began using the Greek term *hiereus* to designate the main leaders of the Christian community. All of this represents a major restructuring of Christian leadership, using terms and rituals that one does not find either in the New Testament or in the earliest histories of the Jesus communities.[10]

---

10. An older but still useful accounting of the early vocabulary for church ministry is found in *The Sacrament of Holy Orders* (Collegeville, Minn.: Liturgical Press, 1962). This volume includes papers and discussions concerning holy orders presented in 1955 at Centre de Pastorale Liturgique. From

It is necessary, however, to say that in the first use of the term "order," in the first extant ordination ritual, and in the initial use of the term *hiereus*, the structural church orders and the related ordination rituals continued to stress the issue of service as the primary and operative task of the designated church leaders. Only in the course of time, during the fourth to twelfth centuries, do the theological discussion of holy orders and the more developed rituals for ordination take on a different form. They slowly began to express the meaning of priesthood and episcopacy in terms of power rather than service. The historical development of this change in emphasis occurred at first in a slow and localized way. One area of the Christian world took certain steps which another area only later accepted. Other moments of change may have taken place in a different area, and these moments were perhaps not replicated at all in other Christian communities. In other words, some local changes in ritual simply died out, while other local changes remained and became more generalized. The process, however, was basically brought about by a local church doing one thing, which gradually was picked up by another local church, which was then replicated in yet another local church, and so on. Slowly, changes became regional in nature, and in time became universal in the Western church. Throughout this process, from 200 to 1100, there was no central church administration which had oversight of these changes. The processes took place at the local level in many places. They then became evident when accepted in wider, regional levels. Local and regional leadership was certainly involved in all of this, but there was no central church administrator that managed or approved these theological and ritualistic changes. During those centuries, the papacy did not direct, allow, reject, or shape these processes of liturgical and theological development on a universal church-wide basis. On the other hand, the church of Rome was in contact with churches in surrounding areas and had influence on how what we now think of as central Italy adapted to life there.

Medieval and Later Developments in Theology and Terminology

In the twelfth century, a common Western theological meaning of ordination, order, and priesthood was established, which centered on three distinct issues, order, highest order, and power.

---

these presentations and discussions one sees how tenuous the early data truly are, and how there was a gradual development both in ordination rituals and in theology itself regarding the meaning of *episkopos*, *presbyteros*, and *diakonos*, and their Latin counterparts. See especially P. M. Gy, "Notes on the Early Terminology of Christian Priesthood," 98-115.

Order

Sacred orders included a chronological and hierarchical process of movement. A man began with tonsure, which generally was not considered an order. Only then did he move through the stages of sacred orders. First, there were successively the orders of porter, exorcist, lector, and acolyte. These were commonly described as minor orders.[11] After these four orders, a person moved to the major orders of subdeacon, deacon, and priest. There were seven orders in all. It was this development of four minor orders and three major orders that dominated a theology of order and priesthood from the end of the twelfth century to Vatican II. This view of order and priesthood, during that long stretch of time, came to be seen as the ordinary teaching of the Roman Catholic Church.[12]

The Highest Order

For the majority of scholastic theologians, priesthood was considered the highest of all sacred orders. Being a bishop—or exercising "episcopacy"—was not considered a sacred order. In the scholastic view, episcopacy was an ecclesial office or the conferral of higher dignity on a priest. In the medieval context, it should be recalled, the level of dignity one enjoyed was not a small matter. In the late twelfth century and at the beginning of the thirteenth century, this view of ordination was challenged and debated. By the mid-thirteenth century, for all practical purposes, the theological position that priesthood was the highest of all sacred orders had become the common or standard theological teaching. In the *Four Books of Sentences*, written by Peter Lombard (ca. 1100-1160), the theological position that priesthood was the highest order and that episcopacy was an office that conferred dignity was strongly advocated. In the theological departments of the medieval universities, Peter Lombard's book became the textbook, and therefore his view of sacred orders became the accepted theological view. Thomas Aquinas, Bonaventure, and the majority of other scholastic theologians adopted Peter Lombard's approach, and their status made the position that priesthood was the highest order the dominant view. Three hundred years later, the bishops at the Council of Trent officially subscribed to the view of priesthood as the highest sacred order.[13]

---

11. The selection of four minor orders did not develop in a uniform way. Some regional areas had more than four such orders, while other regions had fewer. Slowly, the Christian church settled on the four minor orders, and by the eleventh century the four minor orders had become fairly standard.

12. For the minor orders and the way they developed, see John St. H. Gibaut, *The Cursus Honorum: A Study of the Origins and Evolution of Sequential Ordination* (New York: Peter Lang, 2000).

13. The Council of Trent did not define this view that priesthood was the highest of the sacred

In the late medieval period in the Western, Roman church, episcopal office came to be seen as ideally conferred by the pope. Nevertheless, in practice, emperors, kings, and princes had a major say in who could become a bishop. As a dignity, episcopacy was often conferred in the Western church by the pope, but, in many cases, bishops were still chosen by the political governmental leaders. Since the office and dignity of episcopacy were conferred by a human being—the pope—episcopacy was viewed as different from the sacramental priesthood as such. In the sacrament of holy orders (the common English translation of the Latin *sacramentum ordinis,* which literally means "sacrament of order"), the common and standard teaching is that God gives the grace and the tasks. Theologians have a technical name for this divine action of God, *vi sacramenti,* that is, "by virtue of the sacrament itself." In a sacrament it is God's own action that confers priestly commission and power. The ordaining bishop does not confer this priestly power. As a God-given commission and power through *vi sacramenti,* no human being, not even the pope, can change, minimize, or remove such a commission and power.[14]

Since an installation of a bishop was not considered part of the sacrament of holy orders, the dignity and office that one received were given not *vi sacramenti*—in virtue of the sacrament—but rather *vi delegationis*—by way of delegation. In this situation, a human being has delegated someone to an office and dignity. As a result, human beings, such as the pope, can change, minimize, and even remove the person from the office and from the dignity. In the history of the church, papal removal of a person from episcopacy has occurred, but only on the rarest of occasions. A bishop's power, commission, and dignity, however, have on many occasions been reduced and minimized.

Vi sacramenti, in theological teaching, means that what is given by God in a sacrament cannot be changed by any human being. Thus, when one is baptized and confirmed, no human person can "de-baptize" or "de-confirm" him or her. What God has done, God has done. So, too, in the case of priesthood. It is God who ordains, not a human being, and this is an action of God *vi sacramenti.* Once a person is ordained, he has the power to celebrate the eucharist and the power to forgive sin. An ordained priest might be excommunicated and even expelled from the church, but if the excommunicated priest celebrates the eucharist, the Mass is still valid. If he celebrates the

---

orders; rather, the bishops presented the view only as the ordinary view of the Roman Catholic Church. After the Council of Trent, theologians remained free to argue that episcopacy should be seen as the highest order.

14. *Vi sacramenti* became a standard approach in the manuals of theology; see Joseph A. de Aldama, "De Sacramentis," *Sacrae Theologiae Summa,* vol. 4 (Madrid: BAC, 1962), 50ff.

sacrament of penance, a person's sins are truly forgiven. Naturally, he has celebrated both sacraments without permission, but the validity of the sacraments has been steadfastly maintained in official church teaching. The reason for this is *vi sacramenti*. What God confers through a sacramental celebration can never be taken away or minimized by any human being. The power given is sacrosanct.

This is not true, however, in the case of *vi delegationis* ("by the power of delegation"). "Delegation" depends on the giver, and what is given can also be taken back. Following this view of the conferral of episcopal office, the understanding was one of giver and the gift. After the twelfth century, the delegation of a bishop by the pope took on a life of its own. The bishop slowly but surely came to be considered a vicar of the pope. He received episcopal rank from the pope, a rank in the feudal social order that was thought to be received *vi delegationis* (by delegation) from the pope. Consequently, the bishop was thought to represent the pope in the district where he was bishop. Even the Council of Trent in the sixteenth century did nothing to change this theological perception. Episcopacy, according to the Council of Trent, was not an aspect of the sacrament of holy orders as such. The bishops at Trent did not define what a bishop is. Rather, the council fathers allowed the theologians to continue their discussion on the theological meaning of bishop. After the Council of Trent, most Western theologians continued to see the bishop as one who had received an office and a dignity from the pope. In the post-Reformation period, bishops more and more were considered vicars of the pope, and many bishops deliberately nourished this self-identity as personally representing the pope. For many bishops, their greatest sense of identity was this close and vicarious union with the pope.

The bishops at Vatican II followed subsequent theological and historical insights when they took a different direction in explaining episcopal office. What occurred at Vatican II is rooted in historical studies that began early in the twentieth century and reached maturity in certain conclusions in the middle of the twentieth century. In this emerging consensus, a large number of theologians and historians believed that episcopacy ought to be considered the highest order in a threefold understanding of the sacrament of holy orders (the *sacramentum ordinis*). At first, their view was simply considered a new theological "opinion." The bishops at Vatican II, however, adopted this new approach and officially stated that episcopacy was the highest order— the fullness of priesthood—in the sacrament of holy orders (LG 21). The council fathers at Vatican II did not argue or elaborate on the grounds for their teaching. Rather, they state that this view is basic to the council's teaching:

The Sacred Council teaches that by episcopal consecration the fullness of the sacrament of orders is conferred, that fullness of power, namely, which both in the Church's liturgical practice and in the language of the Fathers of the Church is called the high priesthood, the supreme power of the sacred ministry. (LG 21)

The statement of Vatican II on bishops is the first authoritative teaching by the magisterium on the nature of episcopacy in relation to the sacrament of holy orders.

We can diagram this changing role of bishop in the Western church as follows:

Theological Status of Episcopacy through the Ages	
From 200 to 1150:	In the West, episcopacy was generally considered the highest ranking in the sacrament of holy orders.
From 200 to the present:	In the East, episcopacy was always considered the highest ranking in the sacrament of holy orders.
From 1150 to 1962:	In the West, episcopacy was not considered part of the sacrament of holy orders.
Since 1962:	In the West, episcopacy is recognized as the highest order in the sacrament of holy orders.

Conferring Power

In the Western theology that developed from the twelfth century onward, the essence of the sacrament of holy orders was understood to be as a conferral of power.[15] Each order provisioned a person with a certain power in the church. For example, in the case of the so-called minor orders, the power to open the church doors was conferred on those ordained to order of porter; the power to cast out devils, on those ordained to the order of exorcist; the

---

15. The clearest expression of the idea that the sacrament of order chiefly involves the conferral of power prior to Vatican Council II is to be found in the canons of the Council of Trent (1545-1563). See "Canons on the Sacraments in General" (DS, session 7, nos. 1601-13; session 23, nos. 1763-78). For an English translation of these texts, see DN, 413-15 (on the sacraments in general) and 543-47 (on the sacrament of order).

power to proclaim the Word of God, on those ordained to the order of lector; the power to assist at the altar during Mass, on those ordained to the order of acolyte. In the so-called major orders of subdeacon, deacon, and priest, the powers conferred were understood in relation to the centrality of the eucharist. In the case of priesthood, powers to celebrate the eucharist and to forgive sins were conferred and were the powers that defined priesthood. In other words, power became the primary theological understanding of the sacrament of orders, whereas in the early church and throughout many centuries thereafter service had been the primary theological focus.

By contrast, the bishops at Vatican II restored *service* to God's people as the focal image in relation to which priesthood is understood. The same was true for the office of bishops, as episcopacy is seen as an integral aspect of the sacrament of order. We have seen this focus on service above in the citation from the *Catechism of the Catholic Church,* which insists that ministry is intrinsically marked by the character of service (CCC 876). In this citation, the *Catechism* echoes the documents of Vatican II.

With the primary identification of power as part of the structure of orders and of the meaning of the ordination ritual, the Christian church itself as a society began to separate its membership into two major groups. The first group included clerics, that is, those who received through ordination a spiritual power over various churches. The second group, the remainder of the Christians, was similar to the Roman people, the *populus*, as mentioned above.

From the fourth to ninth centuries, however, the Christian community was never divided into two groups: cleric and lay. During these centuries, the divisions in the Christian community were far more complex. There were indeed clerics, and they belonged to an order. However, there were also the emperors and the emperors' family and close blood-related associates. They too belonged to an order: the imperial order. The emperor claimed his position as an appointment from God. From the coronation of Pepin down to Pope Gregory VII (1073-85), there was a powerful and almost universal affirmation of the divine right of emperors and kings. There is an abundance of theological material justifying this imperial divine right. During the early Middle Ages, the emperor was never considered in any way a layperson. This applied both to the eastern emperors and, later, to the western emperors. In the next section of this chapter, I will present in more detail the historical issues involved in this imperial theology.

Moreover, the rise of monasticism brought about a whole new group of Christians in spiritual leadership, whose contemporary successors we call "religious." Again, in the first millennium monks and nuns were never considered lay. Only from the twelfth century on was the Western church canonically and then theologically divided into two groups: cleric and lay. Prior to the twelfth century, the division of the Western Christian population was fourfold: emperor, cleric, monk/nun, and Christians generally. Any attempt to reduce these four groups to two is simplistic. From the first centuries of the Christian church to the twelfth century, there were four groups, not two, and this fourfold grouping can be seen in the way the church operated during the entire first millennium. The canonical nicety of lay/cleric is an imposition that came into the church only at the beginning of the second millennium.

Although ministry, or service, is the original linguistic description of Jesus' life and teaching, and although the original descriptive or iconic picture of Jesus, which reflected this understanding of ministry, was that of Jesus washing the feet of the disciples, the gradual use of order in the structures of the Christian church altered both the focus and the intent of church leadership. Power, not service, slowly began to be seen as the primary theological mark of distinction between those who were in positions of Christian leadership and those who were not. This change did not happen all at once. It took a long period of time and development, from the third century to the twelfth century, before power became the common theological distinguishing mark of the cleric.

This development indicates only one of many theological changes in the meaning of bishop, priest, and deacon.[16] Instead of an apron, a towel, and a bowl of water, the iconic image became manifold: there was, for instance, a giving of the book of the Gospels to those who were ordained. This indicated that they should preach, but it also came to be seen as a sign that the clerics were the official interpreters of the Word of God. In some ordination rituals, there was another sign. The candidates for ordination knelt in front of the bishop and placed their hands into the hands of the bishop. They then audibly pledged their obedience to the bishop. This was a sign of collegiality and unity, but it also came to be seen as a sign of episcopal authority. There was, in ordination rituals, a handing over of chalice, paten, wine, and bread, and this was clearly a symbol of eucharistic centering. But it also came to be seen as a power to consecrate, a power that no one else in the church had. Both words and icons indicate a slow but changing understanding of church leadership.

---

16. See Kenan Osborne, *Priesthood: A History of the Ordained Ministry in the Roman Catholic Church*, (Eugene, Ore.: Wipf & Stock, 2002), 200-218.

Over the past two millennia the meaning and the description of both order and ministry have continued to change. Today, Roman Catholics generally associate the term "order"—when it is used in a church context—with bishops, priests, and deacons. These three groups of people, and only these three groups, are the ones who, in the Catholic Church, are considered ordained Christians. Their ordination takes place through one of the seven sacraments, the sacrament of holy orders. Today, in the Catholic Church, bishops, priests, and deacons are also considered to be the hierarchy and the clergy. All other Catholic Christians are generally referred to as lay or the laity. For many contemporary Catholic people, the Roman Catholic Church has only two classes of members: the clergy and the laity.

In reality, however, there exists *de facto* if not *de jure* yet another group of Catholics, as was mentioned above. These are the Catholics we call the religious. This term "religious" includes, at least in a general understanding of the term, nuns, sisters, monks, and brothers. Even this grouping of religious has further divisions that are more specific. These further and more specific divisions of religious include, for instance, Jesuits, Franciscans, Dominicans, Benedictines, etc. These groups are officially called either religious orders or religious communities. If the Roman Catholic Church has only two classes of members, the clergy and the laity, one can easily ask: How do the religious fit into the twofold division? For many Catholics, these religious seem to be a sort of half-way group between clergy and laypeople. Male religious are commonly called clerical, since most members of orders, such as Jesuits, Franciscans, and Dominicans, are priests. Such religious priests are indeed clergy. But other members of such orders are not ordained, and logically these religious men should be called lay. Such religious orders and communities are, accordingly, a hybrid, clergy-lay form of approved life.

In canon law the division becomes immensely complicated. Some religious communities are canonically considered only lay. This canonical, lay-only group includes all women religious (sisters, nuns, and cloistered women). Even though they are called religious, they are in a canonical sense laypeople, not clergy. The reason for this has nothing to do with their status as women religious. It is not their status as religious that makes them canonically lay. Rather, it is their status as *women* that make them canonically ineligible to be called clergy. Canonically, no women can be called clerics or be part of the clergy, for the clergy is an all-male group within the Roman Catholic Church.

Some religious groups of men are also canonically considered lay religious groups, since in their regulations all members must be lay. These religious groups do not accept ordained men into their religious communities. The

Christian Brothers are an example of this kind of canonical religious group. All Christian Brothers are canonically laymen. The Christian Brothers do not accept priests into their religious community. On the other hand, some religious groups of men who are canonically considered lay religious groups include a few men religious who are indeed ordained. The nonordained men in these lay religious groups are lay, while the ordained men in these same lay religious groups are clergy. The group as a whole, however, even with its clerical members, remains canonically part of the laity.

Nonetheless, some groups of male religious, such as the Jesuits and the Dominicans, are officially called "clerical religious orders." Nevertheless, although they are called clerical orders, these religious communities often include a large number of fully vowed male members who are canonically a part of the laity. The opposite also holds. There are some groups of male religious who are not called clerical orders, for example, the Marianists. Nonetheless, these nonclerical religious orders have a number of men in their group who are Marianist priests.

Although a religious order or community is called a clerical order, this same religious community has fully vowed members who are not clerics. A layperson, in this instance, officially belongs to a clerical order but personally is not a cleric. The opposite is also true. Canon law has ways of making the twofold division very complicated. By this time, the reader may be certainly mystified. You are not the first to feel this way. From the earliest beginnings of monasticism among the Egyptian monks, the leadership of the church found it difficult to define the place of religious men and women in the church.[17] The above description of religious life is canonical. In the next section, I will indicate in more detail the historical issues involved with the rise of monasticism and religious life.

With this basic but oversimplified understanding of orders and the ministries of the ordained members of such communities in mind, let us consider more carefully two specific understandings of order and ministry. Both positions have been and still are, to some extent, major theological and canonical positions regarding order and the ministry of order. This twofold way of considering order and ministry was very popular from the twelfth century to Vatican II. Since Vatican II there has been a second, but less clear understanding of the terms "order" and "ministry."

---

17. For background on the issue of religious orders and congregations, see Philip Sheldrake, "Religious Orders and Congregations," in *Encyclopedia of Catholicism*, ed. Richard McBrien (San Francisco: HarperSanFrancisco, 1995), 1099-1102; also Juliana Casey, "Religious Life" and "Religious Orders," in *The New Dictionary of Theology*, ed. Joseph Komonchak, Mary Collins, and Dermot Lane (Wilmington, Del.: Michael Glazier, 1987), 868-75.

Understanding Ministry from 1100 to Vatican Council II

Between 1130 and about 1140, John Gratian, a monk teaching canon law in the Italian city of Bologna, compiled a series of important canon laws and related sources and texts, to which he added his own comments. This book was probably the most complete and the most scientifically organized collection of church laws ever written up to that time. Gradually, in the decades following 1140, Gratian's book, entitled *Concordia Discordantium Canonum* ("The Concordance of Discordant Canons"), became the standard canon law textbook. It was used as such in Catholic colleges, universities, and seminaries, until the publication of the first official *Code of Canon Law* in 1917. In his book, Gratian took the stance that there are only two classes of Christians: clergy (hierarchy) and laity. Since his book was the authority on legal matters from the end of the twelfth century to the beginning of the twentieth century in the Western or Roman Catholic Church, it is possible to say that for nearly eight hundred years his canonical construction dominated the practical theology of the Catholic Church. In his conception, the church is two-tiered: clerical (the corps of the ordained) and lay (everyone else). In that view the minority in the clergy was considered to enjoy authority over the others and there was minimal involvement of the laity in the official ministry of the church. Neither the clerical/lay vocabulary nor the two-tiered view of the church is to be found in the New Testament or in the earliest Christian communities. This is the first thing to note.

The second thing to note is that the development of monasticism in the fourth century began to influence the understanding of both Christian ideals and the way in which leadership ministries were exercised in both the Eastern (Greek) and Western (Latin) church. We consider first the development of male and female monasticism. Saint Anthony of Egypt (d. ca. 356) is generally considered the founder of monasticism. Nevertheless, before Anthony of Egypt, there were already Christian men and women who removed themselves from everyday life and devoted themselves almost exclusively to prayer, meditation, and good works. These Christians led a celibate life. In several fourth-century papyri we find, for the first time, the Greek word *monachos*, from which the term "monk" is derived. The Greek word *monos* means "alone" or "solitary." These individuals generally lived alone as hermits and over time gradually formed themselves into communities. Thus began the move toward "monastic" life, in which monks ("solitaries") who lived close to other monks became a group living in what we today call monasteries. In them, a number of celibate persons live a life apart from ordinary social life and dedicate themselves almost exclusively to prayer and manual labor. Many other religious traditions have similar groups, including Buddhists and Daoists, each of which has male and female monastics. At the time of Jesus, there was an analogous form of life in which Jewish Essenes lived a communal life and dedicated themselves to a life based totally on the Torah, cultivating ritual purity in expectation of God's appearance on earth.

In terms of Christian monasticism, Egypt became the center of an extremely powerful and important monastic movement. Numerous monasteries in the desert areas of the upper Nile housed several hundreds of monks. In the first five centuries of the Christian church, the monastic movement spread rapidly throughout Egypt, Palestine, Syria, Asia Minor, Italy, Spain, North Africa, and Gaul. From the fifth century on, monasteries grew in Ireland, Wales, Scotland, and England. By the ninth century the movement had spread into modern-day Germany and onward into central Europe. In fact, these monasteries became the center of the missionary expansion of the church. In many areas, in fact, the erection of dioceses with their own bishops followed the foundation of the church by monks.

Monasteries served as local churches. Once you entered the monastery, your entire life was spent within the confines of the monastery, and even if your work might take you outside the monastery for long periods of time, the monastery was your real home, and monastic life taught you what Christianity was about. The monastery, in effect, was your church. It is important to realize that at the beginning of and even late into the 700s, almost all monasteries were organized, administered, and structured by laypersons. The few clerics who became monks celebrated the eucharist for the monastic community, but for the remainder of their time, the clerics were simply monks, working as all did, with no special consideration. Second, in most cases, the bishops had no control over the monasteries, and thus the monasteries were independent churches within a diocese. Needless to say, the bishops were not always happy with this arrangement.

In reading the history of early monasticism, one might ask whether monks were considered clergy or laity. Such a question is, of course, being asked of an earlier period from the point of view of the present situation. The danger is that we read into the former situation conditions from our own day, presuming the categories of a later, two-tiered, clergy/lay church. In the earliest period, monks were not considered either clerics or lay. They were *monks*. Christian people themselves did not regard the monks as either clergy or lay. They were monks and they were holy people. In reality, monks and monastic nuns were thought of as a *third category* or *division* within the Roman Catholic Church. The word *ordo* (English "order") would be applied to them and would evolve eventually to the modern use of the term to designate communities such as the Sisters of Mercy as "religious orders." This is one of the reasons why Gratian's twofold division is not an adequate reflection of historical realties during most of the first millennium of Christian church history. That history is far more complex than theology influenced by canon law suggests.

There is a second fact that further complicates the cleric/lay categorization —the *position of the emperor*. His exalted position was acknowledged not only by society generally, but also by the Roman Catholic Church from very early on. At first, the focus was on the Byzantine emperor, who had his western residences in Ravenna and Milan and his eastern residence in Constantinople. He was regarded as the divinely chosen person who ruled both society and church. In the eighth century, after years of honoring the Byzantine emperors, Pope Gregory II (715-731) wrote to the then Byzantine emperor, Leo III, stating that the center of gravity of the Western Christian world had begun to shift to the inner west. This did not imply that in the eighth century a split had occurred between East and West or that Gregory II was urging such a split. Rather, the western part of the empire had been left to fend for itself and defend itself. Since the eastern emperor had enough to do taking care of the east, the major issues of the western part of his empire were not high on his agenda. In the same eighth century, the Merovingian kings had begun to assume leadership in Gaul (France). Pope Gregory III (731-741) began dealing with the Frankish kings rather than the emperor in Constantinople. This in itself did not occasion the eleventh-century split between East and West. But it was a signal of the way in which the pope, the bishop of Rome, was centering his concerns on developments in the West. Over time, the *practical* drawing apart of the two halves of the empire became formal.

The emperors, both in the east and in the west, were considered to reign by divine right, as ones chosen by God to exercise an office that was both sacred and secular, although no one at the time would have used that exact terminology. In this view, the emperor was certainly not a layperson, nor was the emperor a cleric. He was in a class by himself. In the imperial coronation liturgy, found in the *Ordo* of Mainz (ca. 960), we read that the emperor ascends the throne because of his right of inheritance and also more importantly and more directly by the authority of almighty God. It was God who selected and consecrated the emperor; he was emperor by divine right. There is an abundance of literature on the divine right of emperors and kings, written by scholars from 800 to 1100. The coronation of the Holy Roman Emperor almost became one of the sacraments of the Roman Catholic Church. The emperor's position both in the Eastern churches and in the

Western churches further complicates the twofold division of all Catholics into clergy and lay.

In actuality, during the first millennium of the Catholic Church, there was a fourfold division: cleric, emperor, monk, and layperson. It is for this reason that one can say that only from 1100 to Vatican II was the twofold division of all Christians generally accepted. From about 1100 onward, the role of the emperor, especially in the West, was challenged by the papacy. At the same time, Europe began to split into a number of kingdoms, and at times the Holy Roman Emperor, who was one of these kings, had little control over the wider European world. The year 1100 should not be taken as the exact date in which the fourfold division of members of the Christian world ended and the twofold division began. One can only say that around 1100, circum stances began to change and that two to three centuries later, a Western king or emperor was not seen as appointed by divine right to rule over the church. The transition was long and painful. It moved faster in certain areas of Europe and at a snail's pace in others. During this period of struggle, the papacy wanted to dispel any competitive divine-right positioning of a social and political leader having authority over the church. Only the pope had been given that power by divine right. Two divine-right leaders could not help but engender a bitter contest, which has been called the lay-investiture contest. In reality, the issue went deeper than investiture. The deeper issue was the struggle between emperor and pope and their respective claims to have universal authority by divine right. Investiture was only a symptom of the controversy over the divine right of the papacy and that of the emperor-king When one investigates the period carefully, it is clear that popes were not above trying to extend their authority into matters we today consider secular. Neither popes nor kings nor emperors willingly gave up power they had become accustomed to exercising.

The Understanding of Holy Orders Emerging at Vatican Council II

By an overwhelming majority, the bishops at Vatican II decided to construct the first four chapters of the Dogmatic Constitution on the Church, *Lumen Gentium,* by entitling its major parts as follows: Chapter 1, on the Mystery of the Church; Chapter 2, on the People of God; Chapter 3, on the Church as Hierarchical; and Chapter 4, on the Laity.

Before the final voting, the bishops had long and heated discussions on the precise structuring of these four chapters. All the bishops agreed that chapter 1, on the mystery and identity of the church, should have first place. That chapter's initial position was never in doubt. Chapters 2 and 3 became the focus of debate, discussion, argument, and controversy. A minority of bishops wanted the present chapter 3 on the hierarchy to be chapter 2. In this way, they argued, chapter 2 would be a direct step from the theological mystery of the church to Jesus' institution of the church through his selection of the Twelve as bishops and his positioning of Peter as the supreme leader to the entire church. Clearly, their view was the more traditional. Some bishops also cited Gratian's position, which, as we have seen, had dominated theological and canonical thinking on the structure of the church's membership from 1140 to 1962. The majority of bishops, however, wanted first to describe what *all* Christians held in common before discussing how the ordained hierarchy and the laity were to be distinguished. Chapter 2, on the nature of the people of God, is precisely a statement on what all Christians are from their baptism on. It teaches that all the baptized are, first of all, the people of God. Only on this basis can one move on to speak about ordained clerics and laypeople. To place the chapter on the people of God in the third spot, the majority maintained, would indicate that the hierarchy or clergy are not first, foremost, and most importantly *a* part of the people of God before one thinks of their ministerial role as something exercised *from within* the people of God. Angel Antón writes:

> [In this essay] we have insisted on another profound change—called Copernican by Yves Congar—that was introduced by the Council with the insertion in *Lumen gentium* of Chapter II on the People of God before Chapter III on the ecclesiastical ministry. The reach of this decision, taken when the writing of the *Lumen gentium* was almost finished, did not find adequate expression in the Constitution itself . . . In Chapter II, the *Lumen gentium* outlines a whole theology of community in which [one sees] the fundamental equality of all its members and the communion that unites them all in one identical Christian vocation and one identical hope of eternal salvation.[18]

One can see that a major change occurred in this debate and vote. The new code of canon law, which went into effect on November 27, 1983, codifies the position of *Lumen Gentium*, chapter 2. All Christians are to be considered members of the people of God, prior to any division into hierarchy-cleric and

---

18. Angel Antón, "Postconciliar Ecclesiology: Expectations, Results, and Prospects for the Future," in *Vatican II: Assessment and Perspectives*, ed. René Latourelle (New York: Paulist Press, 1988), 1:413.

laity. The bishops at Vatican II changed the theological and canonical under-standing of the twofold division of the Roman Catholic Church. When one extrapolates from this, the understanding of the church and its ordained min-isterial leadership is as follows:

- By baptism, confirmation, and the eucharist, *all* Catholic Christians are members of the "People of God," the "faithful of Christ," and members of the "universal priesthood of believers."
- Of these members, only some are called to be ministers either as clergy or as laity.

In this vision of the church, the original unity of all Christians in Christ is stressed before there is a question of specialized roles and ministries within the church. Only when one sees the originating unity of all Christians in Christ can one properly move to consider the two issues that are central to this present volume, namely, ministry and orders. Within the entire body of Christian men and women, some and only some are clergy-ministers, and some and again only some are lay-ministers. In the documents of Vatican II, the terms "clergy" and "laity" make sense only if they are interpreted from within the perspective of the original communion in Christ that is granted to all Christians in baptism.

For a definition of order today, within a global perspective, the reestab-lishment of orders and ministry on the foundation of the equality of all Christians in Christ is the first major step to answering the question, What do the terms "order" and "ministry" *mean?* In other words, in today's global perspective, order and ministry have a justifiable significance only if the two titles are seen through the lens of the equality of all Christians. This includes Christians who are European and North American, as well as Christians from Africa, Asia, South and Central America, or any other part of the world. Ideally, where one is born or what culture one belongs to or what lan-guage one speaks confers no privileges. Nor does "white privilege" derive from any gospel value. It is a historical accident and needs to be purged from the way in which the church is ordered. *All* Catholic Christians are founda-tionally equal, and, as we shall see, they are all equally called and commis-sioned by God to share in the mission and ministry of Jesus. If today this fundamental equality is not reflected in the way orders and ministry are understood theologically and carried out practically, the theology of orders and ministry that authorizes it is built on false premises and deserves no sup-port in today's global church.

There is a second basic, foundational issue that must be attended to and explained carefully. There are major voices in the Roman Catholic Church today who disagree with this second point, and their voices remain strong and to some degree authoritative.[19] This second viewpoint can be stated in a forthright and clear way: <u>*There never has been a single, universally accepted theology of order and ministry in the Christian Catholic* Church.</u>

One can historically document a distinct growth and development of the meaning and the practice of both order and ministry. The French Jesuit theologian Jean Galot has become one of the major opponents of this second, historical viewpoint. In many of his recent writings he has repeatedly stated that Jesus established a form of order and ministry that cannot be and has not been changed. One of his statements on this matter deals with this institution by Christ of order and ministry. Galot's essay appears in the same volume as that of the essays of his fellow Jesuit theologian Angel Antón, whom we quoted above. Both men are talking about the Second Vatican Council, and both are giving an assessment and a future-oriented perspective regarding the impact of the council. Galot, however, presents a very different approach from that of Antón. Galot writes:

> The council rejects any conception of a Church that has developed by moving beyond, or even correcting, the intentions of Christ, and that has given itself its own hierarchical structure, independently of any will of the Savior. It is Christ who willed the essential structure of his Church, and who specifically wanted it to be an "episcopal" one.[20]

Galot uses terminology that indicates that he clearly rejects any radical reformulation of the church in terms of orders and ministry. Historical data clearly indicate, however, that changes in church structures were indeed made. What contemporary scholars have pointed out is that there is not a twentieth-century new formulation or reformulation of orders and ministry. Rather, there is a realization that historically the way Roman Catholic leaders have presented the standard approach to orders and ministry is itself the new way, since contemporary historical research indicates the novelty of the standard approach. In other words, the standard approach was accepted only in the post-Reformation times. It is an approach that was used to bolster the position that only the Roman Catholic Church is and was the one true

---

19. See Jean Galot, "Christ: Revealer, Founder of the Church, and Source of Ecclesial Life," in *Vatican II: Assessment and Perspectives*, 385-406. Daniele Menozzi ("Opposition to the Council," in *The Reception of Vatican II*, ed. Giuseppe Alberigo, Jean-Pierre Jossua, and Joseph Komonchak [Washington, D.C.: Catholic University of America Press, 1987], 325-48) lists in detail the opponents of Vatican II.

20. Galot, "Christ," 391.

church of Jesus Christ. Contemporary historical research questions the very presuppositions on which this standard approach rests.

The historical material shows that an overarching episcopal structure was not present in the New Testament text. In the New Testament, the term *episkopos* is never used in any consistent way. Rather, the term is used only for leadership roles in some communities and is never mentioned as the leadership in other major Christian communities. In the majority of church communities as described in the New Testament, the term *episkopos* is not used at all. The obvious conclusion is this: Jesus did not establish *episkopoi*. Had Jesus established *episkopoi*, then all of the New Testament communities would have leaders with exactly the same name, that is, *episkopoi*. The term *episkopos*, therefore, is a term that gradually came into common use among the various Christian communities, and this process took at least two hundred to three hundred years.[21]

Contemporary Roman Catholic biblical scholars do not claim that an ordination ritual can be attributed to any of the New Testament texts. In fact, no ritual is even alluded to in the New Testament. Admittedly this clashes with later traditions that see Jesus ordaining the Twelve at the Last Supper. Finding a way to resolve this issue is not going to be easy, since the tradition of Christ ordaining the first "bishops" at the Last Supper had become so prevalent by the modern period that to cast doubt on its historicity can be upsetting. Nevertheless, even New Testament texts that deal with the laying on of hands, which does have some ritualistic symbolism, cannot be interpreted as an ordination ritual for either episcopacy or priesthood.[22] The lack of a clear New Testament attestation calls into question the entire issue of order as it has been presented in standard approaches to the institution of church order by Jesus Christ.[23]

History by itself does not create church doctrine and dogma. However, historical data certainly play a major role in contemporary attempts to interpret church teaching and to seek solutions to problems that arise at a later date. It may be wise to state a basic principle that avoids saying either that ancient tradition is absolutely binding or that it can be abandoned if found inconvenient: *If scriptural and historical data are thin, then their capacity to bind subsequent generations should not be overstated.*

By the same token, if scriptural and historical data are extensive, then later generations must take heed and rethink the expression of ordinary or stan-

---

21. See Osborne, *Priesthood*, 40-88.
22. Osborne, *Priesthood*, 70-75.
23. See Francis A. Sullivan, *From Apostles to Bishops: The Development of the Episcopacy in the Early Church* (New York: Newman Press, 2001), 35-38, 51-52, 78-80, 100-101.

dard church teaching, no matter whether it involves maintaining or abandoning traditions. A rethinking of the standard view is permissible, perhaps
even necessary today, because we are in a position to consider order and ministry in the light of extensive data, both in the New Testament and in the history of practice in the period from 50 C.E. to the beginning of the third
century. In summary, the documentary evidence of these 150 years makes it
clear that the earliest Jesus communities do not offer solid data for an ordination ritual. At a minimum, there was no universal practice in the East and
West, which one would expect if Christ and the apostles had given clear
teaching on the matter. Only with the discovery of ordination rituals themselves—and the earliest extant ritual is found in the *Apostolic Tradition*, dat-
ing to the beginning of the third century—do we have a text that clearly
speaks of ordination. At this point, until the discovery of a more ancient text,
all interpretations are conjectural. D. Dupuy has summarized this position in
a very clear way: "How someone in the early Church is called to ecclesial
ministry is not described in the New Testament, so that theories relative to
ordination have in part a hypothetical quality about them."[24]

The fact that both sacred orders and understandings of ministry have
changed over the course of the church's history is important for the focus of
this present volume on the theology of orders and ministry from a global perspective. The importance lies in the fact that unless changes can be legitimately made in orders and ministry in various non–Euro-American cultural
situations, then, whether one employs a global perspective or only a Euro-
American perspective, nothing can really be done. A global and multi- or
equicultural framework demands that leadership itself be given a culturally
native character and not be simply a cloned leadership imposed from without that exhibits a totally different set of cultural dynamics. Let us consider
this historical material on changes regarding orders and ministry.

Historical Changes in the Practice and Theology
of Order and Ministry

Although many Catholics believe that the tasks of the bishops, priests, and
deacons are the same now as they always have been since the days of Peter
and Paul, twentieth-century historians and biblical scholars have reached a
different conclusion. The consensus of scholars who have studied both the

---

24. D. Dupuy, "Theologie der kirchlichen Ämpter," in *Mysterium Salutis*, IV/2 (Einsiedeln: Benziger, 1973), 507. For a listing of New Testament data on anointing, see Osborne, *Priesthood*, 70-83.

New Testament and relevant parts of the Old Testament concerning the biblical understanding of bishop (*episkopos*) and priest (*presbyteros*) is that the meanings of these two terms, both in the Greek and the Hebrew equivalents, does not correspond to the contemporary understanding of "bishop" and "priest."

Moreover, in the twentieth century, major Catholic scholars of early church history began researching the data of the early church on the issue of leadership. These historians found that the naming of Christian leadership, from the years 30 to 500 C.E., was at first very diverse and not at all uniform. The terms *episkopos* and *presbyteros* were included in these diverse names, but they were neither dominant throughout all Christian communities nor did they describe the same role and ministry in a uniform way. From the year 215 to roughly 315, the Greek terms *episkopos* and *presbyteros* gradually became dominant; however, the role and ministry of the *episkopos* and the *presbyteros* were different from what bishops and priests do today. Historically, there has been a development in the identification of what bishops and priests have done both in various groups of early Christian communities and at various times of early Christian community living.

Development in the practice and theology of the role and function of bishops and priests took place gradually. The changes began to appear whenever early church communities were confronted with major *pastoral needs*. Such needs required the tasks of *episkopoi* and *presbyteroi* to be altered. Rarely did the changes occur, as we would say today, from the top down, that is, from the higher echelons of church leadership down. Serious pastoral needs were the main catalysts of change. A local or regional Christian community perceived a serious need for a more specific type of ministry, and the local or regional church leaders did the best they could to meet these spiritual and pastoral needs of the Christian communities, even if this meant changing to some extent the role and function of an *episkopos* or a *presbyteros*. Some of these changes did not last, and some were even discredited by regional councils. Other changes, however, began to be accepted by a wider group of local and regional Christian communities, and some of these changes eventually were accepted officially by the highest leadership of the church. We will not understand the meaning of orders and ministry, unless we seriously study the history of their development. Today a majority of Roman Catholic biblical scholars, early church historians, and systematic theologians agree that there is no single definition or essence of *episkopos*, *presbyteros*, and *diakonos* that stretches from the time of Jesus to the beginning of the third millennium. Rather, these scholars accept change and development in what we call ordained ministry.

In the study of lay ministry in the church, we find a similar trend toward change and development. This is clear in our present Roman Catholic Church. Since the Second Vatican Council, lay men and women have become official ministers within parishes and regional structures of Catholic life. Today, lay men and women are ministering in the church in ways that would have seemed impossible fifty years ago. Change has indeed taken place in lay ministry.

In the first five hundred years of church history, laymen and some laywomen were also very active in the ministries of the churches of that time. After 500 C.E., historical data indicate that lay ministers were to some extent deliberately moved to the sidelines by clerics, and the hierarchical and ordained people in the church took over almost all of the ministerial work of the church or at least closely governed it. Non-lay involvement began to change around 1000 C.E., but in very slow fits and starts. When the Protestant Reformation took place, there was another clerical reaction to lay involvement in church leadership. The ordained hierarchy of the Roman Catholic Church once again took a rigid stand against laypeople in ministerial positions. The Roman Catholic leadership of that time did not want to be like the Protestant churches, in which lay ministry began to flourish. Both the American Revolution (1776) and the French Revolution (1789) were, in different ways, anti-Roman Catholic. This revolutionary wave of opposition to the Catholic Church and the wave of "liberty, equality, fraternity" that enlivened these two revolutions once again caused a tightening of hierarchical control of all ministries in the Catholic Church. A call for more freedom for the lay Catholic began to be heard in the last quarter of the nineteenth century, in which many lay congresses were held in the United States and in Europe. The call of lay men and women at the conferences, though loud and at times shrill, was stifled by the European and American hierarchies in the last decade of the nineteenth century. However, the activities of these lay Catholic leaders remained throughout the first half of the twentieth century, but only in a sort of muted and even underground framework. These lay voices became louder from about 1950 onward, and many of the lay issues were openly taking place just as Vatican II was being planned and finally inaugurated.

In the history of lay ministry, we can see that lay men and women played *some* role in the ministry of the Catholic Church in almost every age, but that its positioning and its mandate changed time after time. Eventually their role was reduced, practically speaking, to assisting bishops and priests, and even nonordained religious were consigned to the same subservient role. One finds no essential or unchangeable understanding of lay ministry in the church that can be traced from Jesus to the third millennium. Instead, change and development are the better words to describe the fluctuations of lay ministry in the Catholic Church, all in a pattern of seeing the lay role as one of following the commandments and working toward salvation. This, sadly, is the state of affairs—with a number of happy exceptions, for example, the life of St. Vincent de Paul—but a full-fledged attempt to integrate lay ministry into the essential mission of the church in the world would wait till the twentieth century. And, as we shall see, even the work of Vatican II on the subject has been accorded a mixed reception.

At this juncture, we should ask ourselves the following question: Why did we have to clarify what the terms "order" and "ministry" mean before considering the theology of order and ministry from a global perspective? The answer is that, unless we see that "order" and "ministry" are terms whose functions *can be changed*, we will be forced simply to present the largely static, clergy-dominated meaning of order and ministry. We need to do better, and a discussion that attempts to understand a global perspective on these themes must go beyond the traditional approaches. If the meaning of order and ministry is viewed as essentially immutable, the needs of our globalized church will always be subordinated to past patterns. We will be able only to clone the shape of ministry in patterns we inherit from the past. To recall the views of Edward Schillebeeckx on the subject, it is much more fruitful to see the evolution of ministry and office as "divinely guided" (*de jure divino*) by the Holy Spirit in the past in ways that do not block the church in succeeding ages from adapting to new circumstances in subsequent ages.[25]

If unchangeableness is divinely willed, would there be a reason to write a series of books like this one, discussing theology in global perspective? It is clear that some Catholic scholars maintain the view that order and ministry are immutably defined. Nevertheless, both the New Testament and documents from the early history of the church indicate that there has been considerable change in names and functions in ministry. This evidence is not simply a matter of a few subaltern and rejected strands of understanding. Rather, the evidence for the conclusions on change and meaning for church ministry is multiple, widespread, and geographically diverse. A view that does not acknowledge these data and clings instead to a nonhistorical and nonscriptural presentation generally favors maintaining the status quo.

But moving beyond the status quo is necessary if we want to rethink the meaning of ministry and orders today within the wider, global context. We can do so because the reality of changes in the past that have been ratified by

---

25. Edward Schillebeeckx, "The Catholic Understanding of Office in the Church," *Theological Studies* 30 (1969): 569-71.

popes and bishops necessitates at least the possibility of listening to those who are convinced that changes are necessary in today's globalized, equicultural church. Changes were once made when serious pastoral needs arose. The Roman Catholic Church today faces several serious pastoral needs. They appear as necessary in the old homelands of the church as in the global South.

THREE ISSUES CONFRONTING A GLOBALIZED
WORLD AND CHURCH

Three major characteristics of our contemporary globalization affect both the entire world and Catholicism. The first is that globalization is a major part of contemporary existence. The second is that contemporary communications and travel technologies make it possible for an overbearing form of micromanagement both in civil society and in the Roman Catholic Church. The third characteristic is that globalization and micromanagement in organizations such as the World Bank and the Roman Catholic Church have the potential of enforcing visions of how things should be done that claim to be essential and universally valid but in reality are simply the views of a financial or ecclesiastical elite. These are sensitive issues. I have the impression that they are more openly discussed in regard to the mentality of international corporations and the World Bank than they are in regard to the church. We shall try to raise the issue in relation to Catholicism below, well aware of how sensitive these matters are.

Since we cannot honestly discuss globalization without encountering these three characteristics, we need to take time to identify them and, in a small degree, to analyze them. All three characteristics require treatment far beyond the scope of this volume, namely, to present a complete theology within a comprehensive global perspective. Nonetheless, these characteristics are so important that they must be reviewed in their own global form, before we focus more narrowly on their presence in a global theological framework.

Globalization as a Major Part of Contemporary Existence

At the beginning of the third millennium, globalization has increased both intensively and extensively. Every corner of the earth reflects some aspects of this drive toward globalization. The Roman Catholic Church is a major player in globalization. Indeed, as we said above, Christian mission (carried on by both Catholics and Protestants) was one of the first and strongest movements that was truly global in scope. At the level of both bishops and the papacy, and their close cooperation, the church is one of the most cohesive international actors in the world and as such is a strong player in globalization. The recent pageant of the death of Pope John Paul II brought into dramatic relief the way in which the occupant of Peter's Chair has been given by Christians and others the *de facto* position of the world's moral and spiritual leader. This occurred both because of technological advances in communication and travel and because of the unique personality of John Paul. How much of the exalted position he was accorded will pass on to his successor is hard to say, but never in human history has the head of any religious body had the global influence of a contemporary pope.

There is another, more ambiguous side to this story. The pope and his Vatican officials can send document after document and letter after letter to the church leaders in all parts of the earth. These communications arrive almost instantaneously. Bishops' conferences and general, provincial, and local superiors of religious communities can be asked to explain these communications. An ill-considered word or phrase put into a document by a lowly Vatican functionary and not caught by a cardinal in charge can give instant offense to members of other churches, governments, or followers of other religious traditions. Such lapses can take away the possibility of a local bishop dealing tactfully with a delicate matter that he and, say, the mother superior of a local convent are trying to resolve gracefully. A disgruntled layperson in Cincinnati can complain about a theologian whose views she misunderstands, and a Roman congregation quickly asks an archbishop to see to it that that theologian never talks again from a Catholic podium. A pastoral gesture that might be appropriate at the funeral of a family made up of various kinds of Christians and maybe a Muslim or a Native American is reported, and the bishop of Delhi is told to suspend a good priest. The potential for such micromanagement is virtually endless, and it is without parallel in the history of Christianity.

At the local level, a diocesan bishop can use the same tools of rapid communication to instruct parish priests and directors of religious education on exactly how parishes should handle specific issues, because he fears that the Congregation for Divine Worship will rap his knuckles if he does not. Religious superiors follow the same pattern. In the latter case, since the majority of general superiors live in Rome, they too through Internet, fax, and telephone have rapid contact with local leaders in their religious communities. Novice masters of the same religious community in places as different as

Buenos Aires, Nairobi, and Dublin can be told to implement immediately an instruction from the Congregation for Religious, yet it is not clear that the congregation has taken local conditions into account.

Rapid communication, of course, works in the opposite direction as well. Situations at a very localized level can be instantly communicated to the top leadership levels. Sometimes local bishops may fear to make mistakes and ask for advice. They often find that people in Rome are quite willing to give it, when patient dialogue and testing how best to solve a problem would be better used. As we have said, at other times, local dissidents take minor issues to the top, when the Christian thing to do would be to have good local dialogue. The dissidents override normal channels of parochial communication and get their views ratified by authority, causing enormous and irreparable bitterness. Instant global communication, then, has changed life no matter whether one identifies with making or obstructing changes—and it is not uniformly a blessing. Instant global communication is profoundly ambiguous. Robert Schreiter has written at length on globalization and its effects on the Catholic Church's mission of evangelization. The following is worthy of remembering:

> Thanks to the new communications technologies, messages and information can now be sent around the world with near instantaneity. Air travel makes the movement of persons and cargo rapid and relatively inexpensive . . . The communications technologies make possible a networking that increasingly eludes hierarchical control; network has replaced hierarchy as a social model for communication.[26]

Schreiter observes that communication works in both directions and reminds us that instant global communication can also provide ways for resisting micromanagement, because certain kinds of decisions made in private, when they become known in the light of day, prove impossible to sustain. The clerical sexual abuse crisis in the United States and other parts of the world is a case in point. A long-time policy of denying the seriousness of this issue in the college of the ordained mushroomed into a global resistance movement when reports of abuse in Louisiana and Massachusetts sent reporters in Dublin and Sydney looking for similar behavior. Despite a view of some that such matters need to be kept under wraps lest the church suffer damage, the church today has had to revise its presuppositions on how the ordained are to be protected. A great deal of the reason this happened is globalization.

---

26. Robert Schreiter, *The New Catholicity: Theology between the Global and the Local* (Maryknoll, New York: Orbis Books, 1997), 8.

Globalization is simply a fact today. It has some very excellent benefits. It also has some very devastating consequences. In the seventh plenary session of the Federation of Asian Bishops' Conferences, held in Samphran, Thailand, the Asian bishops publicly took issue with the negative results of economic and political globalization. They wrote:

> Though Asia is free from external colonization, and most Asian countries have some sort of democratic government, they do not follow the same model of democracy . . . Most of the [Asian] governments come to power through the alliance of various parties, often without a clear mandate from the people. Further, there is a tendency towards centralization of power and decision-making . . . [However] . . . Governments are forced to adopt policies and practices such as the Structural Adjustment Policies [SAP] dictated by the IMF [International Monetary Fund], the WB [World Bank] and the WTO [World Trade Organization]. These policies are devoid of a human face and social concern. The model of economic development promoted by the transnational corporations in Asia is not acceptable.[27]

In the act of criticizing negative aspects of globalization, the Asian bishops are making a statement that they know will be broadcast over the entire world by one of the technologies that makes the forces they criticize possible. Church leadership throughout the world has also found that instant communication can be and is used in intra church situations. Catholic lay men and women in the United States today have openly voiced their views regarding the current sexual abuse crisis, and their voices have been heard in the Vatican, in the offices of the National Conference of Catholic Bishops in Washington, D.C., and in diocesan chanceries across the nation and throughout the world, as the local American crisis became a world news item. American bishops, who once had immense moral authority, quickly found themselves with little moral authority.

When it comes to the topics of order and ministry, it is evident that those in orders—bishops, priests, and deacons—are not immune from the force of globalized communication. Their ministry, as well as that of the entire hierarchy of the Roman Catholic Church, has come under a cloud. But it must also be said that the spotlight shed on Rome during the death of John Paul II and the election of the telegenic Benedict XVI seemed to reverse that effect. This reveals another of the ambiguities of global communications

---

27. *FABC*, 3:7.

technologies. They can be used for propaganda and can cause instantaneous shifts in fickle world opinion. Although the problems of the world and the problems of pastoral responses to the needs of people should not be decided merely on the basis of ever-shifting worldviews, leaders are faced with the reality that propaganda-influenced public opinion often makes them take steps that will not wear well over time. A serious pastoral need demands serious thought and openness to the possibility of substantial change.

Micromanagement as a Problem in Church Life

The possibility of instant intervention by top-ranking corporate, military, government, and church leaders in the daily life of grassroots groups they lead has become a contemporary reality with immensely ambiguous results. Ignoring the truth that allowing decisions to be made as close to the level at which they are going to be carried out creates responsibility and feelings of ownership in large organizations. Micromanagers can destroy such qualities if they do not use global communications technology warily. In the case of a manufacturing company, it's true that headquarters in, say, Amsterdam may have knowledge about how one of their factories solved a rust problem in Kuala Lumpur and may be able to help the Nairobi branch save time by e-mailing the experience of one part of the company to another. But for every such fruitful use of global communication, there is probably another in which a top manager tells a local manager how to do something that may stifle development.

Is this the case in the relationship of the pope and the Vatican curia with local dioceses? Intervention from the top has been perceived as improper micromanagement of regional and local Catholic communities. Micromanagement by the Vatican curia, however, is in the eyes of many a fact of church life today. Not to mention it, at least as a possible danger, could lead to a view of order and ministry that ignores an important principle—decisions should be made with local input that is as broad-based and consultative as possible. Should the Vatican curia oversee order and ministry in its global perspective? Of course. The real issue is, What kind of oversight can avoid an improper micromanaging of ministry? There is nothing in the Gospels or in church history and theological tradition that requires a detailed and minute oversight. Avoiding it is clearly a legitimate ecclesial and theological goal. From a sociological point of view, it is important to bear in mind the issue Robert Schreiter has so well summed up in his book *The New Catholicity* when he speaks of globalization generating paradoxical effects. Among other effects, attempts to enforce global patterns often generate resistance at the local level.[28] In the same way that a plethora of McDonald's restaurants can lead local peoples to become more conscious of the values of their traditional foods and to resist foreign imports, so trying to enforce patterns of ministry that are alien to a given people's cultural traditions can bring about a sense that the church does not care about local resources. At a minimum, the central administration of the church needs to be sure that the things it demands truly arise from gospel exigencies and are not just the preferences of those who share a traditional Roman outlook.

Because of the ease of communication and travel, people at a distance from the local scene can underestimate cultural differences, viewing them as accidental to the core of doctrine, liturgy, leadership, and life. Viewed from below, however, impositions can be seen as an improper homogenization of the non-creedal areas of Catholic Church life. The need felt at the top as "unity" can be seen from local areas as an insistence on uniformity and conformity. It is not just a problem in relations between Rome and the global South. Ministering in rapidly expanding exurban areas of the United States, for example, may require as much cultural sensitivity as is demanded in Nigeria. American Catholics are part of an individualistic culture where the demands of suburban, rural, exurban, and urban living are different from anything experienced in the history of the church. The most vital form of church life in all these environments appears to be that of evangelical and Pentecostal communities. Should the church in the United States have the opportunity to study how such churches are flourishing and perhaps adapt the lessons that fit? Cannot the same question be posed in, say, Nigeria, where African Instituted Churches are spreading?

The way in which the ordained and other ministries are arranged is viewed by one group of Catholics as requiring an improper uniformity, while people on the other side see insistence on international "standards" as an important way to maintain unity. How is one to sort this out. At present, those in favor of uniformity clearly control the levers of power. Is this legitimate? On the one hand, contemporary church leadership at every level wants to foster, encourage, and assist ordained and nonordained ministries. These ministries are clearly leadership ministries, and the regional and local churches will grow, develop, and become centers of deep spiritual growth only if the regional and local leadership is active, energetic, and sanctifying. On the other hand, the central offices of church leadership want to regulate regional and local forms of these ministries. They see a world where chaos threatens order

28. See Schreiter, *New Catholicity*, 12-27.

and basic elements of Catholic identity are at risk. A uniform and unified regulation of ministry throughout the world—so official church leadership seems to indicate—is the best way to preserve intact the one, holy, catholic, and apostolic church. Proposals to deviate from this basic ministerial system have been quickly rejected. This is an aspect of current Roman Catholic life, and to the extent that persons in different parts of the world do not perceive it to be driven by gospel exigencies, to that extent resistance can be expected. In matters religious, resistance is often expressed by people leaving one church and going to another. It is no secret that this is occurring in North America and Latin America in different ways, and that in Africa various forms of African Initiated Churches have an enormous appeal.

The word "micromanagement" is very strong. We do not seek here to impugn those who believe uniformity in the structure of ministry is necessary to bring about unity. But we do ask the question whether "micromanagement" of liturgical, ministerial, and social-justice stances is a characteristic of current policies and whether it is having negative affects. Aylward Shorter has indicated that whenever there is a major discussion of liturgy, the authority card is quickly played. Shorter writes:

> The ardent desire for liturgical inculturation—a new liturgical creation— has to compete with the view of liturgy as a field for the exercise of hierarchical power. In so far as the bishop sees his role as the principal guarantor of an authentic liturgy circumscribed by Church law, inculturation cannot fail to be discouraged. As E.-J. Pénoukou has rightly pointed out, an up-dated model of the bishop must be linked to an up-dated model of the church.[29]

In the documents of Vatican II, there was great concern for cultural differences, particularly in the liturgy. In fact, we read in the Constitution on the Sacred Liturgy (*Sacrosanctum Concilium*) that the bishops of the area are the main leaders in this adaptation of liturgy.

> In some places and circumstances, however, an even more radical adaptation of the liturgy is needed, and this entails greater difficulties. For this reason: (1) The competent territorial ecclesiastical authority . . . must, in this matter, carefully and prudently consider which elements from the traditions and cultures of individual peoples might appropriately be admitted into divine worship. Adaptations which are considered useful or necessary

---

29. Aylward Shorter, *Toward a Theology of Inculturation* (Maryknoll, N.Y.: Orbis Books, 1994), 194.

should then be submitted to the Apostolic See to be introduced with its consent. (SC 40)

Many bishops at Vatican II believed that this was recognizing the need for radical change. This radical change, they felt, was particularly needed to make the liturgy meaningful in different cultures. They were thinking then (1962–1965) mainly of areas such as Melanesia, Polynesia, Africa, and Asia. Forty years later, however, as liturgical participation rates plummet drastically in Europe, where weekly attendance rates of 10 percent and below are common, and in the United States, where attendance has gone from 67 percent in 1965 to 47 percent in 2004, questions of inculturation are being raised for older Catholic churches as well.[30] The perspective of Vatican II was focused on the third world, but it turns out that the principles enunciated then have global relevance today. In the citation above from the document on the liturgy, the bishops also indicated that the local leaders have the better expertise and competency on the issues of cultural change. Their voices and opinions should be heard with deepest reverence.

Nevertheless, even today, all local and regional decisions on such issues must be made in Rome. A translation of the Mass, for instance, into Mongolian must be ratified in Rome, where there may not be a single expert. This and a host of examples that could be raised indicate that the issue of who ought to be competent to make such decisions is vital in today's Roman Catholic Church.

Racial, Gender, and Cultural Discrimination in the Church

The three-pronged question of racial, gender, and cultural discrimination is not often raised in relation to civil society, business, or religious bodies. We will not deal with it at length in this book, but it is important that we raise it. Discrimination clearly goes against the memory of Jesus himself as someone who reached out to men and women at the boundaries. It goes further against one of the earliest and still classic statements of what Christian fellowship is to be—Galatians 3:26-29:

You are all children of God through faith in Christ Jesus, for all of you who were baptized into Christ have clothed yourselves with Christ. There is

---

30. For international figures, see the statistics gathered by the Center for Applied Research in the Apostolate (CARA) at http://cara.georgetown.edu/bulletin/international.htm. For figures on the United States, see http://cara.georgetown.edu/bulletin/index.htm.

neither Jew nor Greek, slave nor free, male nor female, for you are all one in Christ Jesus. If you belong to Christ, then you are Abraham's seed, and heirs according to the promise.

The early church was a community of open fellowship, and this is one of the things that most impressed the pagans about it. Group and class loyalties are natural to human beings, and there is no easy way to overcome them, but the principle operative in the church is crystal clear. Any kind of discrimination on the basis of race, class, culture, or gender is out of place. It is also clear from an examination of church history in matters such as the church's willingness to tolerate slavery that the practical working out of such principles is not easy in a world where cultures differ so mightily and even biblical texts treat slavery ambiguously. All people are also to some degree culturally discriminative if only in their preference for certain foods, being able to speak with people who speak the same language and have the same basic assumptions about how people older and younger are to be treated, how men and women are to relate in public and domestic situations, and so forth. Still, the principle should be clear: although culturally based discrimination is to some degree natural, it is never proper to advocate any form of racial or cultural supremacy and privilege.

Although it is painful to raise the next question, it cannot be avoided. Does a certain form of preference for classical clerical culture amount to a form of cultural discrimination? Do both the historical and contemporary composition of the church's leading authorities lead to a form of white privilege in deciding how the church must be formed? Popes and cardinals may not be conscious of how their social location has formed and privileged them, but having a global perspective on order and ministry today demands attention to the possibility that forbidding full discussion of the kind of adaptation and inculturation we have treated above may indicate that the Roman clerics are not fully conscientized in matters of cultural and racial privilege. Is it impossible that someone who uses theological reasoning to justify the exclusion of, for example, women or persons who have not gone through a standard, "full" education program, is embracing privileges patterns he is familiar with rather than seriously considering different patterns that may be more effective?

It is important to raise these issues forthrightly, because whether one likes it or not, there is a suspicion among many that fundamental questions of adapting structures of ordained and lay ministries to contemporary historical and cultural conditions come from a preference of the Catholic leadership to ordain men who share their celibate culture and values with them, and, equally important, not to recognize the need for laity to be involved at every level of inner-church and outreach ministry. Until such suspicions are allayed, it is likely that a remnant of reflexive Marxism will engender suspicions that the ordained leaders of the church are acting to promote their desires to have a church in which only men with their own cultural values exert power and authority.

While we raise these issues only as questions for consideration, many theologians and other persons active in church life suspect that official church positions, be they in the Code of Canon Law or in liturgical rules, express the cultural and theological attitudes of a certain social class within the church. Such positions do not honor the valid practices or principles that can be deduced from Scripture, tradition, and sociohistorical and theological reflection. Indeed, there is much in these official documents that cannot be considered matters of faith.

Does some of this result from disdain for matters that look different if one considers the same subject from the point of view of gender, racial, cultural, or class analysis? This does not mean that such issues are officially addressed, or that they are directly stated, or even that they are fully conscious.

In the globalization of the Roman Catholic Church, the interrelationship between the politically dominant white Roman Catholic world and the demographically dominant nonwhite Roman Catholic world raises enormous issues. Some Catholics, for instance, have spoken negatively about a paternalistic or patriarchal church leadership. Others have spoken negatively about an androcentric church leadership. The terms "paternal," "patriarchal," and "androcentric" have gradually been tolerated to some degree or accepted to a lesser degree as contemporary theological terms. This does not indicate that all Catholics are eager to speak about Roman Catholic leadership as paternal, patriarchal, or androcentric. Rather, Catholics for the most part reluctantly admit that theological discussions that involve these terms are indeed going on. The higher levels of church leadership, however, rarely use these terms, nor do they discuss them.

Nevertheless, there can be no honest discussion of globalization within the Roman Catholic Church today unless the issues of gender, race, and class are faced. Nor can there be any honest discussion of order and ministry from a globalized perspective unless such questions are faced. Unless they are faced, the suspicion of many will be that the upper leadership of the church seeks to deal with fundamental racial, gender, cultural, and class issues as if local churches could be cloned from trees planted in medieval and early modern Europe, or as if solutions reached after long periods of experimentation in medieval Europe and early modern Europe and North and South American history are always valid and obligatory.

Finally, in raising these questions as we do, we are not predetermining that the outcome of the questioning and study will be something that will please liberal or progressive Euro-American theologians and activists who have already made up their mind. It is ultimately a matter of taking soundings to see what *sensus fidelium* may have developed or be developing.

THE THREEFOLD DIMENSION OF ORDER AND MINISTRY
IN THE TEACHING OF VATICAN COUNCIL II

The first three parts of this chapter serve as background for what follows, which is the main theme of this chapter. We seek to understand the mission and ministry of Jesus, and to see this as the foundation and model for all subsequent Christian ministries. To do so we need to consider the way in which the documents of Vatican II describe a certain threefold dimension in Christian order and ministry. No attempt to come to grips with the global issues can succeed unless this threefold dimension of ministry is taken into account.

To begin with a short summary of the matter being explicated, consider that the Dogmatic Constitution on the Church, *Lumen Gentium,* dealt with the so-called triple task of ministry (*tria munera* in Latin) in the light of the theological understanding of: (1) all baptized and confirmed people; (2) the meaning of priest and therefore bishop; (3) the meaning of deacon; (4) the meaning of lay ministry. The *tria munera,* or the three foundational tasks of all church ministries, are those of prophet, priest, and king. Since these precise terms have a certain aristocratic tone about them, many writers prefer to speak of a single "ministry" that is exercised in and through the tasks of (*a*) preaching and teaching, (*b*) sanctifying, and (*c*) leading. Let us consider each of these aspects of Christian ministry more carefully.

1. Prophet. This ministry is considered by many to be the most important of the three. Under that title, the documents of Vatican II discuss the ministry of preaching and teaching. All Christians, through their baptism and confirmation, share in this ministry. The individual, distinct ministries of Christians—for example, the ministry of the ordained and that of the laity—exercise this role according to the nature of their position in the church.

2. Priest. This ministry is most often placed second in order and is centered on the sanctifying aspects of church ministry. All Christians, according to Vatican II, share in the priesthood of all believers, and this priestly task has been given to them by the Lord himself in virtue of their baptism and confirmation. Everyone in the church, therefore, has a ministry of sanctifying. This role, too, is exercised in different ways by ordained and lay ministries, and both the ordained and the laity have roles to play in the sacramental and liturgical life of the church.

3. King. This is the ministry of leadership. Generally, this royal or leadership ministry is listed third on the list of the three ministries or tasks. Everyone in the church shares in this ministry of leadership, and once again the call and commissioning to this leadership ministry come from God and are entrusted to each member of the church through baptism and confirmation. There are also specific areas of leadership ministry that are entrusted to specific ordained and nonordained ministers.

It will be helpful to quote the exact passages of Vatican II that indicate that all Christians share in the threefold dimension of ministry. (The entire paragraph in which each short quotation below appears ought to be read to garner the full meaning of the text.) We look first at texts that show that the general call to ministry is given by God to all the baptized:

Through baptism and confirmation all are appointed to this apostolate [the church's saving mission] by the Lord himself. (LG 32)

All the faithful, that is, who by baptism are incorporated into Christ, are constituted the people of God, who have been made sharers in their own way in the priestly, prophetic and kingly office of Christ and play their part in carrying out the mission of the whole Christian people in the church and in the world. (LG 30)

Second, there are texts that show the call to share in the prophetic ministry of Christ:

The holy people of God shares also in Christ's prophetic office: it spreads abroad a living witness to him, especially by a life of faith and love and by offering to God a sacrifice of praise. (LG 12)

He (Christ) made them his witnesses and gave them understanding of the faith and grace in speech. (LG 35)

All disciples of Christ are obliged to spread the faith to the best of their ability. (LG 17)

Third, there are texts that call all Christians to share in the priestly ministry of Christ:

To all the baptized the Lord "also gives a share in his priestly office of offering spiritual worship for the glory of the Father and the salvation of humanity." (LG 34)

Christ the Lord, high priest taken from the midst of humanity (Heb. 5:1-5) made the new people "a kingdom of priests to his God and Father" (Rev. 1:6). The baptized, by regeneration and the anointing of the holy Spirit, are consecrated as a spiritual house and a holy priesthood that through all their Christian activities they may offer spiritual sacrifices and proclaim the marvels of him who has called them out of darkness into his wonderful light. (LG 10)

Fourth, we note texts that articulate the call to share in the leadership ministry of Christ:

Moreover, it is not only through the sacraments and the ministries that the holy Spirit makes the people of God holy, leads them and enriches them with his virtues. Allotting his gifts "at will to each individual" (1 Cor. 12:11), he also distributes special graces among the faithful of every rank. By these gifts, he makes them fit and ready to undertake various tasks and offices for the renewal and building up of the church, as it is written, "the manifestation of the Sprit is given to everyone for profit" (1 Cor. 12:7). (LG 12)

The threefold ministerial tasks were selected by the bishops at Vatican II because these three correspond to the threefold "office" or "work" of Jesus that was identified in the Gospels from earliest times as expressing the ministry of Jesus in relation to humanity. The bishops are saying that Jesus himself engaged in a ministry of preaching and teaching (as prophet), of sanctifying and healing (as priest), and of leadership (as "king").

As prophet-preacher-teacher, his words and his life proclaimed the good news of God's favor and forgiveness of sins to humankind. Jesus began his public ministry, first by his baptism, then by his forty days of prayer, and finally by his major work of preaching the kingdom of God. His preaching-teaching cannot be confined to his parables, to the Sermon on the Mount, and to other words that we find in the Gospels. Rather, he preached equally by his actions, which include his miracles, his life of prayer, his journeying for the kingdom of God, and his compassion for all. His activities as prophet or revealer include his journey to Jerusalem, the final supper with his friends, his arrest and trial, and ultimately his death. The followers of Christ, according to their vocations, are to take this aspect of Jesus as a benchmark for their ministry today.

As Jesus acted as priest, sanctifier, and healer, his entire life can be summed up as an offering dedicated to God. Although it is in the New Testament writing called Letter to the Hebrews that we find Jesus formally called priest (*hiereus*), and although it is never formally applied by the New Testament to the apostles or to other people in the community, the act of dedicating one's entire life to God is at the core of Christian life. The role of cult is as a *liturgical act* that symbolizes what members of the community are attempting to do in their actual daily lives, lived in the power of the Spirit—that is to say, dedicating themselves and their world to the creator from whom they come. Thus, priesthood in the Christian church helps members of the community bring the meaning of their life to consciousness and liturgical celebration. The act of offering one's entire life is summarized especially in the death of Jesus, who commits his entire being to God in trust in the act of undergoing an unjust condemnation. We are saying, in other words, that the most important priestly acts in Christian life are this daily attempt to live a life consonant with our vocation, a life that makes the gospel of and about Jesus present in the world.

To understand the importance of this, recall that the Greek word *hiereus* is used in only three ways in the New Testament writings. First of all, *hiereus* denotes the Jewish priests and high priests. Second, *hiereus* is used to describe the life of all followers of Jesus. Third, it is used to describe Jesus in the Letter to the Hebrews. We will see below that the early Christian communities rejected the Greek term for priest as a name for Christian ministers. Even with this caveat, this ministry, specifically called priest in the documents of Vatican II, refers to the ministry of sanctifying or making holy. Etymologically, "sanctification" refers to setting something apart for offering to a god. Jesus clearly brought to the many people he met a consciousness of how life lived in its fullness is lived intentionally "toward" God and the coming "Kingdom," a dimension of reality that is found in the midst of the everyday. The sanctification of the Christian, in other words, is a process of growing in consciousness of this divine dimension in the midst of the everyday. The "setting apart" of sanctification is not an abandonment of life in the world, but points to the inner state of one who knows she belongs to God and tries to live the teaching of Jesus in ways that will bring others to see this spiritual treasure. How often Jesus said to someone: "Your sins are forgiven," or "You are loved by the Father." The very presence of the person of Jesus assured them that God loved them, even though they had sinned or even if the authorities of that time had placed them on the margins of acceptable society, in effect "excommunicating" them (as was the case for lepers, Samaritans, and those working for the Roman government as tax collectors or other officials).

Healing is also part of holy-making or sanctifying. The assurance of God's love, which Jesus often brought to people, healed them. So, too, his miracles of healing brought not only wholeness to people but a holiness as well. When one sees that he or she has, at least to some degree, a personal holiness, one is healed. In the Jewish world at the time of Jesus, God was the main physician, and healing included this physical blessing by God, the Physician.

As king, Jesus is a royal leader, but in a way strikingly different from the leadership of the kings of this world. We see this when Jesus says: "I am the good shepherd." Jesus leads by shepherding. Jesus also says: "I have not come to be served, but to serve." Jesus leads by serving. Jesus gets up from the table and puts on an apron and washes the feet of his disciples. Jesus leads by washing the feet of others. The leadership of Jesus was a humble leadership. The one word that describes the leadership of Jesus is service. The one icon that truly manifests the leadership of Jesus is the washing of the feet. This word and this icon stand as the benchmark for all order and ministry in the Christian church.

The *Catechism of the Catholic Church* also uses the threefold schema to characterize the ministry of Jesus and as the benchmark for all ministries in the church. In the *Catechism* we read the following: "Christ is himself the source of ministry in the Church" (CCC 874). In another place, the *Catechism* says, "The priesthood is ministerial. That office . . . which the Lord committed to the pastors of his people, is in the strict sense of the term a *service*" (CCC 1551, citing LG 24). The Code of Canon Law says the following:

> The Christian faithful are those who, inasmuch as they have been entrusted in Christ through Baptism, have been constituted as the people of God; for this reason, since they have become sharers in Christ's priestly, prophetic and royalty office in their own manner, they are called to exercise the mission which God has entrusted to the Church to fulfill in the world, in accord with the condition proper to each one. (CIC, 204, §1; see LG 31)

The *Catechism* returns to this in no. 875, and 876 spells out the implications clearly:

> Intrinsically linked to the sacramental nature of ecclesial ministry is its *character as service*. Entirely dependent on Christ who gives mission and authority, ministers are truly "slaves of Christ," in the image of him who freely took "the form of a slave for us." Because the word and grace of which they are ministers are not their own, but are given to them by Christ for the sake of others, they must freely become the slaves of all. (CCC 876)

It deepens these insights later in saying:

> The baptized have become "living stones" to be "built into a spiritual house, to be a holy priesthood" (1 Pet 2:5). By Baptism they [the baptized] share in the priesthood of Christ, in his prophetic and royal mission. They are "a chosen race, a royal priesthood, a holy nation, God's own people, that [they] may declare the wonderful deeds of him who called [them] out of darkness into his marvelous light" (1 Pet 2:9). *Baptism gives a share in the common priesthood of all believers.* (CCC 1268)

A basic question occurs: Why is Jesus the source of all ministries, and why should the three aspects of his ministry be meaningful for Roman Catholics today? This question attempts to bring together all of the material we have considered in this third section of the chapter. The question can be answered clearly. First of all, one begins with Jesus, or, more specifically, one begins with the question, How can one describe the ministry of Jesus? Vatican II has used the threefold description of all ministries, including that of Jesus, in a comprehensive way. Since this use of a threefold form of all ministries is part of the teaching of Vatican II, the threefold form of ministry can and must be seen as the ordinary teaching of the Roman Catholic Church today. Can it be changed? Of course. As with most attempts to summarize immense amounts of biblical material, any short summary is a candidate for rethinking and rearranging. But as of this moment, a threefold understanding of all ministries has been selected as a balanced theology of order and ministry.

Is it a better way to say in a few words what was once intended when the church spoke of "power" or "authority" to act in the name of Christ as what is conferred in ordination? Was the older understanding wrong in the light of shifting the focal image of the nature of ministry to the triple office or task? Since theology is always dealing in images and metaphors, even when it is using conceptual language, it is important to realize that selecting a new image or metaphor seldom means that one that was used fruitfully in another age or that was meaningful in another cultural milieu is now wrong. It is more fruitful to speak of a new approach being potentially *better* today than the approach that emphasized power and authority. The latter words were very important when legal metaphors were central and the question was primarily one of who validly and legitimately was acting with the authority of Jesus the Christ. One should recall the chaos of the medieval period, when clear lines of authority were a gift in a turbulent world. And in the post-Reformation world, Catholicism was preoccupied with establishing clear lines over against the Protestants. In addition, one must say that placing the accent on service (*diakonia*) in all forms of church ministry is a major issue in an age when people who insist on the authority and dignity of their office are more likely to be laughed at and lampooned than taken seriously. It is no accident, I think, that the two most popular "saints" of our era are the twelfth century's Francis of Assisi and the twentieth century's Mother Teresa of Calcutta. Exemplifying a spirit of service has risen to the level of a modern-day *sensus fidelium,* marking what moderns are prepared to call a "legitimate" execution of a church office. Therefore, service needs to be visible and tangible in every form of church ministry, and the image of Jesus washing the feet of his disciples is a powerful icon of the meaning of ministry.

THE MINISTRY OF JESUS AS THE ICON AND FOUNDATION OF EVERY THEOLOGY OF ORDER

The second, third, and fourth sections of this chapter have focused on issues that reinforce the main theme of the chapter: the ministry of Jesus as the icon and foundation of the theology of order and ministry in the Catholic church. Jesus' own ministry is the icon, standard, and foundation of *all* ecclesial ministries. That's easy to say, but when we consider a globalized world, we perceive a multiplicity of cultures and ethnic diversity. We see a multiplicity of philosophies and worldviews. We hear a breathtaking multiplicity of languages. Differences abound. Because of this multiplicity, one can readily ask such questions as: Is there only one way to be a Roman Catholic minister, given all this diversity? Is there a principle that will help us decide whether there is also room for a multiplicity of lay and liturgical ministries and perhaps even diverse liturgical rites that reflect diverse cultures of the people of God? It is easier in the case of lay activity in the world. No one would insist that there be a food pantry in a church in an area where there is no hunger, or outreach to sex workers in an area where there are no prostitutes. How one runs an education ministry in an area where few have even a primary-level education will be different from how that is carried out in a church where most people have graduated from tertiary-level programs. There seems to be little controversy, then, that room needs to be provided to adapt social-action ministries to the diverse cultural and ethnic-social situations of the people of God.

The real controversies arise when it comes to (1) the shape of liturgical rites and (2) the question of whether ordained ministries can differ widely from place to place. It is my own theological judgment that there can and

should be great diversity in both liturgical ministries and in liturgies themselves, which reflect the cultures and the way in which the ordained ministry
and the church's own life are shaped to deal with ethnic and cultural diversi-
ties amid the many groupings of the people of God. Clearly, though, we must
listen to voices on the other side of this argument. While we are attempting
to be balanced in this book, it does have a perspective.

We seem to be caught between two poles. On the one hand there is cultural diversity, and on the other hand there is the centering in Jesus. Is centering on his example not likely to lead to sterile imitation of first-century
cultural practices? Viewed from another perspective, there is the contemporary judgment that equiculturalism is a valid principle, yet there is the age-
old experience of the church that there is also a valid conserving function in
leadership and that in rapidly changing times, maintaining continuity can
itself be an important ministry. How can a church in a globalizing world deal
with such binary oppositions?

Let us begin with Jesus. If there is one book that every minister in the
Roman Catholic Church, ordained or lay, female or male, Thai or Irish,
should read again and again, it is the book of the Gospels. If in the library of
a church minister there is one book that has dog-eared pages and finger-
stained sections, this book should be the Gospels. Too often in ministerial
circles, both ordained and lay, only the latest books on ministry, the latest
how-to-minister books, are the ones that are dog-eared and marked up. By
reflecting on the Gospels, however, we are reflecting on the ways in which
Jesus himself ministered. And it is common experience that if a group con-
fronts a present-day issue by prayerfully discussing the example of Jesus, his
example proves to open that group to the needs of the community, if an issue
internal to the community is controversial, and to the needs of the wider
world, if outreach ministries are being contemplated.

Admittedly, legitimate questions arise: Why do we have to study the ministry of a Jewish man, when my work takes place in the middle of Ghana?
What has the Jewish world of the first century in common with the new-
millennial world in Peru? Is the Catholic Church stuck on a Jewish way of
thinking, a Jewish way of operating, or a Jewish way of ministering? Why
Jesus, who was Jewish? How can Jesus be the foundational base of a multicultural world, even more pointedly for an equicultural world? In this way,
aren't we likely to end up with absurd questions like, What would Jesus drive?

An answer to these questions must be carefully formulated. What are we
looking for when we read the Gospels? I think it is important to realize that
Bible reading does not give us a how-to lesson on the best way to minister. If
we are looking for such solutions to problems, we are reading the Gospels in

the wrong way. A study of Jesus' own ministry tells us something about God, who is neither Jewish nor Russian, neither Swedish nor Argentinean. Whatever ministry we are in; wherever we might minister; and to whom, with whom, and for whom we might be ministering, the key principle we encounter is how to help bring God into a person's, group's, or community's life. We study the ministry of Jesus to see how Jesus opened others to the loving and forgiving presence of God in that person's life.

One of the first things we encounter there is his openness to the Holy Spirit and the way in which God's presence in him made him present to others. All genuine ministry begins, in other words, with the minister having let in the Spirit of Jesus. She opens us to God's presence, so that we may find the treasure buried in the field (Matt. 13:46) and share the discovery with our fellows. In ministry, we are led by Jesus himself to become God oriented, not Jewish-Jesus oriented. Jesus' message, as also his life, death, and resurrection, reveals God. Many people today are searching for a credible God in whom they can believe. As Christians, we believe that the God we see in Jesus is credible. In our own personal lives, this God is and has been credible, and we want to share the credible God that Jesus revealed to others. The human nature of Jesus is the medium in and through which we can see, hear, find, and love a credible God.

There are many works of art that express Jesus' humanity and incarnation in every race under heaven. For instance, there are pictures of Jesus as Chinese or Nigerian. Pope John Paul II, speaking in Canada in 1984, said, "Christ, in the members of his body, is himself Indian." In this dynamic is created a multicultural body of Christ which validates the equicultural principle. In art and in the community, Jesus as the Christ becomes a man for all cultures and for all ethnic groups. But this is not the historical Jesus who lived two thousand years ago. The historical Jesus was an ordinary human being whom few people ever met. Until he began his public life, he was basically a nobody. He lived in a town that had little or no fame. He was not at all wealthy; in fact he was poor.

When we say that God became human, we focus on a central mystery of Christian and Catholic faith, the incarnation. God becomes human. How can that be? Our human minds cannot put the two—God and human—together in any logical way. But logic plays no role in the incarnation; only in and through faith do we accept the event of incarnation when the Spirit moves us to say yes and entrust ourselves to Jesus, still living. The incarnation is a mystery in which we believe, but believing in it is not merely assenting to a concept. It is saying yes to a person made present by the Spirit.

Writers, painters, sculptors, and musicians go far beyond the historical, human reality of the event itself, when they write, paint, sculpt, and express in music, art, and literature the meaning of the incarnation. Popes, bishops, and theologians speak eloquently about the incarnation, portraying the Christ-event as the central moment of all cosmic and human history. On Christmas eve or Christmas day, ordinary priests and deacons bring these images into play. Christmas is a marvelous time of year for Christian communities. There are crèches with gossamer angels singing over the manger; pious-faced shepherds are kneeling in awe in front of Joseph, Mary, and the baby Jesus; and elegantly attired wise men (the magi) are present with expensive gifts of gold, frankincense, and myrrh. Sometimes even the animals are made to look as if they are trying to kneel in front of baby Jesus. Glory to God in the highest and peace to all people of good will! Christmas carols are full of tenderness and amazement.

In the Franciscan intellectual tradition, a different side of the incarnation is emphasized, and it tells us a great deal about order and ministry. This interpretation emphasizes the humility of the incarnation.[31] Instead of pomp and glory one sees in the birth of Jesus a humble moment in world history. An incident in the life of St. Francis can help us understand the humility of the incarnation. When Francis was about twelve or thirteen—in 1194 to be exact —the empress Constance was on her way to Sicily to join her husband, Holy Roman Emperor Henry VI. At the time of her journey she was pregnant. The retinue of horses and soldiers, carriages and servants had made its way to the environs of Assisi, when Empress Constance realized that the baby was going to be born very quickly. Some historians say that she came to Assisi, where she gave birth to the child. Other historians say that she went to a nearby village called Jedi. No matter where she went, she took up residence in the home of very wealthy people. The child was a boy, the future Frederick II. Assisi at that time was not very large and Jedi was much smaller. For a small town to have the empress come and give birth was major news. Her every move was noticed and many of the details were released to the public. When the boy was baptized in the cathedral of Assisi, the whole town was astir. The teenager Francis must have seen much of this, and he certainly heard people talking about it.

Several years later, Francis left his father's home and father's wealth to become the poor man of Assisi. He had often prayed and meditated on the incarnation. He also loved nature, and Assisi, settled on a hill with panoramic views, was a place where nature-lovers could not help but revel in the sunshine, the river in the valley below, and the moon and stars at night. One day,

---

31. Kenan Osborne, *The Franciscan Intellectual Tradition* (St. Bonaventure, N.Y.: Franciscan Institute, 2003), 34-39, 53-68.

Francis realized something very special. God had come to the very same earth on which he was standing. The incarnate God, Jesus, looked at the same sun, the same moon, and the same stars. But when God came, where were the horses and chariots, the soldiers and maids of honor? Where was the grandeur? The empress Constance was treated royally. Her infant was honored and revered by all the people, rich and poor, noble and serf. What a difference there was when God came in humility. No Jewish person, except for some shepherds, was present, and shepherds were looked down on by ordinary Jewish people. Shepherds came on your property, fed and watered their animals at your expense, and stole whatever they could, and then disappeared. To have shepherds at the birth of Jesus was no big thing. Even the wise men or magi were no big thing. They were not even Jews; they were Gentiles. In reality, the actual birth of Jesus was far more humble than we find in our ordinary Christmas cribs.

Fast forward once again. It is a few years later, and the place is Gubbio, a town not far from Assisi. Historically, Francis of Assisi is credited for constructing the first Christmas crib in this town of Gubbio. A few weeks before the feast of Christmas, Francis had said to some of his friends in Gubbio: "I wish to enact the memory of that babe who was born in Bethlehem; to see as much as is possible with my own bodily eyes the discomfort of his infant needs, how he lay in a manger, and how, with an ox and an ass standing by, he rested on hay."[32] The first Christmas crib was a humble one. Francis wanted to create a version of this humble crib in the small humble village of Gubbio.

The empress Constance arrived in Assisi, and anyone who was anyone greeted her. When the Word became flesh, no one of any worldly renown was there. What does this tell us about God in Jesus and in Christian order and ministry? At least this—as you have discerned my purpose in this digression: order and ministry based on Jesus and the God whom Jesus revealed entail a humble ministry and a ministry to the humble. You don't have to go to far-off Asia, Africa, or South America to find men and women living in humble circumstances. Indeed, the overwhelming majority of people on earth today are poor. The humility of the incarnation itself informs us that God came in humility to serve the humble.

In the incarnation, we see a benchmark, namely, Jesus the icon of humility and exemplar of ecclesial ministry. This consideration of the incarnation emphasizes the issue of service, which the Gospels, the documents of Vatican II, and the *Catechism of the Catholic Church* clearly call the foundation of all

---

32. Thomas of Celano, *Life of St. Francis of Assisi*, Eng. trans. in *Francis of Assisi: Early Documents*, ed. Regis Armstrong, Wayne Hellmann, William Short (New York: New City Press, 1999), 254-55.

order and ministry. In the incarnation, God becomes human in the humanness of Jesus. The humbling incarnation is the icon of ministerial service. We hear God's own words in this incarnate Jesus: I have come not to be served but to serve. We see God's own service in Jesus' washing the feet of his disciples.

It is in Jesus' public life that we see Jesus, who is God-made-flesh, as a minister in action. In the public life of Jesus, six characteristics of his ministry stand out in a remarkable way. In some ways, these characteristics can be considered benchmarks, but in some ways they are *not* benchmarks. In other words, these characteristics of ministry offer us today qualities that should in a profound way characterize our own contemporary ministerial activities. On the other hand, these characteristics of Jesus' own ministry were lived out by Jesus in a different culture, a different time, and in different circumstances from our own. Today's followers of Christ are not called to imitate Jesus' ministry in a slavish way. In this sense, the characteristics of Jesus' ministry are *not* benchmarks. Nonetheless, these characteristics of Jesus' ministry, insofar as they basically reflect God and do not reflect a different culture or a different historical time line, offer us a way in which we, too, might bring a credible God to the peoples of our cultures and our time lines. Let us briefly highlight each of these six characteristics.

SIX CHARACTERISTICS OF MINISTRY EXEMPLIFIED IN JESUS

1. *The Vocation of Jesus Shows That Ministry Is from God*

Again and again key Gospel passages indicate that God sent Jesus and that Jesus was conscious that God had called him to a ministry of prophecy, sanctification, and leadership. This ministry is not self-initiated; rather, it depends totally on God. There is an effacing of the human ego in Jesus and a dependence on and deference to the will of God. The community did not select Jesus, nor did Jesus select himself for his ministry. Christian ministry, likewise, is not initiated by the community, nor does Christian ministry have use for self-appointed ministers, for that way lies the hybris of self-appointed prophets, which brings disrespect on the community of Christ. Before appointment to office, there is need for genuine discernment by the community, and what we call ordination involves affirmation that God has called someone to ministry for the evangelical ordering of the community. When Christians who hold office forget this call from God, they slowly and surely become "career ministers." They do their job; they put in their time; but the real core of Christian order and ministry—hearing and following God's call—is not there. The real core is the call of God to an individual. God is saying to an individual person: be my minister. This call from God echoes in an individual as a sense of vocation.

We are, accordingly, at a point where one of the truly universal elements of ministry can be discerned and brought into relief for our globalized church. *That element is the primacy of determining that the call, especially the call to official public ministry, is a matter for discernment by the church*. Such positions are not professions that an individual can enter into because he or she wishes to. There needs to be a process of ratification of the claim that a person makes that God has called him or her.

There are two corollaries to that element. The first one needs careful consideration of how it can be implemented and is one on which the present-day Catholic Church is vulnerable to criticism. "Discernment by the church" does not mean merely "discernment by those ordained to priesthood and episcopacy." Some method of creating a more widely participatory process is necessary.

The second corollary is that sociocultural factors need to be taken into account both in determining how ministry is to be carried out and into how discernment is carried on.

Discernment of God's call and how it is to be carried out is crucial in the quite different circumstances of a globalized world where, paradoxically, local cultures are becoming more important. There may be some general guidelines regarding a process of discernment, but in the concreteness of human life, it is important to do justice to the existential moment of the community and the individuals to whom entrusting leadership is being considered. Only in a concrete, existential situation does God call an individual to be a minister or to be in orders. Regulations by human beings, even by those who are considered church leaders, cannot and should not limit what God can and cannot do. Our human task is to discern what God is doing. Our human task is not to tell God whom God can call and whom God cannot call.

At this juncture, I would like to point out that the documents of Vatican II make God's action the basis of all ministries. Whether one reads *Lumen Gentium*, *Ad Gentes*, *Presbyterorum Ordinis*, or *Apostolicam Actuositatem*, God's sending Jesus is the primary theological basis for all ministry and order. God sends Jesus to us with a mission and ministry. Every ministry and order in the church is only a sharing in this God-given mission and a ministry of Jesus. To overlook this foundation of God's primary action in Jesus renders both order and ministry in the Christian communities worthless. All Christian order and ministry are rooted in God's action. The Gospels clearly indicate that <u>Jesus himself realized that God had sent him</u>. Jesus himself was fulfilling God's own action. Whenever this basic foundation is lost, then men and women in both order and ministry become simply "<u>career</u>" ministers. Slowly but surely they cease to be ministers whose call is to share in the ministry and mission of Jesus, and the human Jesus was sent by God with this same mission and ministry.

2. *The Ministry of Jesus Is a Ministry of Service (*diakonia*)*

I discussed above how often the Greek terms for servant and service (*diakonos, diakonia,* and *diakonein*) appear in the New Testament. In the New Testament, there are 102 occurrences of this word and its cognates scattered throughout all the books. Too often the English translations use a variety of terms for this one Greek word, including "to take care of," "to tend," "to wait on," "to help," or "to aid." The English translations prevent us from seeing the wide use of *diakonia* in the New Testament writings. If there is one quality of Jesus' life that made a tremendous impression on the followers of Jesus and the early Jesus communities, it was the image of Jesus as the servant, the deacon, the *diakonos*. The "word" is service; the "icon" is Jesus; his washing the feet of his disciples is a prime example of how the author of the Gospel of John remembers that command (see John 13:12-17). In this word, icon, and exemplar, we see the second foundational characteristic for Christian order and ministry, one that cannot be ignored just because our globalizing world and church are complex. A Christian in any order and ministry <u>is a servant</u>; he or she <u>must be of service</u>. He or she must wash and dry the feet of others. To lose this characteristic is to lose the very meaning of Christian order and ministry.

From a global perspective, this characteristic of Christian ministry, if truly embodied, would probably <u>do more to bring credibility to the church</u> than anything else that can be imagined. The way that service is carried on may vary, but the reversal of values brought about by Jesus, according to which the most important thing in church order is <u>to distinguish oneself by being the servant of all</u>, we can be sure, will speak in the language of every nation, much as the Spirit did at Pentecost (Acts 2:1-13). To be of service is an essential part of church order and ministry, and in a good servant the church and the broader community to which the church seeks to minister will find a man or woman who can be trusted. In Chinese, a phrase one might use to compliment another is: *ni yo hsin* ("<u>you have a caring heart</u>"). A Chinese person who has "heart" is a good person, and the care of such a person is a heart disposed to serve. Jesus had a caring heart: *ta yo hsin*. Christian ministers, likewise, must be men and women who have a caring heart. A caring heart leads one to service of others.

3. The Ministry of Jesus Is a Ministry of Love (agapē)

In the Gospel of John, the most important word in the first twelve chapters is the word "life." It is used again and again. From chapter 13 to the end of the Gospel, the dominant word is "love" (Greek *agapē*), which is used again and again. (This is the word used twice in John 13:1: "Before the feast of Passover, Jesus knew that his hour had come to pass from this world to the Father. He *loved* his own in the world and he *loved* them to the end.")

In these final chapters John includes the Last Supper, the washing of the feet, the farewell discourses, the struggle in Gethsemane, the arrest and trial, the journey to Golgotha, the crucifixion, and the death of Jesus. Even the resurrection can be seen in John as part of God's love. Raymond E. Brown wrote in his *Commentary on John* that if we wish to understand John's interpretation of the suffering and death of Jesus, we must understand the washing of the feet.[33] The washing of the feet is a parable in action, telling us, as John so eloquently states it in words, that Jesus loved us to the very end. Christian order and ministry in a global perspective gain another characteristic in Jesus' own ministry of love. Through Jesus' love we see God's love, who loves us unto the end. The Christian vocation is to carry this message of love to the far ends of the world and to embody it to those who are burdened and weary, to those who are blind and deaf, to those who are disheartened and alone, and to those who see no future and have no hope. What a marvelous characteristic this is! If on the stone above one's grave, only one's name was there and the following words: "He (or she) loved the people," such a characteristic would speak a million words. From a global perspective of order and ministry, this does not mean loving only those who are Christian. In countries in which Christians are only 1 or 2 percent of the population, order and ministry still mean loving all who need love, whether they are Christians or not. Such ministerial men and women who reach out to all who need love, regardless of their religion or cultural differences, are truly sharing in the mission and ministry of Jesus, who had received precisely this kind of boundary-breaking mission and ministry from God.

---

33. See Raymond E. Brown, *The Gospel According to John: Introduction, Translation, and Notes*, vol. 2 (Garden City, N.Y.: Doubleday, 1970), where the commentary brings the centrality of *agapē* into relief in many places.

4. The Ministry of Jesus Is a Healing Ministry

That Jesus was a healer is found in all four Gospels. Jesus, however, not only healed illness and pain; he also healed the heart and the memory. He healed the pain of the victim as well as the sin of the victimizer. In Korean there is a word, *Han,* and it has to do with the pain of the victim. Almost all the languages of East Asia have a word similar to the Korean *Han. Han* is not simply the evil and wrong that one person inflicts on another. It is the painful scarring that remains after the evil deed. It is the still bleeding heart and still aching body. Jesus healed the sickness, which caused pain, but he also helped to heal the lingering pain, *Han,* once the sickness was gone. This lingering *Han* is clearly a pain that those in Christian order and ministry can heal at least to some degree. The healing of evil is certainly part of Christian ministry, but even more the healing of the victim's long-lasting pain. *Han* is a characteristic of Christian order and ministry within a global perspective.[34]

5. The Ministry of Jesus Is a Preaching and Teaching Ministry

Jesus did not build churches or synagogues. He did not construct schools and hospitals. Good as these buildings and their ministries are, Jesus primarily preached and taught. But what did he teach? The primary message of Jesus was the "Kingdom of God is at hand now." This means that God is present in the here and now, not in the above or in the future. God is a loving and compassionate presence in the lives of those who thought that even God did not care. Jesus taught also that Spirit of life and holiness is present now, bringing holiness to the unholy and life to the lifeless. Jesus also taught that evil is not the final answer. The final answer in every situation, no matter how distressing and wrenching the situation might be, is God's goodness, care, compassion, and grace. Finally, Jesus also taught that the good news of God's love, the gospel of mercy and hope, is especially found in the marginated and the outcasts, the lepers and the politically, socially, and religiously incorrect. This message of Jesus about God's presence in the here and now is a major characteristic for Christian order and ministry in a global perspective. Christian ministers are called on in word and deed to preach what Jesus preached and to teach what Jesus taught. The four points of his message that we have just listed should be the characteristics of our own global ministerial message in our teaching and preaching.

---

34. An intriguing book on the Korean word *Han* is that of Andrew Sung Park, *The Wounded Heart of God: The Asian Concept of Han and the Christian Doctrine of Sin* (Nashville, Tenn.: Abingdon Press, 1993).

In all cultures and countries, there are marginalized people, outcasts, and lepers. There are people whom the "correct people" call "incorrect," and the "religious leaders" call "irreligious." A person who is involved in Christian order and ministry, no matter what his or her culture might be, no matter what his or her race might be, and no matter what country he or she is a part of, must be a person for whom the characteristic is care and compassion for those on the edge and for those who are voiceless.

6. *The Ministry of Jesus Is Political*

At the time of Jesus, there was no separation of religion and politics. Human life involved the political and social realms and the religious dimension of life as well. It would have seemed odd for a Roman, a Syrian, a Jew, or a Greek to separate them. In addition, there was a general tolerance for the many religious belief systems and traditions in the Roman empire of Jesus' time. The exception was that Roman authorities were alert to signs that any religious group was hostile to the empire. Palestine was ruled in a bifurcated manner. Rome had ultimate authority, but it ruled through the Herodian kings and preferred not to have to step in directly. Jesus, though, was fearless in his criticism of King Herod, the Sanhedrin (who regulated Temple life and public religious observances), and some Pharisees, who were local teachers, revered for teaching the Law and summoning their fellow Jews to observe it carefully. As is typical in such bifurcated power arrangements, maintaining a semblance of order so that each group could function smoothly and have its needs met meant that justice for the marginalized took a back seat. To speak out for justice and to call attention to hypocrisy among religious leaders, as Jesus did, was—in the words of our time, if not his own—political activity.

The need to realize that justice is a higher goal than stability is one of the legacies Jesus bequeaths to the people who follow him. When society's civil, political, or religious leaders condone injustice or foster injustice, the followers of Christ need to follow their Lord in a forthright manner. This is an important form of Christian service, no matter where one resides. The God revealed in prophets such as Amos has little tolerance for leaders who think they need not listen to God's option for justice and the poor. Although Jesus did not seek confrontations, they came his way, and he did not avoid them.

Today's globalized world is one in which the goal of creating justice is low on the priority list of the world's political, economic, or military leaders. The world is driven by inequalities and a system rigged to benefit those who have access to capital. Greed and power are given wide berth in the efforts to shape the ever-widening patterns of globalizing production, banking, and trade. If it is not always easy to discern practical ways to bring about a more just world, it is clearly a fact that today's global communication technologies make it possible for members of the world Christian church to learn what is happening and to speak out clearly. Yet that word will be effective only to the extent that its global voice truly speaks for vital grassroots communities. To the extent that the voice speaking is simply that of a small percentage of activists whom one might call "an attentive elite," the powers that benefit from present arrangements will find it easy to turn a deaf ear. To be a truly effective *global voice*, in other words, the church needs to be a *communion of vital local communities.* The global Christian ministry cannot avoid taking risks in the political sphere, and no church has the channels from grassroots to the international leadership and from central leadership to thousands and thousands of local communities that Catholicism has. Are we using those channels as wisely as we should? Are we seeking ways to add our voice to that of sister churches and the followers of other religious traditions to communicate Catholic experience across the globe in the effort to find solutions to world problems? What is required are solutions that can be globally inspiring yet also adapted to local conditions in observing the glocalization principle.

In Matthew 5:14 Jesus calls his disciples "the light of the world." In Luke 2:32, an ancient text is applied to Jesus, giving him the title, "light to the gentiles." In John 8:12, Jesus says, "I am the light of the world," thus bringing into relief the cosmic nature of the claims made about him in John's prologue (John 1:1-14). At Vatican II, Jesus was called, "the light of the nations," which is also the title of the Vatican II Dogmatic Constitution on the Church (*Lumen Gentium*), which we have quoted often in this book. Jesus is also, as the Nicene Creed tells us (ND 7), "Light from light." The phrase "light of the nations" reminds us that the sun makes the light that enables us to see, and Jesus the Son of God is analogous to the sun. The moon, on the other hand, has no light of its own. It can only reflect the light of the sun. Christian ministry in the world is like the light of the moon. The Christian minister has no light of himself or herself but seeks to reflect the light of Jesus, who, in his humanity, reflects the Light we call God. Jesus, in his humanity, reflects the Light from Light, the loving God who has created all things and loves all people with an infinite love.

This, then, is what the present chapter is all about: Jesus, as the Light from Light, is the foundation and characteristic for all Christian order and ministry, even as today the phrase "light of the world" takes on new meaning in our new global perspective.

QUESTIONS FOR REFLECTION

1. Given what has been said, how can one best describe a bishop, a priest, and a deacon?

2. How do members of religions orders, that is, nuns, sisters, brothers, relate to church order in general? Are they independent actors or subordinate to bishops?

3. What has been the dominant understanding of ordination, office, order, and ministry church from the twelfth century to the mid-twentieth century? How did *Lumen Gentium* differ from that understanding? What difference could the new understanding make?

4. In your view, what are the main difficulties facing ministry in the Catholic Church today? What do you think are the main issues facing the church in shaping ministry in its new global situation?

5. List six aspects of Jesus' ministry that should be characteristics for all Christian ministry. Do you believe these six are found in your local church? If so, how? If not, what would you recommend to your bishop, pastor, and pastoral councils to make them real?

6. Hold an open discussion on multicultural or equicultural life with the members of your class and explore the attitudes that you and your associates have in regard to the proposition, "All cultures are equal."

7. What does the term "globalization" mean in general? Give some examples of globalization's impact on your own immediate world? How should the Roman Catholic Church respond to globalization on a worldwide basis? What are the benefits and dangers of globalization in the world at large and in the church?

8. What does the term "micromanagement" mean in general? Give some examples of micromanagement today in the economic and political world? Do you believe there is micromanagement in the Catholic Church? If so, give some examples.

9. Are Catholic policies on who is admitted to the ordained ministry an example of discrimination or a genuine example of discerning what God wants for the church? Give reasons for your ideas. Is there racism and gender and cultural discrimination in the church? What are the principles that make such discrimination improper?

10. What is the teaching of the Second Vatican Council on the threefold tasks (the *tria munera*) of *every* ministry? Why is it important?

11. Why is the prophetic (teaching and preaching) ministry of Jesus placed first? Discuss whether explicit teaching and preaching are the best way to proclaim the Gospel? Find examples of Jesus' teaching ministry exercised verbally and in action in the Gospels.

12. What is the priestly (sanctifying) mission of Christians? Find examples of Jesus "sanctifying" people in the Gospels? What does it mean "to sanctify daily life?"

Is the priestly ministry of the ordained bishop, priest, or deacon primarily a liturgical role?

13. What is holiness? Can a nurse, a teacher, or a military officer be "holy"? Explain how.

14. Is "leadership" an adequate modern word to explain how Jesus is "King"?

15. Whom do you think is a true leader in today's church? Do you think the offices of pope, bishop, priest, and deacon are genuine leadership roles today?

16. Can or should leadership ministries be carried out in different ways in different cultures? If, for example, the law of celibacy were dropped and if women were ordained, what would be the effect on leadership in the church as you know it?

SUGGESTIONS FOR FURTHER READING AND STUDY

Bevans, Stephen B., and Roger P. Schroeder. *Constants in Context: A Theology of Mission for Today.* Maryknoll, N.Y.: Orbis Books, 2004. An account of the church's concept of its mission from its beginning to the contemporary period.

Irvin, Dale T., and Scott W. Sunquist. *The History of the World Christian Movement.* Vol. 1, *Earliest Christianity to 1453.* Maryknoll, N.Y.: Orbis Books, 2001. The social history of Christianity in its many cultural environments from its beginning to the late Middle Ages. Volume 2, from 1454 to the contemporary period, is forthcoming in 2007.

John Paul II, Pope. *Pastores dabo vobis*, Apostolic Exhortation, On the Formation of Priests in the Circumstances of the Present Day, March 25, 1992.

O'Meara, Thomas. *Theology of Ministry.* Mahwah, N.J.: Paulist Press, 1999.

Osborne, Kenan B. *Priesthood: A History of the Ordained Ministry in the Roman Catholic Church.* Eugene, Ore.: Wipf & Stock, 2002.

Stark, Rodney. *The Rise of Christianity: How the Obscure, Marginal Jesus Movement Became the Dominant Force in the Western World in a Few Centuries.* San Francisco: HarperSanFrancisco, 1996.

Sullivan, Francis A. *From Apostles to Bishops.* Mahwah, N.J.: Newman Press, 2001.

3

Priestly Order and Ministry

Their History and Meaning Today

THEME AND GOAL OF THIS CHAPTER

THE PURPOSE OF THIS CHAPTER is to present a clear description of three different issues regarding bishops and priests. First, I will present the *popular* view of both bishop and priest prevalent today in the media and popular culture. Second, I will present a brief but, I hope, accurate *historical* picture of the Roman Catholic bishop and priest. In this historical overview, we deepen our appreciation of the fact that there has not been a single, dogmatically defined view of the office of either bishop or priest in the Roman Catholic Church. The prevalent view of today became standard in the church after the Protestant Reformation in the sixteenth century. The concern from then until the mid-twentieth century was the practical one of wanting conformity both in doctrine and in leadership to differentiate Roman Catholic from Protestant positions on office in the church.

The third theme of this chapter is the need for openness to the possibility of a diversity in how the leadership is carried out in a globalizing world in which, as we have noted, even as communications technology and political-economic factors are drawing people closer together, tendencies that accent diversity are intensifying. Our question is what this intensification of forces that accentuate local cultural and ethnic identities means for the world church.

The overarching goal of this chapter is to offer the readers a motivation to work for gospel-centered forms of church leadership that may vary from culture to culture. It would be less than honest not to admit that I am personally convinced that the upper leadership of the Roman Catholic Church should endorse the principle that a variety of culturally appropriate ways of exercising office must be adopted if the church is not to suffer grave harm. In that context, we offer ideas on what may be fruitful to help today's globalized church rethink the standardized, post-Reformation model of priestly and episcopal ministry. A globally cloned model of priestly leadership is inconsistent with an equicultural worldview.

Bernard Lonergan has perhaps captured the essence in the revolution in thinking that is required in his distinction between two views of culture.[1] Lonergan reminds us that the notion that there is one acceptable culture became dominant in the West as a part of the church's adoption of the philosophy of ancient Greece and Rome. Culture, in this perspective, is a *normative* view. What is acceptable is in harmony with the classical writers of the ancient period, and in history, it is the role of the guardians of classicist culture to ensure that their standards are maintained. We have moved today, Lonergan says, into an age marked by a *historical* view of culture. The mindset of anyone who has partaken in contemporary education is ruled by a *genetic* and *historical* consciousness. Things, including cultures, are the result of a certain kind of genetic inheritance that is the basis of its fundamental structure and historical experience, which leads to an evolution of that inheritance. For those who are historically conscious, to know something is to study its structure and history. Its history is the story of growth through contact and sharing with other cultures. William McNeill and others are right to say that there has been contact between and a level of influence exerted by the major cultures of the world on one another.[2] To the extent that one becomes aware of the historical nature of cultural development, one is historically conscious. From that point of view, the problem for an organization like the Catholic Church, with its two-thousand-year history, during which time it believed the classicist notion of culture was correct and saw itself as the guardian of this a-historical viewpoint, is this: How can it preserve what is perennial in the gospel while opening itself up to changes required if it is to inculturate itself and the gospel into radically different cultures?

In no area of church life is that question felt more than in the area we examine in this book. How does one inculturate offices of leadership while ensuring that the church does not abandon the heritage given it by the founder of Christianity?

---

1. Bernard J. F. Lonergan, "The Transition from a Classicist World-View to Historical Consciousness," in his *A Second Collection*, ed. William F. J. Ryan and Bernard J. Tyrell (Philadelphia: Westminster, 1974), 1-10.

2. William McNeill, *The Rise of the West: A History of the Human Community* (Chicago: University of Chicago Press, 1963). Despite its title, McNeill's book is an important volume documenting the mutual influence of the great civilizations and cultures on one another. It is not about the triumph of the "West over the Rest."

THE "POPULAR" VIEW OF PRIESTS AND BISHOPS TODAY

In recent years, there have been many movies in which well-known film stars have played the role of Catholic priests or bishops. In addition, there have been scores of novels in which bishops or priests appear in major and minor roles. It is probably not overstating it to say that these images have influenced more people about the nature of priestly and episcopal office than all the official documents ever written. Critics and viewers alike consider these portrayals of priests and bishops to be depictions of the real thing. As art they are evaluated on how well the role is played, but even when they are bad art and bad theology, viewers or readers believe they are seeing and understanding the ministry of priests and bishops. *The Exorcist* was about a Catholic priest, and even though the movie revolved around Satan possessing a girl, the role of the priest seemed to most people to be an accurate portrayal of the standard priest. In both the book and the film *The Godfather*, priests played significant roles. Dan Brown's novel *The Da Vinci Code* has several priests and bishops in it. All these characters seem to be in line with what priests and bishops are considered to be about—protecting the power of the church at any cost.

Sometimes a film portrays a priest or bishop from centuries ago. *The Mission* had sympathetic pictures of Jesuit missionaries and an almost diabolical, cynical picture of a papal legate cardinal. *On the Waterfront* has a priest in a heroic role. The *Bells of St. Mary's* introduced a kind but curmudgeonly pastor and an up-to-date associate—Bing Crosby, playing opposite Ingrid Bergman as Sister Superior.

Standard in all these examples from art is a notion that yesterday's and today's priests and bishops are basically alike. For many it goes so far as believing that the role of priests and bishops has been the same since the beginning of the Christian church. Bishops and cardinals wear red flowing robes and miters and carry ornate crosiers. Priests, on the other hand, wear black cassocks or black suits with Roman collars. In the minds of many, priests have always worn such clothes. And they are always celibate, although such films often portray them as unfaithful to their vows.

Is it too much to say that such images are virtually global? I suspect not. If one travels anywhere, be it to the Americas, Europe, Asia, or Africa, such popular images seem firmly ensconced. Although bishops in the tropics may wear white cassocks instead of black, the very difference calls attention to the "standard" black with shades of red and purple indicating the rank of the wearer. The contemporary and common view of bishop and priest is, in a word, "stereotypical," and those who wear the clerical garb are some of the most recognized figures in the world.

Two issues stand out as we consider order and ministry from a globalized perspective. The first is that the ordinary Roman Catholic is comfortable with this Euro-American image of the priest or bishop. In marketing terms, this image is an extremely successful branding of the two most visible officials of the church, to the extent that even those who exemplify the brand and betray it reinforce the ideal in their very failure to live up to the positive image.

The ordinary Roman Catholic, in other words, is comfortable with this image and with the function of priests and bishops in conformity with that image. Even if one moves to a hybrid culture like that of Latin America, this is the case. Moving farther afield, say, to Africa, Oceania, or Asia, this image is taken as the standard for what a priest or a bishop is to be. Anyone who thinks, for example, that the masses of Catholics in the Highlands of Papua New Guinea or the deserts of Namibia are clamoring for a different kind of priest is mistaken. On the whole, Roman Catholics not only think that priests and bishops *are* the same worldwide, but they also *want* their priests and bishops to conform to that image, an image that has been enforced by the artifacts of popular culture in film, TV, and, for the literate, books.

If the ordinary parishioner in Wisconsin thinks that bishops and priests have always looked and acted like this, the same is true elsewhere in the world. A radical change in how priestly or episcopal leadership is constructed and exercised would be suspected of challenging the true nature of the church as intended by Jesus. Culture, ethnicity, and other similar factors are considered secondary issues when it comes to considering the "standards" to which Catholic bishops and priests must conform. What bishops and priests are in the church (that is, their position and role) and how they act (that is, their function in the church's sacramental life and their government of both parish and diocese) are and should be the same worldwide, in the view of most.

For these Roman Catholics, globalization does not necessitate any basic or fundamental change in understanding the role of or how Roman Catholic bishops and priests should act. If we want to open the church to diversifying the understanding of ordained ministry, altering the way it is carried out, or making any change, we need to realize that for the most part, it is only an educated elite attentive to what *could* be done better who favor changes.

The second thing to be aware of in terms of this effectively globalized image of ordained ministry is this. On the whole, Vatican leadership and the leadership of some (perhaps "many," maybe even "most") local churches are on the same page in wanting priests and bishops to conform to this standard image, no matter where they are in our world. True, in Europe and North America, where Catholics are alarmed at the declining numbers of priests and religious, there are many who favor changing structures to allow married priests and women priests. But such opinions are rare and, as the number of Catholics grows in the global South, Euro-American voices arguing for change increasingly appear to be marginalized, while Vatican leadership grows more and more suspicious that those calling for change have been seduced by Western culture and seek to make changes so they may adapt the church to their level of comfort, not because they feel an evangelical imperative. These are, I know, very hard words for Euro-American progressives to accept, but they are not truly listening to the voices of their critics if they don't realize that these are increasingly common views. In addition, there are strong minorities in both Europe and North America who do not want to see married men and women priests. Some form of schism would likely occur if changes to the standard model of priesthood and episcopacy were to be pushed through.

Today, both the pope and the Roman curia want the global Catholic priesthood and episcopacy to remain basically the same, in conformity to the standard model of celibacy, tertiary-level education, and visible continuity in how such offices are carried out globally. In addition, conformity to the standard pattern is not only desired by Rome; it is mandated by Rome.[3] This church's central leadership bases its position on a theology of order and ministry that it infers goes back to the earliest periods. The very apostolicity of the Roman Catholic Church is portrayed in official documents as being in conformity with ancient patterns of priestly and episcopal leadership. Treating these two issues as givens—that is, the *factual basis* for this portrayal and the *divine mandate* to which the standard model of priestly and episcopal office are attributed—makes it difficult for historians and theologians to speak and write freely on what their research tells them. Lifting that veil and encouraging honest discussion are, then, the conditions for considering

---

3. See the *Catechism of the Catholic Church*, 1536-1600. The *Catechism* does not mention cultural differences. In 1149, however, one reads: "The liturgy of the Church presupposes, integrates, and sanctifies elements from creation and human culture, conferring on them the dignity of signs of grace, or the new creation in Jesus Christ." In 1204: "The celebration of the liturgy, therefore, should correspond to the genius and culture of the different peoples" (reference is made to *Sacrosanctum Concilium*, the Vatican II Decree on the Sacred Liturgy [articles 37-40]). CCC 1205 states: "In the liturgy, above all in the sacraments, there is an immutable part that is divinely instituted and of which the Church is the guardian, and parts that can be changed, which the Church has the power and on occasion also the duty to adapt to the cultures of recently evangelized peoples." However, there is no mention at all of cultural issues in the *Catechism's* entire presentation on the sacrament of holy orders (CCC 1536-89).

whether any major change in church leadership is possible or could be recommended for any segment of our globalized church. Until the notion that Jesus himself directly gave instructions on how priesthood and episcopacy were to be established and maintained is subjected to historical criticism, the gulf between historians and theologians and the central leadership of the church will only grow.

At this point it may be opportune to realize that in the previous section we did not maintain that there was a large popular groundswell demanding change. We are advancing a position here that recognizes the affection of many for the present order of the church. In effect, we are simply asking whether some adaptation might help the church develop in ways that will better equip both the ordained and the laity to understand their role as ambassadors of Christ. If, as some have maintained,[4] the present model of ministry promotes an idea of the church as a filling station to which the laity comes to be served by clerics, then the standard model portrays a misleading improper image of the ministry of both the ordained and the laity in their roles within the church and to the world. There may, in other words, be *theological* and *missiological* reasons for changing the structures of ministry, even if there is no popular groundswell. But because of the allegiance felt by so many to the standard model, any form of change must be the product of study, dialogue, prayer, and discernment. It cannot come as an imposition from the top down.

Certain major theological and ecclesial issues underlie the insistence on the standard model. First, conformity is regarded as more important than considering the possibility of a need to adapt to quite different circumstances that are often intensifying, despite globalization. Second, this form of conformity leads to the temptation of leaders in Rome to micromanage at the local level, even though they have little or no knowledge of local conditions. Even if these central leaders have knowledge of local cultural conditions, they effectively disallow giving them any substantial role either in the sacramental life of the church or in the way Catholic leadership exists in the different social structures of a globalized world. What needs to be stressed here is this: that culture in this way of proceeding is treated as an accident even if official documents often say the opposite.

In considering culture as an accidental human reality, Catholicism finds itself opposing fundamental insights from social sciences such as anthropology, linguistic sociology, and history. In short, the hierarchy of the Catholic

---

4. William R. Burrows, *New Ministries: The Global Context* (Maryknoll, N.Y.: Orbis Books, 1980), 115-37.

Church runs the risk, since many of Rome's own cherished assumptions can themselves be understood as cultural developments that do not flow from the core of Christian teaching and experience, of using specious reasoning to justify positions they have arrived at on different grounds. To act as if culture is accidental to Christian religious expression and theology indicates that one has already taken an a priori classicist view of Roman ecclesiastical, clerical, or curial culture as a standard that must be maintained.

In order to make this real and not simply abstract, I ask the reader to consider for a moment a real person whom you know personally and who was born and raised outside of the United States. It would be even better if this real person was raised outside of what we call the Euro-American cultural area. In other words, this person should be culturally different from you.

Allow me to use my own imagination in this scenario. Let us say that this real person whom I know personally was born and raised in Mexico. He or she comes from parents, grandparents, and great-grandparents who were also born in Mexico. Most of their family comes not only from Mexico, but from a very specific area of Mexico. Let us say that the family has its roots in Jalisco, and these roots go back over many generations. This Mexican person I know has now come to the United States and has become my friend. Let us even give this person a name: for a man, let us call him Carlos; for a woman, let us call her Maria. Without any doubt, Carlos and Maria are culturally different from myself. On my father's side, my lineage is English; on my mother's side, the lineage is German. You, the reader, if you are not Mexican, can think of your own grandparents or great-grandparents. Perhaps they came from Ireland or Italy. Perhaps they came from Korea or Vietnam. You are, therefore, a first-, second-, or even third- or fourth-generation American. You like MTV; you speak English even if it is your own second language; you play baseball and tennis and generally eat french fries or some other form of potato alongside a serving of beef. Your language, your lifestyle, your diet, your physical activities are typically American.

Carlos and Maria, however, are culturally different. Their first language is Spanish, not English. They enjoy soccer rather than American football. They have a different diet from yours. You might add other cultural differences beyond the ones I have just mentioned. After listing such cultural differences, ask yourself this basic question: through your listing of the above cultural differences have you truly described culture? Is culture simply language, diet, sports preferences, and so on? Your answer will certainly be negative. So what, then, is culture?

At this juncture, we begin to move into the heart of the cultural issue. Ask yourself and ask Carlos and Maria, Is culture an accidental part of your life?

Can one simply drop being an Irish American, a mestizo Mexican, or a Hakka Chinese, and continue living? Certainly, some cultural characteristics are accidental and could be easily dropped from one's life. However, there are many deeper issues in culture that are at the core of one's life. It is even a mistake to call them "essential" as opposed to "accidental" elements, for one of the insights of cultural studies is that culture is a totality in much the same way that an onion *is* its layers. It is in this deeper dimension of culture that the term "accidental" turns ugly. To lose these cultural layers is to lose one's way of expressing one's deepest personal relationships to family, country, and history.

What we have been considering in this section, accordingly, is whether diverse cultural manners of expressing fundamental religious experiences and of offering leadership in such matters can be adopted by the church in structuring order and ministry. In the section that follows, we examine how such structures have evolved in Catholic history and what that history could teach us about the principles of church order and ministry.

PRIESTS AND BISHOPS IN HISTORICAL PERSPECTIVE

From today's globalized perspective, the question of leadership is of major importance. Leadership differs from one culture to another. Not all cultures have kings or emperors, queens or empresses. Not all cultures have presidents, senates, houses of representatives, prime ministers, states, governors, or mayors. We know that societal leadership itself is different from one culture to another. Also different are the ways in which traditional family relationships are handled in civil law. In some societies, for example, tribal law is officially recognized as governing marriage. In other societies, civil law takes precedence over such rules. But both societies can function smoothly, and very diverse rules are accepted. The role of elders is extremely important in certain cultures, while elders have no role whatsoever in others. Elders may actually decide land tenure in one country, while in others elaborate systems of registering titles are used. The specific roles of men and women in leadership also differ from culture to culture. The selection of leaders is not determined by a single method. One quite successful nation can enshrine a book such as the Christian Bible or the Muslim Qur'an as a privileged source from which the principles of civil law are derived. Another can be resolutely secular.

In the Roman Catholic Church, the structure of leadership is a major issue. An episcopal form of governance with all diocesan bishops being in communion with the pope as bishop of Rome is seen as divinely willed (*de jure divino* in the traditional Latin phrase), not a mere tradition that could be altered by a constitutional assembly or ecumenical council. Starting with that basic set of theological warrants and principles, all dioceses and parishes are required to adhere to that practice and to the fundamental rules of the Code of Canon Law that spell out the standard pattern of Catholic life. Catholicism sees believing in Christ as the redeemer of the world as a deeply personal and free decision, but it also sees the basic episcopal-papal structure of church order as a matter beyond individual choice for Catholics. We will see that the standard pattern to which the parishes and dioceses must conform is also a matter of historical development. By this, I mean that the standard pattern has a history and that during its history, major changes have been made again and again. The current conformity standard is by and large a social construct that has evolved in the church's European history. It reflects the church's theologically rooted understanding of that history. The question, then, is whether imposing conformity to that standard is the equivalent of making European cultural history, experience, and theological reflection the sole standard for a world church.

When questions of church order are discussed, it is common to refer to them also as matters of "church polity." In ecumenical conversations among the churches, questions of polity are regarded as secondary to questions of "faith," which touch on fundamental matters of belief in areas such as Christology, soteriology, sin, and grace. In the World Council of Churches questions of faith and order and questions of "polity" are studied by the Faith and Order Commission. Depending on the level of the conversations, there are usually Catholic representatives appointed by Rome or local churches present when the Faith and Order Commission meets. What the linking of faith and order in these discussions emphasizes is that matters of order and polity are intimately connected with overarching matters of faith. For Catholics and the Orthodox, indeed, questions of polity are matters of faith, not mere administrative matters. It is important to realize this, because most cultures in today's globalized world regard civil polity structures as secondary. It is not essential that a president be elected by direct election or by a legislature, as long as the rules are clear and the elections are fair. It is not important for a state to be headed by a king or a directly elected president, as long as a constitution ensures that the government has the assent of the people as a whole. Constitutions can be either formally written or a matter of "tradition" recognizing fundamental procedural guidelines to ensure due fairness.

The question of polity for a global Catholic Church is where matters basic to its identity meet questions about cultural adaptation. Catholicism has been clear throughout the ages on a basic principle that was underlined once again at the Second Vatican Council. The church is not just a voluntary society; it is the body of Christ (LG 7) and the people of God of the new covenant (LG 9). Perhaps most important for understanding how the church is Christ's body and God's people, it is seen in *Lumen Gentium* as a reality composed of both visible and spiritual elements:

> The one mediator, Christ, established and ever sustains here on earth his holy Church, the community of faith, hope, and charity, as a visible organization through which he communicates truth and grace to all. But the society structured with hierarchical organs and the mystical body of Christ, the visible society and the spiritual community, the earthly Church and the Church endowed with heavenly riches, are not to be thought of as two realities. On the contrary, they form one complex reality which comes together from a human and divine element. (LG 8)

For Catholics, then, the basic hierarchical structure cannot be changed.

In what follows, accordingly, we consider historical changes in the priesthood and episcopacy during the past two thousand years. We seek to identify principles that can help us understand how these offices can best be carried out in today's globalizing world. This discussion will show that major changes have taken place. If major changes have taken place in the past, then the question immediately arises why changes are blocked today. Is the reluctance to discuss the possibility of change a form of preference for past European cultural models of ministry? We seek here not so much to construct a theology of dissent from present policy as to explicate principles that may prove helpful in moving a discussion that has been stalled for nearly forty years to grounds where it can be carried on fruitfully once again.

Globalization Requires Mutual Respect among and between Cultures

Showing respect for other cultures is one of the few principles everyone in the contemporary world agrees upon, at least in the abstract. In the secular world, if Toyota wants to market cars successfully in Bolivia, it knows that it has to pay attention to Bolivian drivers, what they have to spend, what cars mean in that society, and under what kinds of road and climatic conditions drivers will be operating their vehicles. The answer a Japanese businessman gave to the question, "What is the most important language for international business?" epitomizes what every astute salesperson knows. He answered, "My customer's."

This illustrates what we said above in discussing the "glocalization" principle in the context of globalization. While globalization means that the world has shrunk and certain major economic, social, communications, and political forces are pressuring every area of the world to adapt to these forces, global inputs are in fact received, interpreted, and adapted. Globalization results in "glocalization." In the commercial realm, this principle is easily understood and illustrated. An automobile may be a vehicle that moves people and goods, powered by an internal combustion engine, a battery, or a gas-electric hybrid engine; what it *signifies* socially in a given culture can be quite different from what it means in another. A successful international automobile company glocalizes its marketing to appeal to the needs an automobile fills in a given culture or to a given segment of the culture.

An international fraternal organization will do the same, as will the alumni association of the Universities of Tokyo, Papua New Guinea, Cambridge, Harvard, and Salamanca when they want to create a network to nurture social bonds among graduates, to raise money among them, and to provide a mechanism for screening and recruiting prospective students. If Cambridge tries to use in Bangalore the techniques that were successful in getting London-based graduates together, it will likely have only fair to mediocre success.

At one level, these same principles apply to the Christian church as a whole and to the many churches. Roman Catholicism, though, has a special set of questions it needs to confront. First, although in principle "catholic" means universal, in fact the Catholic Church grew in Europe for fifteen hundred years. Its current transnational culture, in fact, was one of the major forces that created European culture. This church culture has served as a binding force that, despite the many languages and cultures of the nations that lived between the Caucasus and the West of Ireland, provided unifying principles. In the 1500s, the church began its spread into Latin America and the southern part of North America. In the 1800s it gained a major foothold in North America. Because the dominant population of the United States was European, the church's inculturation went relatively smoothly. It was more complex in Latin America, where the Iberian conquerors subjugated native peoples as effectively as was done in North America. Instead, a Spanish and Portuguese elite ruled over a population of mixed-race or mestizo people and native peoples. From nation to nation in Latin America, the proportions of Europeans, mestizos, and Indians varies, but it is clear that Catholicism there preserved the outer form of European Catholic culture while the vast majority of people followed a popular form of Catholicism that is only now beginning to be understood by social scientists, pastoral theologians, and the hierarchy.

The Latin American pattern is the forerunner of certain patterns that emerged in the church's inculturation in Africa, Asia, and Oceania. It is only now being studied carefully, but it seems clear that grassroots Catholicism is an amalgam of persistent traditional ("local") religious traditions, elements of "world" religious traditions such as Buddhism, Taoism, and Confucianism or Indian religious traditions. There are two sides to this dynamic. On the one hand, people in the Congo, Tamil Nadu, Luzon, Myanmar, and the Sepik were not stooges who took unquestioningly what colonial-era missionaries fed them. Instead they found a liberating, hope-inspiring message, which they translated into their own linguistic thought patterns, as they made Christianity their own faith.

But it is precisely at this point that Catholicism faces the question of respect for other cultures. Until now, the church has insisted that its ordained leadership be trained according to models developed in Europe over centuries. They must become conversant with doctrinal formulas that were developed to answer European questions, and they must follow ways of life pioneered by Europeans. Is its way of operating analogous to that of two great Western nations —France and the United States? These two nations understood (and perhaps still believe) that their political institutions and philosophy are "universal," and they had (have?) foreign policies aimed at extending them. It is clear that France long saw its role in Africa and Asia as a *mission civilitrice* of helping backward peoples adopt its institutions. Since World War II, especially, the United States has felt its values so superior that it has often tried to force them on other nations under a dozen different guises.

The loyalty that Catholics feel to their church probably means that efforts to change the European model are not pursued with the same spirit as would occur in civil society if, for example, the electrical system were malfunctioning. It is important to say, indeed, that research and daily observations show the sincerity with which peoples of vastly different cultures have taken on and appropriated the Euro-American version of Catholic Christianity. Nevertheless, the question implicit in this section has to be asked. *Is the church showing the respect for cultures and attempts to glocalize its local communities that globalization requires?*

Essential Structure and Cultural Differences in Catholic History

In the past one hundred years, scholars have challenged the standard Roman Catholic presentation of the way in which Jesus instituted the church. Theologians who have challenged that version have not denied that Jesus *instituted* the church. Rather, they have questioned how far the details of such an institution by Jesus can be assumed or proved. As we move into the third millennium of Christian history, the two views that I present here both claim that Jesus instituted the church. The question is how detailed his "instructions" on this "institution" were. Let us consider how this question arose. To do this, we must first examine the theological and historical research that Roman Catholic biblical and historical scholars accomplished in the twentieth century. This historical overview will provide us with the context in and through which the issue of institution has come to be unavoidably acute for today's Roman Catholic world.

In spite of the common view that the function and identity of both bishops and priests have been unchanging over many centuries, historical research indicates that over the last two thousand years there have been major changes in the roles of both bishops and priests. Indeed, beginning in the late 1890s and extending to 1959, historical and biblical scholars, both Roman Catholic and Protestant, began to research the history of the sacraments. They eventually produced books that outline the changes in the understanding and practice of each of the sacraments. The sacrament of penance was the first of the sacraments to be studied in such a thorough and historical way. In 1896, H. C. Lea, a Protestant scholar, wrote a three-volume book entitled *A History of Auricular Confession and Indulgences in the Latin Church*.[5] These three volumes radically challenged the Roman Catholic Church's position on the sacrament of penance. Lea did this by unearthing forgotten but unquestionably authentic historical data. Lea's historical research led to questions about the historical warrants that the Roman Catholic Church understood, practiced, and articulated about the sacrament of penance. The practices of sacramental penance at the end of the nineteenth century did not, according to Lea, go back to Christ himself but were additions made at various times in the course of church history. They were not dogma and practices that could be traced to the early church.

When Lea's book was published, major questions arose. Did Jesus himself institute this sacrament? Did priests always hear confession? Did Christians always confess their sins privately and in detail to a priest or bishop? Lea's work indicated that the church had changed the liturgy of the sacrament.

Naturally, this book engendered a high level of alarm in the church. Catholic scholars were urged to write a critique of Lea's work. At that time, the main scholars of early Christian history and literature were called "patrol-

5. H. C. Lea, *A History of Auricular Confession and Indulgences in the Latin Church*, 3 vols. (Philadelphia: Lea Bros. & Co., 1896).

ogists," and they studied the church "fathers" in the discipline called "patristics." Patrologists read early Greek, Latin, Syriac, and Coptic languages in which early Christian literature was written. When they examined the evidence, much to the consternation of many, Catholic reviews tended to agree with the Protestant scholar. This created further anxiety in the Roman Catholic Church.[6]

Because the First World War broke out in 1914 and lasted until 1918, and because the two decades after that were turbulent, the crisis quieted down, since both study and research were in large measure suspended because of the chaos in Europe. Nevertheless, from 1930 to 1965 Catholic scholars produced excellent histories of the sacrament of penance. In these books, the changes that took place in the ritual and in the theology of the sacrament were documented and carefully spelled out. There was no longer any doubt that historically and theologically the sacrament of penance had undergone major changes over the centuries.

The focus on the sacrament of penance in the early part of the nineteenth century engendered an interest in the historical development of all the other sacraments. Interest in the sacrament of penance and the forgiveness of sin through this sacrament raised questions about baptism. As a result new studies began to appear on baptism. The study of baptism, considered the "gate to the Eucharist," led to a broad and lengthy study of the Mass and the eucharist itself. Scholars found many changes in both the rituals that celebrated these sacraments and the ways in which the rituals were understood. The reappraisals of penance, baptism, and eucharist raised questions about the role of priests and bishops, and in the middle of the twentieth century, high-quality historical studies on priesthood began to appear. As with the sacraments of penance, baptism, and eucharist, the studies of the sacrament of orders (the rite for ordaining bishops, priests, and deacons, but also the grace and role of these ministers) showed that there had been major changes both *liturgically* and *theologically* in the understanding of this sacrament.

Changes in the sacrament of order took effect in different cultures and at different times. In the West, the cultures were the Euro-Mediterranean cultures, the Celtic cultures, and the Germanic cultures. In the Eastern churches, cultures also played a major role, as one sees in the various languages of the Eastern churches: the Greek, Russian, Armenian, Chalcedonian, Coptic, Syriac, and Bulgarian Orthodox churches, and so on. The diversity of these churches is not simply language; it is profoundly cultural. It is important to realize that the Roman Catholic Church recognizes the valid-

---

6. For a historical overview of this response to Lea's book, see Kenan Osborne, *Reconciliation and Justification* (Eugene, Ore.: Wipf & Stock, 2000), 52-101.

ity of orders and eucharist in almost all these Eastern Orthodox churches.
This would seem to be a tacit but clear acknowledgment that culture and history can lead to different rituals and theologies. If this principle is accepted,
it would seem to undercut arguments for uniformity within the Catholic
Church scattered throughout the world. In the Vatican II Decree on Ecumenism, *Unitatis Redintegratio,* that principle is clearly affirmed (see UR 15).

Although the historicity of the other sacraments has been acknowledged
and although the historical grounds for recognizing the same in regard to
episcopacy and priesthood are equally strong, arguments for the historicity of
the episcopacy and priesthood have not been well received. Our next step,
then, is to consider in some detail the position that the official leadership of
today's Roman Catholic Church continues to maintain. Let us consider first
the status quo.

A New Look at the Standard History and Theology
of the Sacrament of Order

In the next few pages, we will compare the standard presentation of the history of the sacrament of order (i.e., the functioning of episcopacy, priesthood,
and diaconate) with the results of contemporary historical research on the
same topic. The phrase "sacred order" refers to the threefold order of office in
the Catholic Church, namely, the office of bishop, priest, and deacon. It also
includes the manner in which a person is selected to become a bishop, priest,
and deacon, and the rite in which the sacrament of order is conferred. We
have been using interchangeably two English translations of the Latin *sacramentum ordinis.* The term translated literally is "sacrament of order," but in
English "sacrament of [holy] orders" is more prevalent. The term *sacramentum ordinis,* in fact, has a number of meanings. First, the term refers to a
sacrament that establishes the "order" of those who lead the church—bishops,
priests, and deacons. At another level, the role of holders of these offices is to
secure order in a different sense, that is to say, by ensuring that the "order" is
"apostolic." An apostolic church is one founded on and by the authority of the
first apostles and preserves integrally the teaching of the apostles.[7] In a third
meaning of the term, the *sacramentum ordinis* is the ritual used to confer the
grace of the sacrament and to publicly place the recipient of the sacrament in
the order (i.e., in the "college" or "corps" of bishops, priests, or deacons).

---

7. See Hans Küng, *The Church* (New York: Sheed & Ward, 1967), 344-59, for an excellent summary of apostolicity as an essential mark of the church.

How and when did the Catholic Church's ministers of order come to be called bishop, priest, and deacon? How and when did an ordination ritual arise as the means of conferring this threefold mantle of leadership on certain members of the community. Did the threefold structure (bishops, priests, and deacons) begin with Jesus himself? Was there an ordination ritual for this threefold leadership present from the very beginning of the Christian church that dates to the time of Jesus himself? No

In chapter 2, we considered some of the data; let us now consider even more historical details on this issue. The standard account of the history of the sacrament of order has been most recently and authoritatively summarized in the *Catechism of the Catholic Church:*

> When Christ instituted the Twelve, "he constituted [them] in the form of a college or permanent assembly, at the head of which he placed Peter, chosen from among them" (LG 19; cf. Lk 6:13; Jn 21:15-17). Just as "by the Lord's institution, St. Peter and the rest of the apostles constitute a single apostolic college, so in like fashion the Roman Pontiff, Peter's successor, and the bishops, the successors of the apostles, are related with and united to one another" (LG 22; cf. CIC 330). (CCC 880)

In this view, which is based primarily on the Vatican II document *Lumen Gentium*, Christ chose the Twelve. The Twelve appointed successors who are called bishops. Peter is seen as the head of the Twelve, and his successor (called here "the Roman Pontiff") is the head of the college of bishops. Just as the apostles with Peter as their head formed a college or permanent assembly, the bishops with the pope as their head are a college or permanent assembly.

The *Catechism* presents this position as follows:

> Christ, whom the Father hallowed and sent into the world, has, through his apostles, made their successors, the bishops namely, sharers in his consecration and mission; and these, in their turn, duly entrusted in varying degrees various members of the Church with the office of their ministry (LG 28; cf. Jn 10:36). The function of the bishops' ministry was handed over in a subordinate degree to priests so that they might be appointed in the order of the priesthood and be *co-workers of the episcopal order* for the proper fulfillment of the apostolic mission that had been entrusted to it by Christ (PO 2). (CCC 1562)

In this paragraph, based on *Lumen Gentium* and *Presbyterorum Ordinis* (the Vatican II Decree on the Ministry and Life of Priests), the *Catechism* teaches that Christ instituted the Twelve apostles; the apostles appointed bishops as their successors; the bishops then appointed priests as "*co-workers of the episcopal order*," a phrase that is italicized in the text of the *Catechism* itself.

This standard view has a long tradition in the Roman Catholic Church. It antedates but was strongly affirmed at the Council of Trent (1545-63) both to consolidate Catholic tradition and to differentiate as clearly as possible Catholicism's difference from Protestantism on the question of church order and the three levels of ministry it taught were instituted by Christ. This outline was uncontested until the mid-twentieth century and was used to show the Catholic faithful that the Roman Catholic Church had maintained the order instituted by Christ, while Anglican and Protestant churches had not.

It is important to note that in the two passages from the *Catechism* cited above certain terms are used without any hesitation. The successors of the apostles are simply called bishops. The implication is that from the very first, the successors of the apostles were called bishops. Historically, however, this cannot be proven. Second, the *Catechism* asserts that the apostles, including Peter, formed a college. The Latin term *collegium*, however, appeared at a later date. Third, priests are seen as co-workers of the bishops, but working in a lower level than bishops. Again, such a distinction of levels cannot be found in the New Testament writings, nor can it be found as an integral part of the church order in the West until the third century. What we see in this explanation is a reading of later historical names and functions into the New Testament writings. The reading of later terminology back into the self-understanding of an earlier age is one of the most criticized aspects of the sacrament of order as articulated in the *Catechism*.

Let us go behind *Catechism* two generations and consider several theologians who wrote on the institution of episcopacy and priesthood just prior to Vatican II. Adolphe Tanquerey (1854-1932) wrote several textbooks that were used extensively in seminaries prior to Vatican II. Many, if not most, of the bishops who attended Vatican II had used these books as students. In one of these textbooks, Tanquerey wrote the following:

They [the first Christians] were subject to a holy hierarchy, that is, to the Apostles who exercised supreme authority among all the communities of the Gentiles; indeed this authority was viewed as divinely received. The Apostles oftentimes claimed it for themselves in their epistles, in teaching, in judging, in correcting, in proposing laws or precepts, not just for the faithful, but also for the elders (presbyters = priests) who took care of the faithful. Serving under the Apostles were inferior ministers: deacons, priests or bishops, who in turn took upon themselves some authority in spiritual matters and who thus formed, along with the Apostles, a true hierarchy.[8]

Tanquerey ably summarizes what was taught from the Council of Trent until roughly 1960. It is found again and again in official documents and in other nonofficial but still very influential theological textbooks. Bishops—and this precise name is used—are the direct successors of the apostles. Priests and deacons—again, these precise names are used—are the direct appointees of bishops as lower-level ministers. Tanquerey gives even more specific details regarding the apostles, stating that the apostles proposed "new laws and precepts," "judged" specific issues, and "corrected" certain followers of Jesus for acting or teaching wrongly. Apostolic succession involved very precise matters of authority and structure, and apostolic succession is treated so as to equate the early activity of the apostles and their early successors in a fashion that led the reader to perceive a one-to-one correspondence between the ancient and the present-day office and function of bishops and priests.

Implications of such constructions of identity between the two ages include the following. The authors who hold the traditional view maintain that the very structure and naming of this hierarchy and the essential powers exercised by each of these ministries go back to the apostles themselves. It was not a big step for teachers using such books to state that, therefore, these offices were instituted directly by Jesus. In the post-Reformation context of disagreements with Protestantism, moreover, it was maintained that only the Roman Catholic Church had kept this divinely willed structure intact, particularly because of the wise guardianship of the papacy.

Two related matters need to be brought into relief. First is the theological or faith issue. Under this principle it was taught that God instituted and gave humankind the church. Acceptance of this church is a matter of one's faith. Second, since an interpretation of history purportedly based on evidence is the warrant for asserting that the shape of office in the present-day church can be found in the primitive church, only *historical* data can prove the claim. If, however, reliable historical studies undermine that picture, then the question of what kind of obligation in faith one has to accept the church's *theological* doctrine becomes confused. An important *theological* issue is at stake, namely, apostolic succession and the establishment of the church by Jesus. What kind of church did Christ and the apostles envisage? Do we have evidence they gave *any* orders on this subject?

---

8. Adolphe Tanquerey, *A Manual of Dogmatic Theology*, trans. J. Byrnes (New York: Desclee, 1959), 110.

First, the most rigorous historical studies *do* indicate that being founded by the apostles or by persons appointed by the apostles is universally considered, from as early as the time of the Scriptures, a mark of being a true church. An apostolic church in this era is one that is recognized by other churches as having lineage traceable to the apostles and their successors and preserving their authentic teaching. A second essential part of that teaching was that people are called by God into the church. Human beings do not establish the church as a kind of society that preserves the teaching and memory of its founder. As we indicated above, the core of *Lumen Gentium*'s teaching on the matter is that the church is not and cannot be something that human beings instituted. The church is not human-made; rather, the church is a church established or instituted by God. It is precisely this issue which the standard and official position on the presentation of sacred order wants to and needs to maintain. One can believe or disbelieve that teaching. But the fact that it is universally believed to be the *sine qua non* of the earliest teaching on the church has withstood every challenge even from biblical scholars or historians. Here we are at what Luther in a later age would call an *articulus stantis et cadentis ecclesiae* ("an article on which the church stands or falls"). The Nicene-Constantinopolitan creed says, "We believe . . . in one, holy, catholic and apostolic church." This creed, which we recite Sunday after Sunday, proclaims our belief that God established only one true church, that the church is holy because God is holy, and that this church is catholic, which means that it has a *universal* (always the same in essentials everywhere in the world) message and preserves the *whole* message of Christ. By saying that the church is apostolic, the creed tells us that the church goes back to Jesus himself. Apostolic succession is the main focus of the word *apostolic*, and therefore the church as God's gift to us is part and parcel of our belief in one, holy, catholic, and *apostolic* church. The perennial integrity of the church is involved in this statement of the creed.[9]

The second question we are dealing with forces us to confront the details concerning this institution of the church by Jesus. The scientific historical approach to church origins, which arose in the nineteenth century, was taken up in the twentieth century in a serious way by Catholic biblical and historical scholars. This approach does not undermine the belief in the institution or establishment of the church by Jesus the Christ. It does, however, challenge the adequacy of certain apologetic positions long used to "prove" the direct institution of the standard model of the church and its threefold ministry by

---

9. See Küng, *Church*, 296-319, for a good account of the catholicity of the church.

Jesus. Let us examine the presentation of sacred order developed in the twentieth century by biblical and historical scholars.

Overview of Recent Biblical and Historical Scholarship on Sacred Order

Catholic biblical scholars and church historians began to modify the standard view during the middle of the twentieth century. Protestants had begun to do so already in the nineteenth century and were the forerunners of this new account of church order in the earliest ages. We will consider only the main issues that contemporary biblical and historical Roman Catholic scholars have raised, and we must remember that what we say here is backed by entire libraries of scholarly books

In 1988, I wrote a book entitled *Priesthood: A History of the Ordained Ministry in the Roman Catholic Church*. After presenting some New Testament material in the first chapter of this book, I wrote the second chapter, "An Ecclesiological Presupposition," which is only nine pages in length yet it is undoubtedly the most important chapter of the book. In this chapter, I presented the two views that we are focusing on in this volume. Here is how I expressed this division in 1988:

1. The first approach is to see Jesus during his lifetime, clearly establishing a church, together with its basic structures and ministries. In other words, the gospels are read in such a way as to make explicit Jesus' role in establishing a fairly detailed church community.
2. The second approach is to see the church, together with its structures and ministries, arising after the resurrection. In other words, the church is a post-Easter event, and as such, under the guidance of the Holy Spirit, the early community began to shape the details of structure and ministry.[10]

We have just focused on the first approach, indicating how the *Catechism* and some key theologians have described Jesus' institution of the church and how he provided the actual names for church offices and gave details of their key activities. This view was, as we saw, the standard view from the time of the Protestant Reformation to the mid-1960s. During that period of time, the Roman Catholic Church was deliberately apologetic; that is, the church

---

10. Kenan Osborne, *Priesthood: A History of the Ordained Ministry in the Roman Catholic Church* (Eugene, Ore.: Wipf & Stock, 2002), 30-31.

leaders were determined to show that the Roman Catholic Church was the true church and that the Protestant churches were not truly churches. To do this, this same leadership emphasized that Jesus had established a church, had given the exact names to its principal officials, and had set out in some detail the primary duties of these offices. All this served the apologetic purpose well. Roman Catholics grew up knowing that they belonged to the one, true church that Jesus had established. Any deviation from this belief was considered Protestant.

During this same period of time, the Protestant churches were also very apologetic in their own defense. The Protestant churches maintained that they alone were the true church, founded by Jesus, because they preached the Word of God and had rooted out the historical accretions that had crept into Catholicism. For the Protestant theologians and church leaders, the Word of God was the most important issue. If a group of people did not heed and obey the Word of God, which is found in the Bible, then they could not be the true church of Jesus Christ. In the Protestant view of the Roman Catholic Church, Catholics placed the authority of the pope and bishops over the Word of God. They alone could say what the Bible meant.

Both the Protestant and Roman Catholic Churches maintained these antagonistic attitudes from the mid-1500s to the mid-1900s, four hundred years of mutual distrust, mutual rejection, and mutual anger. The ecumenical spirit that we experience today is a major breakthrough from this former apologetic, defensive, and antagonistic spirit. However, it was not the desire for a more ecumenical relationship that brought about the twofold approach to the institution of the church. Certainly this twofold approach to the institution of the church has aided the ecumenical endeavors between the Protestants and the Roman Catholics, but it was not an ecumenical fervor that began the change in Roman Catholic thinking on the institution of the church.

The change originated from a serious rereading of the New Testament itself. It began with a biblical base, more specifically, a New Testament base. The change began to show itself very clearly in scholarly Roman Catholic writings from around 1935 onward. This change was also brought about by the study of the history of the sacraments, which was mentioned above. The sacramental history began in earnest with the publication in 1896 of Lea's volume *A History of Auricular Confession and Indulgences in the Latin Church*. The response to this book, as we noted above, began with an attempt at historical rebuttal. However, the strength of Lea's case led Catholic scholars to reconsider the historical evidence for all the sacraments. This, in turn, led to the historical studies of priesthood itself. In the mid-1900s, when the earliest books on the history and theology of priesthood began to appear, questioning of the standard interpretation of the direct institution of the church by Jesus himself also began.

1. Historians wrote lengthy articles and books on the historical development of all seven sacraments, with a major emphasis on their origins in the first and second centuries of Christian life. The scholars began to point out that there was strong evidence for baptism and eucharist in the New Testament and that there were abundant documents on them from the earliest period. Then they pointed out that New Testament data for the other five sacraments are almost nonexistent and that Christian writings in the first and second centuries are, to a large degree, silent about these other five ritual sacraments. Naturally, this caused concern in the Vatican and elsewhere.

2. New Testament scholars focused on texts that mention the selection of the Twelve by Jesus, the sending of the Twelve, the variety of names for early church leaders, including the terms *episkopos, presbyteros*, and *ekklēsia* (Greek *ekklēsia* = church, a translation of the Hebrew: *qāhāl* = the called assembly). These New Testament scholars noted how infrequently the terms *episkopos* and *presbyteros* appeared in the New Testament and how they were not found at all in the four Gospels. Commentators began to note also the many other terms used for leaders and ministers in New Testament churches. Naturally, this reading of New Testament texts also caused concern.

3. During this entire period, patrologists, scholars of early church literature, began producing critical editions of the earliest nonbiblical Christian writers, especially those called the apostolic fathers, whose writings were dated to the late first and early second centuries of the Christian era. We depend on the writings of these apostolic fathers for a richer understanding of the beginnings of the church itself. We have, for the most part, no other sources for an understanding of the earliest church communities. The New Testament data and the writings of these apostolic fathers are the source for almost everything we know about the first 150 years of Christian communal life, except for fragmentary references to Christians by Roman or Greek historians, which also offer few details of early Christian existence. Thus, the realization that the patristic data did not give the church the warrants it sought to prove that its structures and ministries could be dated to the second or third generation of Christians caused concern. Why? If there is no written evidence to corroborate a historical claim, it is highly dangerous to trust oral and other traditions beyond a third generation of witnesses. The historical evidence for the standard Roman Catholic model was beginning to seem thin.

The combination of these three areas of scholarly work slowly but surely led to questions about the standard account of the institution of the church. In my own description of the second approach, cited above, I hinted at what has became generally accepted by scholars, namely, that *the church's institution is a post-Easter event.* On the basis of the material that the three scholarly groups developed in the first half of the twentieth century, theologians began to reflect on the standard approach, and out of that study arose consensus that the church is the creation of the Spirit as much as the result of the ministry of Jesus.[11] Belief in the resurrection of Jesus, of course, had long been central to the teaching of the church. But theological work that began to flourish in the years before Vatican Council II began to see the resurrection as much more than a proof of the divinity of Jesus.

According to the *Catechism*, the resurrection is "the crowning truth of our faith in Christ" (CCC 638). It "remains at the very heart of the mystery of faith" (CCC 647) and "constitutes the confirmation of all Christ's works and teachings" (CCC 651). Even more, the resurrection is a work of the Trinity, a "manifestation of God's power through the working of the Spirit" (CCC 648). In speaking of the church as the work of Christ and the Spirit, then, the *Catechism* says:

> The mission of Christ and the Holy Spirit is brought to completion in the Church, which is the Body of Christ and the Temple of the Holy Spirit. This joint mission henceforth brings Christ's faithful to share in his communion with the Father in the Holy Spirit. The Spirit *prepares* men and women and goes out to them with his grace, in order to draw them to Christ. The Spirit *manifests* the risen Lord to them, recalls his word to them and opens their mind to the understanding of his Death and Resurrection. He makes present the mystery of Christ, supremely in the Eucharist, in order to reconcile them, to *bring them into communion* with God, that they "may bear much fruit" (Jn 15:8, 6). (CCC 737)

While the *Catechism*, when one examines its overall orientation, seems to favor a view of the church as instituted by Christ, it also seems to put at least some eggs in the post-Easter basket. Whether both interpretations can be supported is doubtful. Theologically speaking, without the resurrection and the descent of the Spirit, the *Catechism* knows that it is difficult to see how there can be any belief in the church. Certainly the church, in the texts quoted

---

11. See Stephen B. Bevans and Roger P. Schroeder, *Constants in Context: A Theology of Mission for Today,* American Society of Missiology 30 (Maryknoll, N.Y.: Orbis Books, 2004), 10-31, for an especially lucid and comprehensive account.

above, sees the institution as an action involving both the Spirit and Christ. Rather than Jesus being simply the founder of the church, the institution of the church becomes a part of the great paschal mystery of Jesus' death and resurrection and the pouring out of the Spirit. These, then, are issues that theologians began to raise on the basis of the data from historical, New Testament, and patristic scholars. Moreover, these principles are at least adverted to by the church in its *Catechism*, a book promulgated by Pope John Paul II, a work that few accuse of substituting speculation for solid doctrine.

The second approach outlined above has a powerful foundation in the New Testament, in early church history, and in the writings of the earliest fathers of the church. It cannot be accused of being something radically new. The interpretation may be new to our generation's ears, when contrasted with the standard account so rigidly adhered to after the Reformation. Indeed, what this second approach indicates is that the post-Reformation Roman Catholic interpretation is itself new, resulting from too much emphasis placed on medieval canon law and developed in an atmosphere of hostility to the Reformers and their new churches.

Let us look at some of the early texts. One of the most important writings of the apostolic fathers is the *Didache*.[12] In this early work (about 90 to 110), there is no mention of presbyters. Only *episkopoi* and *diakonoi* are mentioned.[13] Johannes Quasten notes: "There are no indications whatever in the *Didache* which would warrant the assumption of a monarchical episcopate."[14] H.-M. Legrand concludes from his analysis of the *Didache* that the prophets celebrated the eucharist along with the apostles as also the *episkopoi*. In the *Didache*, he notes, *episkopoi* are not seen as successors of the apostles; rather the itinerant prophets are the successors to the apostles.[15] Itinerant prophets were not the ones whom, in the standard view, Jesus had selected, but in the *Didache* they are ministers of the eucharist.

One could consider another apostolic father, Clement of Rome, who lived at the very end of the first century. A letter ascribed to him became extremely popular in the early second century. Clement was a church leader in Rome, but it seems that at that time the Roman church was governed by a troika

---

12. As regards the *Didache*, see Robert A. Kraft, *The Apostolic Fathers: Barnabas and the Didache* (New York: Thomas Nelson & Sons, 1965), 3:135-77.

13. *Didache* no. 15: "Elect for yourselves *episkopoi* and *diakonoi*, men who are an honor to the Lord"; see Kraft, *Barnabas and the Didache*, 174. The text does not indicate how they are elected. No mention of an ordination is made.

14. Johannes Quasten, *Patrology* (Westminster, Md.: Newman Press, 1950-53), 1:33; see pp. 29-39 for a summary of the entire *Didache* as regards its contents and text.

15. H.-M. Legrand, "The Presidency of the Eucharist according to the Ancient Tradition," in *Living Bread Saving Cup*, ed. K. Seasoltz (Collegeville, Minn.: Liturgical Press, 1982), 200.

(three leaders). Were these three leaders *presbyteroi* or *episkopoi*? We really do not know.[16] Other writers from the apostolic church and postapostolic church could be cited. What we do know is that the naming of ministries in the church and the functions of individual ministers evolved slowly. At first, there was diversity both in the names and in the descriptions of ministerial functions. Only at the end of the third century did a uniform naming and functioning begin to take over. We call this uniform pattern *episkopos, presbyteros,* and *diakonos.*

We cannot, however, have two coexisting, contradictory teachings of the church on the origins of the church itself. At this moment of time we have two interpretations of early church data. In my book on priesthood, I called the two approaches two ecclesiological presuppositions. There are, of course, heated arguments for each interpretation. The *Catechism* does not advert to the historical research that underpins the second approach. It makes no mention at all of the findings of contemporary New Testament scholars, church historians, and patristic scholars. The *Catechism* seeks to maintain the practical status quo, while using language that undercuts the arguments for the present discipline with regard to the sacrament of order and church structure. Silence on the issues raised by serious historical scholarship, however, cannot be a correct answer.

In a theological account of the sacrament of order and ministry that is written with an eye to today's global situation, the issues involved in these two approaches are of utmost urgency and must be dealt with forthrightly. In a globalized world, which we recognize is multicultural and multireligious, the question of cultural relativity and the origins of the church's theological teaching and discipline in European history need to be confronted.

This is not just my personal opinion. Shortly after Vatican Council II, voices of concern from the third world bishops were already in evidence. Angel Antón observes:

> The Churches of the Third World have also adversely criticized Vatican II for reflecting the situation of the Church as it exists in the social, cultural, economic, and political environment of the developed world. This criticism is not unfounded. The world with which the Church is carrying on

---

16. For the *First Letter of Clement of Rome*, see Robert Grant and Holt Graham, *The Apostolic Fathers: A New Translation and Commentary,* vol. 2, *First and Second Clement* (New York: Thomas Nelson & Sons, 1965). This volume provides the English text and a commentary on this first-century document. A more recent book, which enters into greater detail on the situation in both Rome and Corinth, is Barbara E. Bowe, *A Church in Crisis: Ecclesiology and Paraenesis in Clement of Rome,* Harvard Dissertations in Religion 23 (Minneapolis: Fortress, 1988).

a dialogue in *Gaudium et spes* seems to be identified with the scientifically and technically developed world, at a high western economic and cultural level, whereas the Churches of the Third World could, from this point of view, consider themselves part of the Churches of silence.[17]

Forty years down the road from Vatican II, we realize that the situation is different. Churches that were thought of as young then, are today among the most vital in the world. The churches of the West, meanwhile, are in decline and seem well off in only one area—financial resources—not a quality, one senses, that Jesus would have been particularly impressed with. Philip Jenkins, moreover, maintains that it is precisely the more conservative churches that are most flourishing.[18] All of these churches are fully capable of making up their own minds. There is no justification, however, for denying either thriving churches in the global South or ailing churches of the global North a green light to study seriously how different structures of order and ministry might produce better results if adapted. In particular, it is probably not too much to say that the present manner of structuring these ministries prolongs the service-station mentality that keeps the laity in both the North and the South from appropriating a fully adult consciousness about their vocation to be ambassadors of Christ in the wider world.

Several assemblies of the bishops outlined plans for their churches that can indeed be called innovative. One of these episcopal conferences was the Symposium of Episcopal Conferences of Africa and Madagascar (SEACAM) gathered at Kampala, Uganda, in 1969. There was as well a gathering of the bishops of Mexico, Central and South America (CELAM) at Medellín, Colombia, in 1968, and in Puebla, Mexico, in 1979. There have also been several gatherings of the Federation of Asian Bishops' Conferences (FABC) from 1970 to the present. All of these episcopal gatherings have stressed the contextual, local, and cultural qualities of their respective gatherings. In all of them, "theological ideas of local inspiration were being developed that, while avowing faithfulness to Vatican II as their source of inspiration and constant point of reference, proposed to outline a new model of ecclesiology, more in conformity with the legitimate aspirations of the faithful in their respective Churches."[19] In all this discussion, the limitations of Vatican II have become

---

17. Angel Antón, "Postconciliar Ecclesiology: Expectations, Results, and Prospects for the Future," in *Vatican II: Assessment and Perspectives*, ed. René Latourelle (New York: Paulist Press, 1988), 1:415.

18. Philip Jenkins, *The Next Christendom: The Coming of Global Christianity* (New York: Oxford University Press, 2003).

19. Antón, "Postconciliar Ecclesiology," 416.

more and more evident, and since Vatican II, the stream of directives issued by the Vatican curia have been seen not only as micromanagement but also as further evidence of Euro-American theological colonialization.

A globalized world requires a globalized framework, which does not mean that one size can fit all situations. This holds true for the issue of leadership, even church leadership. With this in mind, let us review the findings of the New Testament scholars, the historians of the first two centuries of church life, and the patrologists who have analyzed in a critical way the writings of the early Christians, particularly the writings of those whom we call the apostolic fathers. These findings can be listed as follows.

Overview of New Testament Scholarship on Order

Nowhere in the New Testament are the Twelve called bishops or priests. If anyone makes a connection of apostles to bishops and priests, that is, if someone asserts that the apostles were ordained bishops and priests, this judgment is a reading backward into history. It is a judgment made not on the basis of the texts themselves, but on the basis of some quasi-dogmatic issue, namely, an intellectual conviction that ordination has always been part of church history.

Nowhere in the New Testament is their any indication of an ordination of the apostles to the episcopacy or to the priesthood. The interpretation of Jesus' words at the Last Supper, "Do this in memory of me" (1 Cor. 11:24) as words of ordination cannot be verified in either the text or the context of the passage. Such an interpretation has been placed on the text and context at a later time in church history. It is *eisegesis*—a reading into New Testament texts—not *exegesis*—allowing the texts to speak for themselves. Nor is it legitimate to see the Last Supper as the ordination of the Twelve. In the light of later developments, it maybe legitimate to use what the early fathers of the church and medieval monks called a "spiritual reading" of the texts and apply them imaginatively in prayer, but they will not bear the kind of weight that certain proponents of the standard account of the threefold order place on them.

After the resurrection, the Twelve play, first, a strong and, later, a modest role. Joseph A. Fitzmyer calls their role "ephemeral," since the apostles, after chapter 12 of Acts, simply disappear from the text and are rarely referred to again.[20]

---

20. See Joseph A. Fitzmyer, *The Gospel According to Luke: Introduction, Translation, and Notes*, vol. 1, Anchor Bible 28 (New York: Doubleday, 1981), 23-27, 253-58. In Acts the last mention of apostles is in 16:4.

The Greek term for bishop, *episkopos,* is not used as the most common name for church ministers. Paul uses this term only twice, but offers many other names for early church ministers. The Gospel of John and the Johannine Letters do not use the term *episkopos* at all. The Letters of John use only the Greek term *presbyteros.* The word *episkopos* is not found in the Gospels of Mark, Matthew, and Luke. *Presbyteros* in these Gospels refers only to Jewish priests. It is never used for any Christian minister, nor is it applied to Jesus himself. Colossians and Ephesians do not use either *episkopos* or *presbyteros* for ministers, although they do use other terms. The letters ascribed to Timothy and Titus use the terms *episkopos* and *presbyteros,* but in the contexts in which we find them, the two titles seem to refer to the same ministry. Thus, in these letters, a bishop or priest is in actuality one and same kind of minister. The tremendous diversity of names for Christian ministers that one finds in the New Testament indicates that no set names existed for determined ministries. If Jesus, through the apostles themselves, had called their successors *episkopoi* and *presbyteroi,* why are these two names not uniform in the New Testament? Evidently, Jesus only used the term "the Twelve" to specify his closest followers. Even the term "apostle" seems to be from the evangelists, not a title that Jesus himself used.[21]

The role of Peter is important in the New Testament, but to see in Peter the kind of pope that emerged after the year 461 is a fanciful reading of later developments into the scriptural picture of Peter.[22] This is a very delicate and at the same time a very important issue. The work done by the Roman Catholic and Lutheran scholars on this matter remains some of the most important research on this subject, and it raises questions about both legitimate interpretations of scriptural texts on the issue of Peter and the "Petrine office."[23]

When we turn to the time just after the writing of the New Testament, namely, the last part of the first century and the early part of the second century, we begin to see faint traces of historical development. This historical development is not universal and occurs differently in different areas of Christian community life. In the following outline we can see the main issues of this development with a focus on the two terms *episkopos* and *presbyteros* as they are found in the New Testament itself.

---

21. Osborne, *Priesthood,* 53-65.

22. See Eamon Duffy, *Saints and Sinners: A History of the Popes* (New Haven: Yale University Press, 1997), 1-86, for a very accessible but thoroughly researched account of the gradual emergence of the papacy into the form that the standard account of ministry seems to believe was established in the first century.

23. See Raymond E. Brown et al., eds., *Peter in the New Testament: A Collaborative Assessment by Protestant and Roman Catholic Scholars* (New York: Paulist, 1973).

EPISKOPOS in the New Testament

- The *episkopos* is a major figure in some parts of the New Testament church but not in all parts. It seems that in some early Christian communities there were ministers called *episkopoi*, but in other early Christian communities there were no *episkopoi* who acted as the main church leaders. These communities used different names for their main leaders.

- The term *episkopos* is not readily identifiable with the term "bishop" as used in later church history. A one-to-one correspondence, in other words, cannot be seen between *episkopos* as used in the New Testament and "bishop" as found Christian documents written at a later time.

- The term *episkopos* is also used in the New Testament as a synonym for the term *presbyteros*. Thus, the later distinction between bishop and priest is not the same as the distinction—if any exists—made by the New Testament authors when *episkopos* and *presbyteros* are used.

- The New Testament does not call the apostles or the Twelve *episkopoi*.

PRESBYTEROS in the New Testament

- The term *presbyteros* means "elder," not "priest," and is primarily related to the role Jewish elders played in the history of Israel. The elders were often the local leaders of a clan or tribe, and they met with various Jewish kings to give advice or to agree/disagree with the king's plans, especially in times of war. By the time of Jesus, "presbyters" was the Greek term used in the Diaspora for leading and respected citizens in a Jewish village or town or a Jewish community living in the Roman world.

- "Presbyter" is not used by Paul or the authors of Colossians and Ephesians. Nor is it found in the canonical Gospels.

- "Presbyter" is found in the Acts of the Apostles, the Book of Revelation, and in the Letters of John, Timothy, Titus, and James. In the Acts of the Apostles, the word "presbyter" is used frequently. Clearly, then, in the communities with a relationship to Luke-Acts, the presbyter was a major residential leader, and often there were several presbyters who, as leaders of a given community, were referred to by that word.

We can draw some conclusions from this brief survey of the terminology of leaders. First, the nomenclature for Christian leadership was fluid, with a variety of terms used from place to place. But the most important personages and names used in the New Testament are the "apostles" and "the Twelve." Except for the Letters of John, these are mentioned, and always with great respect, by every New Testament author. The earliest material in the New Testament are Letters of Paul. There we find an abundance of titles for church leadership: prophet, teacher, deacon (note that a woman is called a deacon), servant, father, overseer (*proistamenos*), and liturgist (*leitourgos*). Paul uses the term *episkopos* only twice. It was certainly not a key title in what we call today the Pauline churches.

In the Acts of the Apostles, Luke honors the apostles and the Twelve, but he barely mentions *episkopos*, and *presbyteros* is used frequently. Here, too, we find other titles of church leaders: evangelist, teacher, prophet, and servant (*hypēretēs*). "Shepherd" is used as a ministerial title in Ephesians, and "preacher" (*kēryx*) is used similarly in the pastoral letters, 1 and 2 Timothy, as well as in Titus.

From the variety of titles in the New Testament, one can say only that there was neither a fixed hierarchy nor an established and uniform pattern of names and tasks. In other words, one will *not* find in the New Testament a bishop and priest whose position and functions are identical to the position and functions of today's bishops and priests. This variety of names and functions and the local differences of nomenclature indicate that the early Christian communities were finding their way toward identifying a vocabulary to denote Christian leaders and their functions.

Other biblical data on these issues of ministry in the New Testament could be added, but the above details are some of the more challenging factors that the standard and official presentation on order and ministry must face. The oft-repeated approach that Jesus chose the Twelve and ordained them bishops, who in turn ordained their own successors *episkopoi*, cannot be demonstrated. Even less can we say that there is evidence in the New Testament for these *episkopoi* calling *presbyteroi* to be their "co-workers of the episcopal order" (as we saw in the *Catechism* above). Given later developments, it may be true that the process was at work that would see *episkopoi* and *presbyteroi* fairly universally stabilized by the middle of the third century. The church's hierarchy brings suspicion upon itself when it uses the standard interpretation today, as if reliable scholarship had not shown that the process was not that simple. A basic pedagogical principle is that even when making the presentation of complicated matters, nothing should ever be written in such a way that later learning will show it to be factually wrong. A more sophisticated explanation can replace a simpler one, but an educator has no license to make the more basic account unfaithful to facts.

Developments from the Second Century to 1000

We have seen that from about the years 90 to 200, historical data for almost every aspect of the Christian church's concrete existence are very meager. Because the data are so thin, all historical interpretations of this minimal data must be made with caution. After the year 200, there is much more historical data that deal with the early Christian communities. From the resurrection of Jesus to 200, the New Testament offers us the most information on early Christian communities. Outside the New Testament, we have important written sources, but they are very few and not very detailed. Any conclusions on the basis of these earliest historical sources must be made with great care. In fact, most conclusions are more hypotheses than solid conclusions.

As a consequence, prior to about the start of the third century in year 200, there is no hard evidence regarding the manner in which a person became a leader in a given church community. Every view presented by scholars or church doctrine concerning the process and the ritual by which someone became a church leader prior to 200 is conjectural. Paul Bradshaw in a recent essay on ordination writes:

> The oldest extant ordination rites as such appear to be those in the so-called *Apostolic Tradition* conventionally attributed to Hippolytus of Rome in the early third century, but the identity, date and provenance of this document have been questioned, and it displays some features not otherwise attested in the ancient sources.[24]

The document *Apostolic Tradition* is the first written account of an ordination to *episkopos, presbyteros,* and *diakonos* that we have.[25] What we today think of as ordination may not have been the way in which a person was installed as a local church leader before that, but, since we have so little to go on, caution must be observed in speculating. We are quite aware of church

---

24. Paul Bradshaw, "Ordination," in *The New Westminster Dictionary of Liturgy and Worship,* ed. Paul Bradshaw (Louisville: Westminster John Knox Press, 2002), 342. Bradshaw has also written a lengthy overview of early ordination rituals, spelling out the key theological elements found in the individual rituals; see Bradshaw, *Ordination Rites of the Ancient Churches of East and West* (New York: Pueblo, 1990), 3-103. See also James F. Puglisi, *The Process of Admission to Ordained Ministry: A Comparative Study,* vol. 1 (Collegeville, Minn.: Liturgical Press, 1996).

25. An English version of the text is found in Bradshaw, *Ordination Rites,* 107-9; see also Osborne, *Priesthood,* 119-27.

leaders during this period, and we have testimony by a few writers regarding the localized naming of these leaders. To say that these Christian church leaders had to be ordained is a *theological* judgment, concerning which we need to realize the danger of reading subsequent developments into an earlier period. The ordination theory for this early period of church history is a hypothesis alongside other hypotheses. It is logical to believe that what we find in the *Apostolic Tradition* is a development of earlier traditions, but it is not possible to say much more than this.

Several later books of rituals seem to have been influenced by the material in the *Apostolic Tradition*, yet again, firm conclusions cannot be drawn about the influence that the *Apostolic Tradition* had on other churches after 200. The *Sacramentary of Serapion*, dated around the middle of the fourth century, is the next extant document after the *Apostolic Tradition* with an ordination ritual. From 200 to 350 the selection of Christians for the offices of *episkopos, presbyteros,* and *diakonos* was made by the local community, and the selection by the local community remained part of the process until the end of the first millennium. Bradshaw notes that unless a community selected an individual for a major ministerial role, the person was not considered validly elected for leadership. A person who did not have community approbation could not take over as *episkopos, presbyteros,* or *diakonos* in the local community.[26]

The titles of the main leaders of a Christian community varied during the period 90-200. In some areas, the main leader was called a *presbyteros,* while in others he was called an *episkopos.* St. Justin Martyr (d. ca. 165) was living in Rome when he wrote his *First Apology.* In this book he briefly describes both baptism and eucharist. He refers to the eucharistic leader as *proestos,* which means a presider. Justin also makes mention of *diakonos,* but no mention is made of either *episkopos* or *presbyteros.*

There are today many authors who still translate the Greek term *episkopos* as "bishop" and *presbyteros* as "priest." This is not only unsatisfactory but very misleading. The position of an *episkopos* in an early Jesus community and the position of a *presbyteros* in such an early community do not correspond to today's description of either bishop or priest. Rather than translating *episkopos* as "bishop" and *presbyteros* as "priest," it would be better, during the period from the resurrection of Jesus to about 200, simply to use the two Greek words *episkopos* and *presbyteros,* lest we give the impression that their meaning is clear. From a historian's point of view, equating the *episkopos* with today's bishops and *presbyteros* with today's priest is untenable.

---

26. Bradshaw, *Ordination Rites*, 21-26.

What does emerge after about 200 is that Christian communities began to exhibit a common form and set of names for their leaders. That is, in a given community there would be a leading figure, called *episkopos*. Helping the *episkopos* in apostolic and administrative tasks, there was usually a *diakonos*. The *diakonos* was most often the most visible pastoral minister in an ecclesial community. He was the one who visited the sick, took care of basic pastoral problems, and was in charge of the finances. The *episkopos* was most visible on Sundays, but during the week there were many other administrative issues that kept him away from pastoral work. As advisors of the *episkopos*, there might be two or more *presbyters* in a given community. They were married, had families, and probably were engaged in some trade. On Sundays they were next to the *episkopos* during the eucharistic celebration, but their main task seems to have been to advise the *episkopos*. One can certainly say that from the first half of the third century on (200–250) there was a growing uniformity of names and tasks.[27]

From about 200 to 400, what we see is that the title *episkopos* was gradually given to the main leader of a Christian community. Such a person at that time resembled today's parish priest more than today's diocesan bishop. This is made very clear by an event that occurred in the year 411, when St. Augustine was *episkopos* of Hippo in present-day Tunisia. An assembly was convoked by the emperor, and one of his delegates, a layperson, was in charge. The meeting was attended by roughly 540 *episkopoi*. That number of *episkopoi* makes one pause. How could so many *episkopoi* have diocesan sees in Tunisia? The answer to this question seems to be that every city, town, and village that had a Christian community also had a leader called an *episkopos*. In some of these cities and towns, there were two or more Christian communities, each of which had a main leader called an *episkopos*. In many there were both Donatist communities and orthodox communities competing with each other. In both Donatist and orthodox churches, the principal leader was the *episkopos*. In other words, every community, roughly equivalent to what we think of today as a parish, had an *episkopos* as its pastor. Each of these *episkopoi* had a *diakonos* and usually one more *presbyteros*. This situation was by no means restricted to North Africa but was found throughout the Mediterranean world. *Episkopoi* resembled today's pastors, not today's bishops.[28]

---

27. In the English translation of the *Catechism*, the Greek words are translated as "bishop" and "priest." Continuing this practice gives the impression that the meaning of the *episkopos* and *presbyteros* in the early centuries corresponds to the contemporary meaning of bishop and priest.

28. Kenan Osborne, "Envisioning a Theology of Ordained and Lay Ministry," in *Ordering the Baptismal Priesthood*, ed. Susan K. Wood (Collegeville, Minn.: Liturgical Press, 2003), 210–11.

The *episkopos* was the main leader of both the community and its baptismal, eucharistic, and, when necessary, reconciliation liturgies. There was no eucharistic concelebration as we know it today, and eucharistic prayers were most often not fixed. Since the presider made up that prayer as he went along, others could not have joined in. Only in the Middle Ages do we see a group of priestly clerics reciting a fixed eucharistic prayer together. In other words, prior to 400 or thereabouts, a man ordained a *presbyteros* generally did not celebrate the eucharist as a contemporary priest would do.[29]

What, then, did a presbyter do? In the ordination ritual that we find in the *Apostolic Tradition*, the presbyter is ordained to give advice to the *episkopos*. Part of the task for the *episkopos* was to adjudicate legal cases. The *episkopos* would hear both sides and then retire to a private room with the *presbyteroi*, and the *presbyteroi* would help the *episkopos* come to a decision about the case.[30]

When Augustine was still a *presbyteros* in Hippo, the aging and sickly *episkopos* felt he could not deliver the homily. He asked his *presbyteros*, Augustine, a noted scholar of rhetoric, to give the homily. When Augustine approached the pulpit, the people did not want a *presbyteros* to preach to them, observing the custom that only an *episkopos* should preach.[31]

During this period many small communities of Christians developed in rural areas. At first, the *episkopoi* attempted to find people who would accept being a *chōrē-episkopos*, that is, an *episkopos* in the rural areas (*chōrē*). Since an *episkopos* at that time was considered "married" to his community until he died or became unable to fulfill his tasks, few men wanted to marry a non-urban community where they would have to spend the remainder of their days. With few volunteers for this role, the *episkopoi* in many areas turned to *presbyteroi* and asked if any of them would want to become the leaders of a small rural community. Many *presbyteroi* agreed to do this, and in these rural communities, the *presbyteroi* for the first time became presiders at the eucharist and preachers. At first, the rural church under the *presbyteros* provided the catechumenate instructions for those seeking baptism, but the rite of baptism itself took place in the main church, celebrated by an *episkopos*. In

---

29. See John Klentos, "Eucharist: Eastern Churches," and Paul Bradshaw, "Eucharist: Early Christianity," in *The New Westminster Dictionary of Liturgy and Worship,* 172-75.

30. Puglisi, *Process of Admission,* 39-46.

31. See F. van der Meer, *Augustine the Bishop: Church and Society at the Dawn of the Middle Ages,* trans. Brian Battershaw and G. R. Lamb (New York: Harper Torchbooks, 1961), 6; van der Meer notes that Valerius, the aged bishop of Hippo, in the case of Augustine went against the proscription that presbyters should not preach. As bishop, Augustine was a popular preacher but not an erudite, bombastic preacher (pp. 412-32).

time, baptisms were also held in the rural communities, and *presbyteroi* were its usual administrators. These changes marked a clear shift in the meaning, the role, and the function of a *presbyteros*. When the *presbyteros* took over the small rural community, there was no new ordination. Nor did he become a *chōrē–episkopos*. He was a *presbyteros* of a rural, mission community who celebrated the eucharist, preached, and baptized, and even later he began to administer the sacrament of reconciliation.[32]

With the development of these outlying communities, the central church in the nearby city and its *episkopos* took on a change of position as well. The central church became what we would call today a cathedral, and the *episkopos* was now a main leader of a number of communities of Christians. The diocese as we now know it had began to appear.[33]

Moreover, the number of regional meetings of *episkopoi* increased. Therefore the *episkopos* was often away from his cathedral church, attending episcopal conferences. From 400 to 1000, the number of these regional episcopal conferences grew geometrically. After 1000, however, the number of regional conferences in the West began to decrease, as Rome began to hold councils at which issues would be determined for larger regions. After about 1000, the independence of regional groups of bishops and of local bishops began to decline, while the role of the papacy began to rise and decisions were made to keep policies standard throughout Europe.[34]

It is interesting to note that the changes in the role and function of both *episkopos* and *presbyteros* appear to have been occasioned by pastoral concerns and changed circumstances as the church grew. There was no determination of roles by the papacy. Instead, changes were made on a local level, and in time regional oversight, analogous to contemporary dioceses, began to predominate. Gradually patterns began to coalesce and grow toward the structure we now know.

Our historical survey indicates that changes in the title, identity, and function of priests, bishops, and deacons did take place. These changes could not have occurred had there been a scriptural record or an oral tradition that Jesus himself had determined the title, function, and identity of the various church ministries. Scholars agree that pastoral needs occasioned most of these changes, not an overarching theology of priesthood or episcopacy. We will see in the next section that there are major pastoral needs today in the area of church ministry that must be addressed, even if this means further changes in an understanding of bishop, priest, and deacon.

---

32. See Bernard Cooke, *Ministry to Word and Sacraments* (Philadelphia: Fortress Press, 1976), 364.

33. See Osborne, *Priesthood,* 179–88.

34. Osborne, *Priesthood,* 179–88.

PRIESTLY AND EPISCOPAL MINISTRY AND ORDER
IN TODAY'S GLOBALIZED CHURCH

The Need for Honest Dialogue and Conversation about Church Order

We have summarized studies of both biblical and historical data on the question of order in the early church. This material tells us much about the past. What relevance does all this biblical and historical matters have for the way we are today? Many conclusions can be drawn. One item stands out and speaks to our contemporary circumstance when globalization and historical consciousness make us conscious of the multicultural nature of the world in new ways. The one I refer to is that with which we ended the previous section, namely, in the first centuries *local* church pastoral concerns were the driving force behind adaptation and, ultimately, the formation of the standard forms of ecclesial ministry and order. We have tended to think of these standard forms as immutable. In fact, they are the result of <u>historical evolution</u> and <u>human judgment guided by the Spirit</u>.

Pastoral concerns and guidance by the Holy Spirit are the key phrases. Guidance by the Spirit must be sought in prayer. From the human side, God relies on us to use our own capacities for analysis and decision making. Every local church has pastoral concerns. It is the nature of a local church to minister to the needs of its member and to the needs of the broader human community in which it lives. As communities and their needs change, reflection on past practice and theological reflection are intrinsic aspects of ongoing church life in a healthy community.

The major pastoral concern of one area of the globalized world is not necessarily the same as that of another despite the world's increased connections. When we look at the church from a global perspective, we notice how great the diversity is between one region and another. In the global South, one major problem may be the impact of change being forced on it from the North or the cycle of poverty that a region (sub-Saharan Africa, for instance) cannot break. A church that is globalized in the best sense of the word would be one in which the church can magnify the voice of those being adversely affected and enlist the help of members of churches in the nations that are causing the problems. Is Catholicism utilizing properly the vertical channels of communication that ought to be its strength in this sort of issue? The kind of consciousness-raising that the members of churches in Euro-American regions would undergo if such communication were taking place effectively could bring such Christians to grow spiritually by understanding who their neighbor is.

On the other hand, when one considers both the Euro-American areas and their pastoral concerns, one runs into churches that may fairly be characterized in many places as "hollowed out." The institutional shell is there, but they are "enfeebled," lacking the requisite cadre of committed faithful to make a difference, tended to pastorally by an aging generation of priests and bishops. Considering such realities, we begin to realize that there is no single, all-encompassing solution to the concerns that apply to both the Euro-American sphere and to the rest of the world. Even more pointedly, we can say that there cannot possibly be a single, all-encompassing solution.

Pastoral concerns are existentially localized. Even if one could identify a solution that is, in principle, valid, its application would be a matter of glo-calizing it, and one is plunged immediately into the realm of having policies that encourage local peoples. Globalization may give the illusion that central bodies such as the pope and his curia can communicate universally applicable policies, but there are human dynamics called "reception" and "acceptance" that are necessary before concrete actors at local levels put policies into practice. For the most part, globalization is better at making possible a one-way communication rather than ensuring two-way conversation. Conversation and dialogue are a two-way street, and practical action is never optimal until both sides are in agreement. The technology for near-instantaneous, global dialogue in the church exists. Does such dialogue falter because habits of mind and heart need to change?

If the necessity of two-way communication is accepted, are there common issues about which a global conversation could be fruitful? At least two issues seem to be candidates for such a dialogue. The first I would propose is inability of many communities to celebrate the Sunday eucharist together. The second is the reality of gigantic pastoral problems throughout the world church. They affect the first, second, and third worlds differently. Each needs special consideration.

What Prevents Sunday Eucharists? Ordination Policies?

In Central and South America and in the Philippines, a major pastoral problem exists today and has for several centuries, namely, the recurring lack of Sunday eucharist for most Catholic communities. In many parts of Oceania and Africa, churches have grown up that have never known regular Sunday eucharists, mainly because the church did not devise forms of ministry that could move from the "missionary chapter" of church development to a full-fledged "local church" chapter. In Europe the problem is growing. In the United States, it looms larger every year. According to the Center for Applied Research in the Apostolate, in 1960 there were five hundred parishes without pastors in the United States; in 2000, there were twenty-five hundred.[35] This is not to say that the problems that cause this scandal are the same everywhere, which is why it demands a global analysis and responses based on local conditions. In Europe or the United States, Catholics can get to churches with Sunday eucharists without much trouble. In many parts of both continents, in fact, people increasingly choose among several, as old territorial parish rules are disregarded. But whether one speaks of a remote Melanesian village or a rural Iowa farm community, the principle ought to be that pastoral ministry is available and communities can celebrate the paschal mystery in the eucharist.

In 1998, when the Vatican's Congregation for Divine Worship published a document entitled Directory for Sunday Celebration in the Absence of a Priest, something new was afoot. Never before had the official Roman Catholic Church published a Directory of the universal church on the theme of the lack of priests for Sunday liturgy. The issue, of course, had been discussed unofficially in theological essays, in ordinary letters from Vatican offices, and in diocesan communications. The Directory, however, is the first official statement from a Roman congregation that officially details what Roman Catholics are to do when a priest is absent on Sunday. There is a disturbing element conceded in this document that has been too little noted, namely, that the congregation accepts the lack of a priest for Sunday liturgy as a "normal" situation for many people. In article 1, the congregation gives a fairly comprehensive account of why this has come about, but the issuance of the Directory indicates that a new kind of normality has been accepted. The document states that the situation is regrettable, but does not analyze the situation or its causes. The solutions offered are placebos to allow Catholics to receive the eucharist on Sunday. In my view, the solutions proposed are untenable.

In the first section of the 1988 Directory, we read that the Directory is meant "to ensure, in the best way possible and in every situation, the Christian celebration of Sunday," which means celebrating the eucharist. "The Mass is the proper way of celebrating Sunday" (Introduction). "The Church of Christ has always faithfully come together to celebrate the paschal mystery on the day called 'the Lord's Day'" (1). The "Sacrifice of the Mass on

---

35. Bryan T. Froehle and Mary L. Gauthier, eds., *Catholicism USA: A Portrait of the Catholic Church in the United States* (Maryknoll, N.Y.: Orbis Books, 2000), 121.

Sunday" is to "be regarded as the only true actualization of the Lord's paschal mystery and as the most complete manifestation of the Church" (13). Sunday Mass is part of God's own plan (12). Other forms of celebrating Sunday have only a "substitutional character" (21). Other forms "should not be regarded as the optimal solution to new difficulties nor as a surrender to mere convenience" (21). At the very end of the document, John Paul II is cited: "All Christians must share the conviction that they cannot live their faith or participate in the manner proper to them . . . unless they are nourished by the Eucharistic Bread" (50). The Directory is clear. It states the priority of eucharist on Sunday in no uncertain terms. When one turns to chapter 2, however, the priority of the eucharist is superseded by two other priorities: the first is the priority of priestly celibacy, and the second is the priority of only male priests. To have married priests and to have women priests would not immediately provide priests for all areas that today are priestless. However, since these two issues play no role whatsoever in the "Conditions for holding Sunday Celebrations in the Absence of a Priest," it is obvious that these priorities are, at least by their absence, seen as greater priorities than eucharist for Christian communities. Celibacy, though urged by many church leaders, became a universal law of the Roman Catholic Church only in 1123, when the First Lateran Council enacted the first law requiring celibacy of all clergy. Pope Paul VI's encyclical *Sacerdotalis Caelibatus* and the *Catechism of the Catholic Church* recognize celibacy of the clergy as either a law or a discipline of the Western church and recognize different disciplines in Eastern Catholic churches, where priests can be married if the marriage takes place prior to ordination. Once a man is ordained, he must remain celibate. In the Eastern churches, bishops are generally selected from the celibate diocesan clergy or the celibate monks. A human law can be changed. The *Catechism of the Catholic Church* says:

> All the ordained ministers of the Latin Church, with the exception of permanent deacons, are normally chosen from among men of faith who live a celibate life and who intend to remain celibate "for the sake of the kingdom of heaven." (CCC 1579)

In the next paragraph, the *Catechism* recalls that in the Eastern churches there is a different discipline or a different form of law in regard to married priests. The difference between the Western church and the Eastern churches on this matter of celibacy is simply one of discipline, tradition, and law. No doctrinal issue is involved. The theology of priesthood does not include the necessity of celibacy. How, then, can a "law," a "tradition," or a "discipline" become a matter of higher priority than a community's need to have Sunday Mass?

Globalization, it could be argued, should lead the Catholic Church to maintain its Western discipline to promote unity. But the absence of the eucharist and structures that encourage the kind of pastoral activities that we know are necessary to form communities also calls for a response. Does a proper respect for the principle of glocalization indicate the need for serious dialogue? If one reads Pope Paul VI's *Evangelii Nuntiandi* and Pope John Paul II's *Redemptoris Missio*, on the evangelizing mission of the church, we see models of lay insertion as gospel agents in the world that will never occur without vital communities, and such communities depend on apostolic-minded persons to inspire them. Many Vatican documents on evangelization proclaim the call to bring the gospel to men and women who have never heard it and to rekindle it in the hearts of peoples who once lived it but have moved away from the church.

We saw above how the early church faced and resolved the pastoral problem of caring for rural communities without a resident priest. As we pointed out above, only few bishops (*episkopoi*) wanted to go to the rural areas. As a result, the leaders sent presbyters to them. They did not at first celebrate the eucharist or preach homilies. Nonetheless, the gravity of the situation in the rural areas overrode the traditional pastoral practices, and the rural communities were provided with Sunday eucharist by adapting to new pastoral requirements. This change in how the presbyterial order functioned did not take place because a central power approved such a decision. The local *episkopos*—who, we should recall, was more like today's local pastor than today's diocesan bishop—realized that there was a need for a new kind of pastoral ministry. In consultation with other *episkopoi*, they began to develop a response to this need. If this was done in the past, can analogous changes be contemplated today?

In the heyday of the modern missionary movement, whole continents and countries were evangelized. The number of baptisms was staggering. Today, the majority of people in Mexico, Central America, and South America are Catholic. The Philippines is a majority Catholic country. In Africa and Oceania, Catholic communities have been planted that range from 20 to 50 percent of national populations. Evangelization, however, cannot mean that we baptize people and then not provide them with the eucharist. If the policy of the church is to baptize, then the church leadership should also provide the baptized communities with the eucharist. While it is admirable that zealous evangelical and Pentecostal Protestants are rushing in to provide pastoral care that the Catholic Church cannot, the question Why not? is unavoidable. The fact that there are today in second- and third-world areas so many baptized Catholic communities who do not have access to Sunday eucharist is a scandal of major proportions. A theology of order and ministry from a global perspective cannot be formulated without an urgent remedy for this scandalous situation.

The solutions will not be universal and applicable everywhere in the same way. Local pastoral solutions need to be considered, and the local churches must have a major say in the way a solution is reached for their own local needs. Micromanagement of a universal center is counterproductive. A globalized perspective demands a mutual resolution to major local pastoral issues. A change in the law of priestly celibacy, indeed, is not the only possible solution to the problem of Catholic communities without a pastor to celebrate the Sunday eucharist.

Dialogue with Women and on Women's Place in Church Order

While acknowledging that the question of women priests or pastors is even more radical than that of ordained married men, the theology and law that all priests must be male has become less convincing over the years in many parts of the world. The ordination of women is not even considered in the Directory, no doubt because in 1976, the Congregation for the Doctrine of the Faith promulgated *The Declaration on the Question of the Admission of Women to the Ministerial Priesthood.*[36] Its Latin title is *Inter Insigniores.* Carroll Stuhlmueller notes in the preface to a book on that document that it was prepared

> by scholars who had read widely on the subject and seriously interacted with this mass of material. Earlier publications, therefore, usually undertaken on the private initiative of theologians, contributed significantly to the document, directly or indirectly, positively or negatively.[37]

The *Declaration* in its introductory section (paragraph 4) states: "The various arguments capable of clarifying this important problem have been submitted to a critical examination." When the *Declaration* was published, a commentary by the same congregation was appended—at least when the *Declaration* was sent to the episcopacy of the United States. In this official commentary, mention is made of works consulted—doctoral theses, articles in various reviews, and pamphlets that defended or refuted the ordination of

---

36. Congregation for the Doctrine of the Faith, *Declaration on the Question of the Admission of Women to the Ministerial Priesthoood* (edition with commentary has been prepared by the United States Catholic Conference, Washington, D.C., 1977).

37. Carroll Stuhlmueller, ed., *Women and the Priesthood* (Collegeville, Minn.: Liturgical Press, 1978), 6-7.

women. The data that the committee studied included biblical, historical, and canonical data. The committee realized that arguments either pro or con were made on the basis of sociology, psychology, and the institutional history. The *Declaration* says the following in paragraph 5:

> In execution of a mandate received from the Holy Father and echoing the declaration which he himself made in his letter of November 30, 1976, the Sacred Congregation for the Doctrine of the Faith judges it necessary to recall that the Church, in fidelity to the example of the Lord, does not consider herself authorized to admit women to priestly ordination. The Sacred Congregation deems it opportune at the present juncture to explain this position of the Church. It is a position which will perhaps cause pain but whose positive value will become apparent in the long run, since it can be of help in deepening understanding of the respective roles of men and of women.

Since the appearance of this declaration and commentary, much has been written, both defending the congregation's position and opposing it. It is not my intent to consider all the pertinent material. My focus is simply on a single issue. Does the prohibition of women from priestly ordination help or hinder the articulation of a theology of order and ministry adequate to today's global situation and the broad perspective necessary to make local decisions in a global context? It is my judgment that this prohibition, in a manner analogous to the insistence on the discipline of priestly celibacy, has major negative implications for a global perspective on the theology of order and ministry. There are two basic reasons for my position. Let us consider each of them carefully but briefly.

A change in the law or discipline of priestly celibacy and opening up to different ways of training pastors is not the only issue in the lack of pastors to help form churches and lead Sunday eucharists. In the view of many, the rule that all priests must be male is equally problematic. The ordination of women is not even considered in the Directory of the Congregation for Worship, or in the *Catechism*. Yet if women were able to be ordained, the pool of prospective pastors would double.

Having said that, however, it is important to note that no issue is more controverted in our world of rapid globalization and cultural change than changes in the role of women. If European and American progressives take it as a universal truth that women's social position must change to reflect the equality of men and women and that gender roles mandated by patriarchal cultures must be ended, there are opposing voices who see this as the worst kind of globalization where Western cultural norms are being forced on the rest of the world. We will not even pretend to try to resolve this global conflict, but we must recognize it and the fact that the discussion that follows is not just theological. It is about some of the deepest and most sensitive cultural controversies in the contemporary world.

In 1994, Pope John Paul II issued the apostolic letter *Ordinatio Sacerdotalis*, "On Reserving Priestly Ordination to Men Alone." He reviews earlier documents and in his fourth and final section says:

> Although the teaching that priestly ordination is to be reserved to men alone has been preserved by the constant and universal Tradition of the Church and firmly taught by the Magisterium in its more recent documents, at the present time in some places it is nonetheless considered still open to debate, or the Church's judgment that women are not to be admitted to ordination is considered to have a merely disciplinary force.
>
> Wherefore, in order that all doubt may be removed regarding a matter of great importance, a matter which pertains to the Church's divine constitution itself, in virtue of my ministry of confirming the brethren (cf. Lk 22:32) I declare that the Church has no authority whatsoever to confer priestly ordination on women and that this judgment is to be definitively held by all the Church's faithful.

It is not the intent of this volume on theology of order in global perspective to contest either the 1976 statement of the Congregation for the Doctrine of Faith or Pope John Paul's apostolic letter. Does the prohibition of women from priestly ordination help or hinder a theology of order and ministry expressed in global perspectives? It is my judgment that the prohibition has consequences similar to the issue of priestly celibacy, which we have discussed above. There are two convictions behind my position. Again, I raise them not to dissent from the Roman magisterium, but to point out that reception has always been one of the marks that history uses to judge the authoritativeness of a Roman document. In the case of not ordaining women, the church's documents have left many unconvinced. Over time, their critics may be proved wrong. Still the two statements have driven other views underground, where their disagreement festers with no sign of diminishing. Let us consider each of the two convictions that lead me to suggest that this entire matter needs a clearer and more convincing case to be made. Two important arguments are to be noted.

The first is raised by Rosemary Radford Ruether, who sees this teaching and its corollaries *rendering the fundamental doctrine of God incredible.* She states the case as follows:

The critical principle of feminist theology is the promotion of the full humanity of women. Whatever denies, diminishes, or distorts the full humanity of women is, therefore, appraised as not redemptive. Theologically speaking, whatever diminishes or denies the full humanity of women must be presumed not to reflect the divine or an authentic relation to the divine, or to reflect the authentic nature of things, or to be the message of work of an authentic redeemer or a community of redemption.[38]

The key words are those in which Ruether places the case on a *theological* plane. She goes beyond the sociological level where secular equal-rights theory demands giving women, in principle, any position men can occupy, for example, leading a nation or a corporation. She goes deeper. Having institutional policies that recognize the full humanity of women is, of course, profoundly important for her, but she grounds this full humanity of women in a theology of God, which must be credible if Christianity is to be credible. If women are not honored and respected, considered equal to men, and acknowledged to be fully human, then the church's doctrine of God (a) does not reflect the divine or an authentic relation to the divine, (b) does not reflect the authentic nature of things and persons in creation, and (c) does not reflect the message or work of Jesus as an authentic redeemer or a community of redemption.

The focus of her argument is that when women are made secondary to men, God is not understood correctly. God as the creator and redeemer of all is misunderstood. In other words, if men are preferred to women and women are not in their human nature basically equal to men, then one's theology of God is challenged. If authentic redemption can only be masculine, then one's theology of God is deficient. The issue is basically a question of who and what God is, not a *women's* issue but a deeply and totally theological one for all Christians. This is key to Ruether's principle.

The church has too often and too easily dispensed with issues raised in liberation and feminist theologies and with biblical and historical challenges to the standard approach to the institution of the church and its structure by saying that the issues raised are *new*. By implication, then, they are not an integral part of Christian tradition. I maintain that they are not new in the sense of being "novel." Instead these movements go deeper than secular social analysis or theories of women's rights. They are based in the nature of *who* God is and *what* the Christian God is about. The conclusion is clear. As our understanding of God has developed, we see more deeply that God is just

---

38. Rosemary Radford Ruether, *Sexism and God-Talk: Toward a Feminist Theology* (Boston: Beacon Press, 1993), 18-19.

and does not prop up oppressive social and economic structures. God is a God who has created us in God's own image, male and female. Men cannot legitimately claim that they are more adequate images of God and women less. The Christian God acted out of love in sending Jesus. God continues the mission of Jesus in and through the ministry of the entire church, not just the clergy. Therefore, to disparage women is to disparage God. The field of feminist discourse and insights into this principle are foundational not peripheral.

The second argument is that *the church's position on women renders the leadership of the Roman Catholic Church incredible*. The *Declaration* on the nonordination of women itself in its opening three paragraphs undercuts its conclusions as it quotes church leaders on the role of women in public life. The first citation is from John XXIII's encyclical *Pacem in Terris* (1963) in which the pope speaks of the part that women today are taking in public life. This development, he notes, has had swifter growth "among Christian nations that are heirs to different traditions and imbued with a different culture." This is followed by a quotation from *Gaudium et Spes* in which all forms of discrimination against sections of human life are to be overcome and eliminated since they are "contrary to God's plan." Discrimination based on sex is given first place.

The third document on the nonordination of women cites Pope Paul VI's address to the members of the Study Commission on the Role of Women in Society and in the Church and to the members of the Committee for the International Year of Women (April 18, 1975). Mention is also made that Paul VI had included Teresa of Avila and Catherine of Siena among the doctors of the church. The fourth citation is from the Vatican II Decree on the Apostolate of the Laity (*Apostolicam Actuositatem*), which states that "it is important that they [women] participate more widely also in the various sectors of the Church's apostolate" (9).

Other official statements can be added to this litany urging the equality and dignity of women. *Lumen Gentium* states clearly that "there is in Christ and in the church no inequality on the basis of race or nationality, social condition or sex" (31). The working document of the preparatory commission for the synod on the laity (*De vocatione et missione laicorum in ecclesia et in mundo*), is cited as follows: "The affirmation of the dignity and freedom of each person, the basis for the dynamic participation characterizes the life of a great many people in our day" (8). And then, "The movement for the advancement and liberation of women is certainly one of the more significant manifestations of the general tendency toward participation. The just struggle in favor of recognizing the equality of rights between women and men at all levels, found upon the assertion of their equal dignity, has not failed to bear fruit" (9).

More recently, John Paul II, in his encyclical on women (*Dignitatem Mulieris*), states:

> Every individual is made in the image of God, insofar as he or she is a rational and free creature capable of knowing God and loving him. The foundation of the whole human ethos is rooted in the image and likeness of God which the human being bears within himself [herself] from the beginning. (7)

One could also cite passages from the Instruction of the Congregation of the Doctrine of the Faith, "On Certain Aspects of the Theology of Liberation," in which the creation in the image and likeness of God is set forth as the basis of the equality, dignity, and freedom of every human being. The subsequent *Instruction on Christian Freedom and Liberation* (March 22, 1986) from the same congregation, in its opening paragraph, speaks of freedom and dignity and the inalienable rights of every human being: "The church of Christ makes these aspirations her own."

The official teaching of the Roman Catholic Church on the principle of the equality of men and women is crystal-clear. Their equality is based on God's creation of every human person in God's own image and likeness. The cumulative effect of these passages is enormous. The fact that these passages again and again go back to God's creation as image and likeness leads us, as it did above, to the Christian God question and its credibility. It also leads us to the credibility of church leadership, which presents this doctrine on equality, freedom, and dignity, only to have the principle seemingly contradicted on the matter of ordination by the *Declaration*. People will rightfully argue that Catholic leaders are giving mixed signals. In one context, they speak of human equality, dignity, and freedom. In the context of ordination, they say that Jesus chose only men.

As stated above, we do not seek to contradict the theology of the declaration of the Congregation for the Doctrine of the Faith on the nonordination of women. We do, though, suggest that the studies that show that the gradual emergence of the order of ministry in the first six centuries may give Roman authorities grounds for rethinking their position. Could it be that the radical example of Jesus treating women as equals and the teaching of Paul on the equality of all in Christ (see Gal. 3:26-29) were so challenging in the early period of the church that they were, as the colloquialism puts it, "placed on a back burner" until the church was better able to accept it? Could texts

such as 2 Corinthians 14:34 ("women should remain silent in the churches.
They are not allowed to speak, but must be in submission, as the Law says")
need further study? At a minimum, it is important to realize that the role of
women is of profound importance for a theology of orders and ministry from
a global perspective. The global exploitation of women is well known. If the
Catholic Church is not a major voice decrying this exploitation, then the
church will be incredible. Indeed, the church's voice in areas like the protection of unborn life is rendered less credible at international forums because of
its position on nonordination of women. Granted that the church's critics
may themselves be exploiting our ordination policies to keep other Catholic
views from being considered, we need to inquire carefully whether our position on ordination will bear scrutiny. Minimally, the church needs to make a
better case or find its credibility undermined.

Liberation theologies, feminist theologies, and biblical and historical theologies challenge the standard account of the institution of the church and its
proto–apostle-bishops. Their proponents believe that these movements go
deeper than ephemeral social analysis or liberation movements being in
vogue. This is what Ruether—one senses she does so with a certain sadness—
is asking us to consider.

The way in which such questions are dealt with, moreover, must be credible or the church's leadership and its teaching will not be taken seriously,
which leads us to our second consideration on how these issues have an
impact on the church. This is the question whether reserving ordination to
males undermines the fundamental credibility of the church. From the side
of traditionalists, of course, that question can be reversed and the following
can be asked: Is the demand that women be ordained supported in Scripture
and tradition, or is modern Western culture's evolution in regard to gender
identity being used to trump tradition without a sufficient period for reflection or a true examination of the many ways gender is constructed culturally
across the globe?

Many people who are imbued with the principles of the human rights tradition, which springs from Christian social principles, need to hear a more
convincing explanation than has been given heretofore. For a theology of
orders and ministry from a global perspective, the issue of women's full equality is of profound importance. We want to underline the importance of
Ruether's basic principle. The exploitation of women is a global issue. If the
Catholic Church is not a major voice decrying the domination of women by
outmoded cultural patterns, then the church will be incredible. If the
Catholic Church has within its own structures a mixed signal on the equal-

ity of women, then the church will be incredible. The global perspective is like a magnifying glass. It can make the beauty of the church more visible and bring out its details; it also brings into relief the shadow side of the church's life.

In considering the history of order and ministry, we have noted that major changes in the structure of order and ministry have taken place in the past. If such changes once took place for serious reasons, then they can occur again.

Dialogue on Delicate Issues in Global Catholic Relationships: Racism and White Privilege

Order and ministry in the Roman Catholic Church involve by their very nature the issue of leadership, and leadership requires credibility. Two delicate aspects of the multicultural and globalized relationship between a Christian community and its leaders begin to emerge when the demography of a local or regional church changes. This becomes most apparent when a formerly cohesive parish community or even an entire national or larger regional church begins to change its ethnic and cultural balance. One kind of delicate dialogue needs to take place when this occurs. A second delicate dialogue occurs when a Christian community finds itself within an overwhelmingly non-Christian world.

What is at stake when a formerly cohesive community begins to include others who are culturally and racially different? This issue has local, national, and larger regional dimensions. There are dioceses and parishes in the United States, for example, in which a cohesive group of people, usually whites of European extraction, have been monocultural and monoracial for decades. In Europe this has often been the case for centuries. In both regions, the credibility of traditional church leadership was built up over a long period of time. Whites in these regions are among the most privileged people in the world. Although poverty certainly exists among certain strata of these societies, most whites in them live economically privileged lives in comparison to the peoples of color both in Europe and the United States and in the rest of the world. Are racism and white privilege a major problem in the global Catholic Church?

Because migration across international borders and within countries has increased greatly since World War II, the situation has changed as culturally different people move in. Mexicans follow jobs to an Iowa slaughterhouse and meat-packing industry. Filipinos move to New York City to take positions in hospitals that are chronically short of nurses. Indians move into areas that require mathematicians, physicists, and other kinds of scientists that the United States and Europe often cannot provide because of the deterioration of their own schools. Jamaicans move to Philadelphia and find themselves in conflict with inner-city African Americans who do not have the islanders' educational backgrounds. Rwandans crowd into Congo to escape genocide, and formerly monoethnic parishes and dioceses in the United States and Europe find that they have thousands of new members who are culturally and racially different.

The demographic change has also affected the universal Roman Catholic Church. Today there are more Roman Catholics in the Southern than in the Northern Hemisphere. According to the 2005 *Annuario Pontificio*, which gives international Catholic statistics, since 1978 African Catholics have gone from 7 to 13 percent of the total number of Catholics. Europeans have gone from 35 to 26 percent. In the year 2000 Europe had approximately 280 million Catholics and Latin America 297 million, but Europe had six times the number of parishes and five times the number of priests that South America had. North America has grown from 57 million Catholics in 1975 to 77 million in 2000, while the number of priests declined by 15 percent from 68,000 to 58,000. In South America the number of priests rose during that same period from 32,000 to 42,000.

We can only hint at the dimensions of race, culture, and privilege that face Catholicism in almost every region of the world. Can the leadership of the universal church remain culturally Euro-American in outlook and in practice when migration and church growth occur on such a scale? On the other hand, when migration is joined to fast cultural change inside each discrete area, is it possible that having the patience to ride out the tides of change to see what will emerge when some form of stability returns is a wise course? In a book such as ours, we cannot pretend to answer such questions. We must, however, insist that the issues at stake are not merely those of orthodox ecclesiology against people overimpressed by the shifting sands of cultural change.

If we look at the recent international synods of bishops for the Americas, Oceania, Asia, Europe, and Africa, it is fair to ask whether the central leadership of the church has treated them as serious deliberative bodies. This question needs to be asked and answered with honesty and transparency.

An entirely different issue emerges when a church is relatively homogeneous from a cultural or ethnic point of view but lives in the midst of a people that is neither Christian nor Catholic. *What kind of order and ministry are required when the local church is in a minority situation.* In this scenario, different issues arise regarding a Catholic people vis-à-vis the non-Catholic but culturally identical community. The different issue is clearly the predominance of a major non-Christian religion. In this area, the response of the host religion can range from showing relative openness and tolerance to regarding Catholics as cultural and religious traitors.

The presence of Catholics within a region that follows another religious tradition has not been extensively discussed, partly because most Catholic theology still operates from within the "Christendom" paradigm, even if a Catholic ascendancy in Euro-American nations has long since passed out of existence. Nonetheless, our mind-set is still largely one formed during the era of Christendom. Increasingly, however, the Roman Catholic community faces situations like those that prevail, for example,

- in Nigeria, where Muslim–Christian tensions threaten to boil over
- in France, where militant secularism seems ever less prepared to accord any public role to the church
- in India, where revivals of Indian religious traditions in the Hindutva movement accuse Christians of being non-Indian
- in the United States, where groups such as evangelicals, long kept out of public life, are now trying to counter the secularization of civil society, thus upsetting both secularists and "mainline" fellow Christians
- in China, where secularism reigns and churches are persecuted if they do not follow the government line
- in Malaysia, where religious communities tend to follow ethnic lines within a general Muslim majority that seeks to find its place in the midst of an international Islamic renaissance that has little tolerance for other faiths

Catholics find themselves in all these situations and many more. Especially in Asia, they are a minority in a non-Christian sea, and even further a minority among Christians, sometimes facing the rapid growth of evangelical and Pentecostal churches, many of which vehemently maintain that Catholics are not fully Christian. Finally, while the numbers of Catholics grow worldwide, their percentage of the total world population slowly declines.

One needs to stress that the issues are not simply cultural, political, social, economic. They are also religious, since the culture of these countries is profoundly religious. They are concrete examples of Tillich's principle, referred to earlier: "Religion is the substance of culture and culture is the form of religion." A secular Islamic country is in many respects an oxymoron. The

Qur'an is meant to inspire one's entire life, and people in most of the Islamic world simply cannot understand how someone could follow another religious tradition when the superiority of Islam is so clear. In Islamic countries, religion is not a private matter any more than it was in Germany in the year 1400, when Catholicism was firmly established, or in 1648, when entire regions were forced to adopt the religion of their rulers. Should a minority Catholic Church in such situations be given leeway to adopt structures of order and ministry that could lessen their burdens?

One deeply rooted aspect that merits a major focus on the bipolar and tripolar relationships between Roman Catholic leadership, on the one hand, and the multicultural multireligion factors on the other hand, is rarely mentioned explicitly. This aspect is extremely delicate. It is not usually brought into the field of discourse. In interreligious dialogues or in intercultural dialogues in which Roman Catholic leadership is a part. Nonetheless, it is on the table, and it is a factor regarding credible Roman Catholic leadership in both bipolar and tripolar situations. The delicate issue is racism.

When the word "racism" is used, there is an immediate tensing of everyone in the room. Yet every ethnic group, every culture, and every nation has some form of racism, which more often than not is not discussed publicly. And not all the bad examples are of white racism against other peoples. An example of racism and interreligious dialogue from 1976 may help us to understand the issues of a tripolar complexity. In 1976, Jack Kornfield, Joseph Goldstein, and Sharon Salzburg opened the Insight Meditation Society's retreat center at Barre, Massachusetts. These three American Buddhist leaders had studied Therevada Buddhism in Burma under Mhos Sayadaw and other Burmese Buddhists. In 1987, they opened the Spirit Rock Meditation Center in Marin County, California. Eventually the form of Buddhism they developed ran into major difficulties. Sylvia Boorstein, one of the leaders of the group, publicly was asked whether she, a Westerner, could be a real Buddhist. Boorstein answered: "I am a real Buddhist. I'm not an *ethnic* Buddhist, but I'm a *real* Buddhist, and I'm also a Jew." The implication was that the Meditation Society's Buddhism was more authentic than (presumably simple) "folk" or "ethnic" Buddhism. Her critics argued that here they saw an example of white supremacy in the judgment that she represented the *real* Buddhism, while Burmese-American Buddhists, some of whom were third and fourth generation, were simply *ethnic* Buddhists.

In his dissertation, Joseph Cheah notes that Burmese who had suffered from Euro-American colonialism and who had migrated to the United States saw racism in these claims of real Buddhism over against a so-called ethnic

Burmese Buddhism.[39] The term "real Buddhism" implied that white Westerners were the only ones who understood and practiced true Burmese Buddhism. The furor was in the news for some time and has not been forgotten.

Roman Catholic leadership at the papal level has been European for nearly two thousand years, and European history has shaped both the papacy and the church as a whole. Does the church need to admit that this leadership often interfaces with Roman Catholic leaders who are culturally from a non–Euro-American venue in a non-condescending way? Does it need today to go out of its way actively to repent of such habits and sincerely ask Africans, Asians, and Latin Americans their opinions on questions of order and ministry? Does the "foreignness" that many Asian Catholics feel require a response? When European and American curia officials interact with Asians and Africans, do they do so on an equicultural basis? The Vatican has made many demands that its positions, formulations, and legislation are the benchmark everywhere. In interreligious interchanges, Vatican documents sometimes speak of religions such as Buddhism in tones that betray a sense of superiority. Yet the Sri Lankan Buddhists who read such documents are conscious of being part of a religious tradition that is far older than Christianity. Are curial officials aware of how their statements will play in Colombo or Bangkok? It is one thing for an Italian curial official to make a statement that may be disliked by the European Parliament. He knows the culture and how debates are carried on. It is another thing for that cardinal to draft a policy for the entire world as if his Euro-American cultural sensitivities equipped him to know how it will sound in Lagos, Kuala Lumpur, or Port Moresby.

The Federation of Asian Bishops' Conferences (FABC) was very honest when it stated publicly that Catholics should learn much more about these other religions prior to any dialogue with them. They indicated that the level of understanding of non-Christian religions by Roman Catholics, even by Asian Catholics, was inadequate. Can the same be said for the top leaders of the Roman Catholic Church? In-depth study of non-Christian religions is the first step toward credibility. There is at present no immediate answer regarding the issue of racism and white supremacy and Roman Catholic leadership in order and ministry, but the issue cannot be ignored.

———

Let us summarize the crucial issues raised in this long chapter. Historical studies of order and ministry indicate that new ways of functioning and self-

---

39. Joseph Chea, "Negotiating Race and Religion in American Buddhism: Burmese Buddhism in California" (doctoral diss., Graduate Theological Union, Berkeley, Calif., 2004), 17-20, 97-116.

understanding have taken shape over the centuries in Roman Catholic order
and ministry. We have been considering primarily the church in the Latin
West, since it became the progenitor of most of what is today world Catholicism. That church first became more and more culturally Greek, because
Hellenistic culture was the gold standard of the Mediterranean world. As the
great migration of the northern nations put pressure on the Western empire,
it first became culturally more Latin and Roman. It then became more Germanic as Roman Catholicism in the Middle Ages both evolved into and
shaped medieval church and culture. Its intellectual culture became scholastic and then, as the Renaissance developed and the Middle Ages ended, it
began to think of Christendom as the heir of Greek and Roman civilization.
When the missionary movement began in 1492, Renaissance ideas that
Greco-Roman-Catholic culture was the gold standard that new Christians
needed to adopt were well established. With nods to cultural adaptation,
Catholicism tried to maintain those ideals into the twentieth century. Vatican Council II was called to deal with problems left unresolved in a two-
century-long conflict of official Catholicism with modernity. The council
fathers, however, were only beginning to be aware of the depth at which
issues of religious and cultural diversity and equality, white privilege, and
racism would face it as it entered the twenty-first century. In some ways and
to some degree, Vatican II succeeded in examining the difficulties presented
by modernity and equiculturality, but the challenge so eloquently stated by
the conciliar document *Gaudium et Spes* remains:

> The joys and hopes, the grief and anguish of the people of our time, espe-
> cially of those who are poor or affected, are the joys and hope, the grief and
> anguish of the followers of Christ as well. Nothing that is genuinely
> human fails to find an echo in their hearts. For theirs is a community of
> people united in Christ and guided by the holy Spirit in their pilgrimage
> towards the Father's kingdom, bearers of a message of salvation for all of
> humanity. That is why they cherish a feeling of deep solidarity with the
> human race and its history. (GS 1)

Since those words were written, the realities of equiculturality, racism, and
white privilege have emerged ever with greater clarity. Our mission as Christians is to evangelize in a process that respects authentic cultural values but
also recognizes the principle that the gospel is a call to individuals to turn
their cultural values to serve the gospel. Again, our goal in this chapter is not
to give answers to all the questions that flow from this, but to suggest that
church order and ministry need to take all cultures seriously and cannot jus-
tifiably give precedence to Euro-American values.

QUESTIONS FOR REFLECTION

1. What is the difference between a normative view of culture and an empirical or historical view of culture? What is the importance of this distinction for questions of order and ministries in the Catholic Church?

2. If culture is personal and communal, what is at stake for Catholicism in its attempt to maintain a universal form of leadership structures across the globe. Make the case for and against the present policy?

3. From your reading in this book and elsewhere, what is your working definition of culture? Is being a Roman Catholic Christian becoming a member of a distinct global culture? How do you understand the "inculturation" task of the church?

4. In terms of principles involved, should cultures have a role in determining how sacramental liturgy and church leadership are adapted? Could there be major differences between, for example, how baptism is celebrated in Barcelona, Spain, and in Beijing? What are the arguments for and against allowing such differences?

5. Could presbyteral office be exercised by several married elders in a Rwandan village rather than by a priest trained in a traditional seminary. What are the arguments for and against such an arrangement?

6. What are the main *historical* issues in question when one advocates or argues against the official or standard presentation of the history of order in the Roman Catholic Church?

7. What are the main *theological* issues when one advocates or argues against the official or standard presentation of order in the Roman Catholic Church?

8. What are the three most important items that biblical research has established on the origin and development of order in the Roman Catholic Church?

9. Discuss the issues that are at play in the question whether church leaders should be appointed by those in a higher rank or chosen with strong input from people who will be under this person's ministerial care.

10. If every Catholic community should be able to celebrate Sunday Mass each week, how should the shortage of priests be alleviated?

11. Clarify and list the church's reasons for ordaining only men who choose to be celibate. Do you think these reasons are convincing in your culture? Can you give examples of cultures where a different policy should or should not be adopted?

12. Clarify and list the church's reasons for not ordaining women. Do you think these reasons are convincing in your culture? Can you give examples of cultures where a different policy should or should not be adopted?

13. What are the key issues in determining how order and ministries should be structured in the Catholic Church.

SUGGESTIONS FOR FURTHER READING AND STUDY

Halter, Deborah, ed. *The Papal "No": A Comprehensive Guide to the Vatican's Rejection of Women's Ordination.* New York: Crossroad, 2005.

Hopkins, Dwight N. *Black Theology of Liberation.* Maryknoll, N.Y.: Orbis Books, 1999.

Lakeland, Paul. *The Liberation of the Laity: In Search of an Accountable Church.* New York: Continuum, 2003.

Mbiti, John. *Introduction to African Religion.* Oxford: Heinemann, 1991.

Park, Andrew Sung. *The Wounded Heart of God: The Asian Concept of Han and the Christian Doctrine of Sin.* Nashville: Abingdon Press, 1993.

Phan, Peter C. *Being Religious Interreligiously.* Maryknoll, N.Y.: Orbis Books, 2004.

Sanneh, Lamin. *Whose Religion Is Christianity? The Gospel beyond the West.* Grand Rapids: Eerdmans, 2003. Shows that Christianity is now a world religion and cannot legitimately be dominated by Western cultural ideas.

Schreiter, Robert J., ed. *Mission in the New Millennium.* Maryknoll, N.Y.: Orbis Books, 2001. Essays from Asia, Latin America, Europe, Africa, and the United States about the mission and shape of the church.

4

Lay Ministry

Its History and Meaning Today

THEME AND GOAL OF THIS CHAPTER

THE THEME OF THIS CHAPTER is to present a brief but clear description of lay leadership in today's Roman Catholic Church. To accomplish this we will consider the three foci that are basic for a study of lay ministry.

The first focus is on the way that leadership in human societies exhibits a twofold feature. On the one hand, there is structural or institutional leadership, and, second, there is charismatic, ad hoc, personal leadership. From a sociological, anthropological, and philosophical standpoint, a study of leadership requires an analysis that can deal with this twofold structure, since such a bidirectional analysis opens up the concrete way leadership functions. If one concentrates only on institutionalized leadership, there is a danger that ideals and ideology are discussed at the expense of what actually occurs. In some studies of leadership, however, structural and institutional aspects of leadership take precedence over the charismatic and personal aspects of leadership. Many history books move in this direction, at least in part because this form of leadership is better documented. Nonetheless, charismatic leadership, as we shall try to show, plays and has often played an equal and important role in church leadership, since people of great holiness, who were not officially ordained or deputed institutional, have often influenced the direction of church life in a given epoch and are an essential aspect of the dynamic captured in the Reformation adage *Ecclesia semper reformanda* ("the church always in need of reform").

The second focus aims to describe the official, post-Vatican II theological position on lay ministry in the church. Much was done by the bishops at Vatican II to ensure that laypeople would achieve a wider and more respected role in leadership inside the church, as well as in the world. As in other aspects of post-Vatican II church life, there are signs that both laity and clergy have found it hard to draw the practical consequences from the coun-

cil's teaching and then to implement them. There appears to be a a singular
hesitation, above all, about the role of women in church life.

The third focus is on a brief historical presentation of lay ministry in the
Roman Catholic Church. This historical survey moves from the New Testament down to the Second Vatican Council and later. During these two thousand years of church history, the role of the nonordained person in the church's
teaching, liturgical, and administrative ministries has not been consistent. I
will present this historical material from four distinct historical periods to
show this: (1) from New Testament times to roughly the year 500; (2) from
500 to about 1000; (3) from 1000 to Vatican II; and (4) from Vatican II to
the present.

We shall see that in the hundred years prior to Vatican II, there was a
global chorus of lay voices that expressed the needs, realities, and hopes of
laypeople who were ministering in a church that they already realized had
become multicultural in a world of cultural, socioeconomic, and political
stratification. How have these insights been put into practice? This is one of
the key questions that needs to be discussed. In Europe, North America, and
areas of the church that have most felt the attractions of liberal, post-Enlight-
enment social ideals, the clash between laity and clergy has been especially
public. The issues there differ considerably from what they are in other parts
of the world.

The Roman Catholic Church, from a global perspective today, struggles to
find a new level of internal cohesion within a multicultural and multireligious
world. Economic and social stratification within given areas is also important, as well as divisions that are felt between different civilizational groups.

The goal of this chapter is to present a factual history of both institutional
and charismatic lay leadership in the church and then, on the basis of this history, to indicate some possible avenues of development for the church today.
This goal can be met only if one considers all three of the foci mentioned
above. To appreciate the complexity of the three foci, the role of the first focus,
with its inclusion of charismatic leadership often operating outside institutional auspices, raises the principle that institutional leaders by themselves
cannot provide direction to all those who are called to minister in the world.

One must also have a basic grasp of the current official position on lay
leadership within the Roman Catholic Church. The orientations that the
bishops gave at Vatican II cannot be ignored, even if they were tentative and
perhaps not fully integrated into traditional understandings in ways that gave
a clear image of what would enjoy priority in concrete situations. Decisions
that enshrine the principle that the church is a community where laity is

formed to work in the world on the world's problems need to be carried through. An inward-looking church that thinks it has done enough when there are lay communion ministers, catechists, and financial advisors will become increasingly irrelevant in relation to the problems of our globalized world.

"INSTITUTIONAL" AND "CHARISMATIC" LEADERSHIP ROLES

Insights from Historical and Social Studies

As human societies develop, the leadership roles tend to take on more organized and more specific shapes. The classic studies of Max Weber (1864-1920) emphasize that in modern societies, the tendency is for institutional leadership to be "bureaucratized" and "rationalized."[1] By these terms, Weber referred to the process whereby institutions of governance that were formerly tied to and legitimated by such concepts as the divine right of kings changed in the modern era as the principles of the Enlightenment and the American and French Revolutions gained ground. Instead of magistrates ruling in the name of the king, who ruled in the name of God, authority structures were set up by parliaments, rested on the consent of the citizenry, and were tinkered with over decades to provide more and more efficient services. Weber and his close friend and colleague at the University of Heidelberg, Ernst Troeltsch (1865-1924), documented how Protestant principles and history were the inspiration for this and how these principles challenged Catholicism. In their day, the church had fought these principles with every instrument at its disposal. Catholicism's traditional claim, viewed from Weber's and Troeltsch's perspective, is that the distinction of institutional and charismatic forms of leadership was not applicable to the church because of its apostolic nature. Using "perfect society" language, the church maintained that it was a mistake to say that the church had changed or was changeable.[2] It had everything needed (institutional and charismatic elements) directly from God.

---

1. Weber's most significant works were published in a three-volume work in German entitled *Gesammelte Aufsätze zur Religionssoziologie,* published in 1920 and 1921. The volume most frequently cited has been translated as *The Protestant Ethic and the Spirit of Capitalism* (New York: Routlege, 1992).

2. See the decree *Lamentabili* of the Holy Office in 1907 (DN 846); see also the encyclical letter of Pope Pius XII, *Mystici Corporis* (1943; DN 848). These teachings were subsumed into *Lumen Gentium,* chapter 3, but the principle is already stated in chapter 1, art. 8.

In fact, as we have seen, a single form of leadership appears not to have been directed by Christ, and the shape of order and ministry developed gradually in the first five centuries and coalesced only after more than one thousand years. Even then, Eastern Orthodox churches did not agree with the Western church, and it is likely that 60 percent or more of the world's Christians lived in the East until at least 1453, when Constantinople fell to Muslim armies. The point that needs to be emphasized is this: the core *doctrinal* truth that the church is guided by Christ and the Holy Spirit needs to take account of *historical* research that shows how much the church has evolved over the centuries. Today Western culture has been profoundly modified by a two-century-long march toward democratization as the standard for legitimacy, and then toward establishing accountable bureaucracies on a rational basis. Without pretending to know whether this principle is globally applicable to the church, we are trying to discuss lay ministry in the church and in the world in the light of globalization and wide acceptance of these principles. To the extent that people have been affected by modernity, they find it hard to believe that the church's monarchical papal and episcopal structure is divinely willed. Such people tend, instead, to suspect that church leaders may use such claims as a way to avoid the kind of modernization that would bring the benefits of greater lay participation into every level of church life. Are such people correctly reading "democratization" as a "sign of the times," or have they been seduced by modernity into skepticism concerning a form of church governance in which bishops and the pope especially receive a special form of divine guidance that keeps the church faithful to its founder's intentions? Or is there some way in which "charismatic" leadership from outside the ordained episcopal corps can be recognized?

Books on the history of human life and civilization use many terms to classify distinctive structures of societal leadership. What we are dealing with here is church leaders' attempt to classify its own leadership structures. Such classifications often include a variety of perspectives, presuppositions, biases, and ideologies. Furthermore, historical studies may classify a given type of authority with relative adequacy, but no one ever writes a definitive work on history. New and more precise research continually calls for an updating of historical accounts. It is always subject to revision in the light of new insights. Nevertheless, there has been excellent historical work on almost all aspects of human life. Anthropologists and ethnologists have found both matriarchal and patriarchal organization principles in the stone-age societies. Their presence in such societies indicates that human leadership was never monolithic. Other historians have traced the origins of kingship and its role in human society. Kingship, however, is not a universal phenomenon, since many human societies did not develop a royal or imperial genealogy for local and regional leadership. Other historians have researched the role of the priest-leader, a combination and even identity of the holy and the secular within a single person. The rise of feudal structures has been a major area of historical research. More recent democratic forms of leadership have occasioned a study of their historical roots. Given all of this, one can conclude that in various parts of the world and at various times in history diverse social forms of leadership took place.

In all these historical and anthropological studies, however, one finds a tendency to develop a twofold structure of leadership. On the one hand, stability is desired, and one kind of leadership emphasizes predictable structures, institutions, and organization. On the other hand, other societies have emphasized charism, personality, and magnetic appeal. And there are blends. A highly organized society based on hereditary kingship may face a crisis that king and court cannot rise to. A charismatic individual may arise, seize power, and lead the transformation of the society that may be necessary to face, for example, an invader or climatic change. When the crisis is over, a new stability is desired and sought. Both forms of leadership, then, can be mixed, and both are in one way or another, at least potentially, present in every human society.

In a certain sense, larger societal structures are modeled after families structures. There, too, there are structures as well as personal charisms. In societies based on monogamous, lifelong marriages, when a couple marries, it takes time for the husband and wife to find equilibrium regarding issues of authority, even when the societal norm is theoretically patriarchal. A great deal of subtle negotiation goes on over the question, Who has the last word? When children become part of such a family, a new set of decision-making issues arises, and these, too, are worked out over time. The family that simply takes a society's norms and follows them mechanically is not going to be a happy family. Still, personal or charismatic qualities of a mother and father, a husband and wife, also play a major role in the working out of familial leadership. Dysfunctionality can also be presenting both structured and charismatic leadership. Dysfunctional aspects leave in their wake problems and scars. So, too, charismatic and personal factors can be dysfunctional and can engender social, psychological, and even physical malformation.

The same interplay of the structural and the charismatic is evident in the government of a country. In the first pages of American telephone books, for instance, there are long lists of federal offices, state offices, county offices, and city offices. In all of these offices, there are thousands of workers. Each of these workers, from the highest to the lowest, is busy maintaining structures, continuing institutions, and sustaining organization. They are Weber's bureaucrats trying to keep the structure moving in an efficient and healthy way. Through this work, people make a living. The first pages of a telephone book are a clear testimony that we live in a highly complex institutional environment. There are also societies that are far less bureaucratized, and difficulties are handled on an ad hoc, highly personalized basis. The Catholic Church exists in both kinds of societies and also in societies that can be put on various stages between the extremes. The Catholic Church is one of the oldest organized societies in continuous existence. It has evolved its own form of bureaucracy that, with minor differences from place to place, is uniform throughout the world.

We need to stress at this point that no matter what model predominates, both charismatic and institutional elements are needed. Charismatic individuals can personalize service in highly structured offices, and their absence often means that such offices fail to operate. Dysfunctionality often sets in if charismatic individuals are not present, yet in neither the Federal Register of a government nor in the Code of Canon Law of the church is there formal recognition of this fact. The kind of people who compile the rules that regulate institutions, in fact, seem unable to realize the necessity of attractive, flexible, intelligent persons to make the adjustments, to bend or ignore the rules that a truly efficient organization needs if it is to serve its members and customers. The church, indeed, seems to find it difficult to admit that its leadership can be seriously dysfunctional and needs charismatic lay leadership to restore integrity. One can understand the desire to maintain faith in the promises of Christ to be always with the church. Nevertheless, a series of events such as the sexual abuse of children by priests, which became public in the late twentieth century, forces us to admit that the sins of individuals can coalesce to the point that church leadership can be seriously dysfunctional.

Relevance for Church Leadership

This above material on family, government, and social-science insights on institutional and charismatic leadership might seem a digression. It leads us, however, directly to a discussion of church leadership. As we have suggested above, churches are not an exception to this dual, institutional and charismatic form of leadership. But in the case of the Roman Catholic Church, where the claim that its abundance of structures—papal, diocesan, interdiocesan, and parish—are themselves performed and instituted with charismatic assistance, the lines become blurred. It can be hard for such highly structured organizations to admit that they can cease to be vehicles through which God's love can be seen. In religious orders of men and women, there are likewise a plethora of organizational structures. Supposedly such orders are founded around a charism such as the gift of caring for the poor, working in cross-cultural missions, or healing. They can become sclerotic, nevertheless, and can impede charismatic individuals from pioneering work because such initiatives do not fit into an organizational chart laying out the steps necessary for approving new ministries.

Structures provide solidity, stability, and even credibility to churches and communities within churches. At the very same time, they must be open to the charismatic innovator or facilitator that sociology sees in every other form of societal organization. Clearly, some popes, cardinals, bishops, priests, nuns, and brothers have been powerful charismatic personalities. Such leaders have affected the church for the good. Frequently, those whom the church declares saints have been charismatic leaders with great influence on the church's life. In many instances, it was precisely their charismatic leadership that led to their being declared saints. But it is equally true that other popes, cardinals, bishops, priests, nuns, and brothers have been so rule-bound that they have been unable to recognize when the rules need to be ignored. Indeed, one wonders if anyone who has scrupulously abided by all the structural and institutional aspects of ecclesial life has ever been canonized. On the other hand, neither is it a sign of sanctity to ignore rules, and it is more normal for a charismatic Christian to work flexibly within and occasionally beyond the structures. Such people know that the letter of the law can be stultifying, and its spirit gives life; because of this he or she is recognized as someone exceptional.

The point is that both institutional structures and charismatic individuals can promote dysfunctionality. And, although the Roman Catholic Church claims that it has been instituted by Jesus himself, not all the specific institutional aspects of the Roman Catholic Church can be traced to an institution by Jesus. The vast majority of customs and rules of the church, in fact, cannot be traced back to Jesus, as we saw in the previous chapter. They derive from the attempt of communities to live faithfully under the inspiration of the teachings of Jesus and the presence of his Spirit. To understand what occurred, it is important, first of all, to distinguish between ministries that are well captured in the old Latin phrases *ad intra* and *ad extra*. *Ad intra* refers to ministries carried on *within* the boundaries of the community and for the benefit of the community. *Ad extra* refers to ministries and activities carried on *outside* the boundaries of the community. Since Vatican II, certain *ad intra* ministries once reserved to the ordained have been opened to lay tenure, as in the case of the official ministry of lector and acolyte. Persons invested in these offices are inducted into them in official rituals. Women, however, are not allowed into these lay ministries. At another level, dioceses and parishes have opened up positions in areas such as finance and interpretation of canon law, administering the temporal affairs of the diocese. Structure is evident. Dioceses also open up positions for lay tenure in the structural leadership of the church. In the diocesan offices there are directors, department heads, tribunal judges, defenders of the marriage bond, advocates, auditors, and so on. A telephone directory for a diocesan chancery office indicates a variety of names for such institutional and structural assignments. One must be appointed to these positions. People do not simply "appear" in these assignments because of personal and charismatic qualifications. Today, laymen and laywomen are indeed institutionally and structurally part of church leadership, and they are entering these institutional leadership positions in growing numbers. All this is well and good, although sometimes questions arise whether people exercising some of these practical roles are, technically speaking, employees or ministers of the church The point to be applauded is that such roles are not limited to priests, deacons, and bishops.

Church leadership within a globalized framework calls for even greater changes than we have seen. In non-Western cultures, one set of issues is presented. In the West another. What is excellent in one culture or family of cultures can be dysfunctional in another, and vice versa. When one is attempting to adapt structures in places that are not only culturally different but formed in another religious tradition that remains dominant, another set of issues is presented.

When we take a long view of leadership in family, governmental, educational, and religious realms, we cannot help but see the predominance of structural elements over the charismatic side. At one level this simply reflects the deep-seated human need for order and predictability. More often than not, leadership is dealing with humdrum, day-to-day structural elements. But what can never be forgotten is that our times are not ordinary. We need openness to the likelihood that charismatic leaders will show the way to fruitfully inculturate church structures in these often topsy-turvy times.

Structural and Charismatic Leadership in Historical Perspective

We can learn a lot about the two types of leadership simply by a quick look at church history books. In many of these historical volumes, particularly those written by Roman Catholics, the authors trace the ups and downs of the church by concentrating heavily on clerical leadership, that is, on the actions of various popes and bishops. By and large, lay catholics play a secondary role in these volumes. The layperson appears in these volumes only to the extent that he or she interacts strongly with the clerical leadership. The momentum in these volumes is often clerical. Laypeople are presented as leaders within the social structures of the church, for example, the emperors, kings, and princes of Catholic Europe exerted tremendous political and economic leadership vis-à-vis the church. On a day-to-day basis, these sociopolitical leaders had much to do with the historical flow of church life. Still, their activities are often described in a way that leaves the clerics, especially the highest level of clerics, the operative center. The church, in these volumes, is considered to be a church with a "clerical center" of structural leadership.

What that top leadership does, gets involved in, omits, and so on, is the inner circle around which all other details circulate. Too often church history is basically a history of clerical "structure," of clerical "institutions," and of clerical "organizations." This structural emphasis contributes, more often than not, to a "normal way" of understanding church: namely, the "church" equals the clerical church.

This attitude the church equals the clerical church—underlies such phrases as "the church teaches" or "the church says." Who is the "church" in these statements? Who is teaching? Who is saying? The answer is clear. When one hears the phrase "the church teaches," one basically hears that the clerical or institutional leadership of the church teaches. When one hears the phrase "the church says," one really hears that the clerical or institutional leadership of the church is speaking. In these and similar statements, the term "church" equals the "church's clerical or institutional leadership."

Even with this overriding clerical centering to church history, we today have been blessed with a series of books on church history, written by excellent scholars. Indeed, one can say that from 1900 onward, the breadth and depth of historical scholarship on church issues have reached a level never before imagined by ecclesiastical leaders and scholars. From the twentieth century onward, we Christians exist in an enviable position. In his time, Augustine did not have such a solid grasp of church history. In their time, Thomas Aquinas, Bonaventure, and John Duns Scotus did not have such a solid grasp of church history. Luther and Calvin had a slightly better understanding of church history, and this is found in their writings in the ways in which they raise their complaints about the Roman Church. However, neither Luther nor Calvin had the intensive and extensive historical resources we have today. The bishops at the Council of Trent, by and large, had only a small grasp of church history. The documents that these bishops developed show that a few of the bishops were aware of historical problems regarding issues of the church, but the bishops' sense of history was thin. Their arguments pro and con various positions are made from an ideological and theological stance, not from a historical stance.

From the end of the Council of Trent to Vatican I, a slow yet sporadic growth in the knowledge of church history began to take place. Here and there one finds a moment of brilliance, but it was not until the very end of the nineteenth century and the beginning of the twentieth century that the Western church—Catholic, Anglican, and Protestant—truly developed studies based on solid research regarding key issues of church history. Today we stand on the shoulders of these scholars. We have a better and sharper understanding of historical issues and problems within the history of Christianity.

Nonetheless, most of the major books on church history, good as they are, still tend to equate church with structure and institution. This overemphasis on the institutional church was addressed by the bishops at Vatican II in a subtle but very telling way. In their careful endeavors to understand the church's very nature and its value as church for the contemporary world, the conciliar bishops focused first on the mystery of the church and, second, on the people of God—chapter 1 and chapter 2 of *Lumen Gentium.*

The Mystery of the Church

We have seen above that the church in its essential depths is and can only be a relative actuality. The church in its very nature is relative to Jesus. It is Jesus, and Jesus alone, who is the light of the entire world. The church has no light of its own; the church is the mystery of the moon. It is church only when it reflects Jesus. The very life and nature of the church are relative to its dependence on Jesus.

Through this relative understanding of the church, the bishops wanted to clarify the phrase that Pope Pius XII had urged: the church as the Mystical Body of Christ. The conciliar bishops emphasized the church as mystery— therefore, the mystical aspect of the church—and the church's essential relation to Jesus—therefore, the "of Christ" aspect. They did this deliberately to indicate that the term "body," which has an institutional and structural connotation, is seen as secondary. To be secondary in no way means accidental; it simply means that one needs to begin with the church as mystery—a mystery of the moon, a mystical relativity to Jesus, and a total dependence on Jesus. Only on this basis can one then speak of structural leadership and charismatic leadership. The meaning of church is deeper, stronger, wider, and richer than any and every structural aspect, even the structural aspect described as "body" of Christ.

The People of God

The bishops at Vatican II wanted to change the centralizing clerical and institutional focus of what the church is all about. They did this in a very significant way. Their efforts and their successes, however, have, to date, not been all that successful. Even today, thirty-some years after Vatican II, whenever one hears a phrase such as "the church teaches," one still catches the meaning: the "clerical or institutional leadership of the church teaches." The non-clerical voice and presence too often play no role in the statement "the church teaches." The documents of Vatican II, however, moved in a different direction.

The documents of Vatican II stressed that the church is fundamentally the people of God and that all baptized, confirmed, and eucharistic Christians have a basic equality in the church. Every baptized, confirmed, and eucharistic Christian has an equal call from God and an equal mission from God to share in the teaching/preaching ministry, in the sanctifying ministry, and in the administrative ministry of Jesus. Such a view is not expressed in the phrases "the church teaches" and "the church says." The meaning of these phrases remains: "the clerical and institutional leadership of the church teaches." If the chapter on the people of God is taken seriously, then there is a different response when one hears the phrase "the church teaches." If, in this phrase, the intent is to focus on the clerical leadership of the church, then the different response is this: "Yes, but what does the people of God teach?"

Foundationally, the church is the people of God. Foundationally, then, there is a voice to this people of God. This voice is present, before a division between clerical and lay is made. There is a voice to this people of God that is not only more foundational, but, as a foundational voice, it provides the reason why there can also be a secondary clerical or lay voice. This can be expressed in another way. Members of the church are gospel people. The Word of God has been proclaimed, and a people who have heard God's Word have come together. The gospel, the Word of God, is foundational to the gathering of the people. The gospel, the Word of God, did not first call clerics. Nor did the gospel, the Word of God, first call laypeople. The Word of God was addressed to people as people. The gospel called together a people. Only on the basis of this foundational gospel call and on this foundational proclaimed Word of God does a people of God exist. Only when there is a people of God is there even the possibility of having a division of lay and cleric. The foundational people of God have heard the Word. Then, they have shared the Word with each other and with others outside this "people of God." The very Word of God is the initial and primary voice that speaks. The sharing of this voiced Word of God is the second level of voice communication. The people of God have heard and they speak. They are not a voiceless people of God. Thus, when we hear the phrase "the church says," we should ask what the people of God are saying, since this voice is the foundational voice upon which and because of which the church can have a clerical voice and a lay voice.

The documents of Vatican II developed a strong foundation for this foundational voice on the threefold ministry of Jesus. The threefold ministry of Jesus, in the documents of Vatican II, exists in a basic manner in every baptized, confirmed, and eucharistic Christian. Each and every Christian is called—a voice calls, or the Word of God calls—and each and every Christian is commissioned—a voice commissions, or the Word of God commissions. Only on the basis of Jesus' threefold ministry and the threefold ministry of the people of God does all other leadership have meaning and viability. Today this position of the bishops at Vatican II has not yet been fully acknowledged and accepted by the major leadership in the Roman Catholic Church. In this fundamental threefold ministry of all baptized, leadership is both institutional and charismatic. In our second focus of this chapter, we will study this position of Vatican II in detail.

Conclusions

From our consideration of leadership in every major aspect of human society, we have arrived at the following conclusions:

- All human leadership is structural, institutional, and organizational, on the one hand, and, on the other hand, charismatic and personal. The two are not either-or but both-and.
- All human leadership, either in its structural aspects or in its charismatic aspect, has, on the one hand, a certain excellence, and, on the other hand, a certain dysfunctionality.
- The leadership of the Roman Catholic Church, over the centuries, has exhibited and still exhibits a structural, institutional, and organizational side as well as a charismatic and personal side.
- In the leadership of the Roman Catholic Church, both in its history and

in its present format, there has been and there remains an excellence in both its structural and charismatic leadership, and there has been and there remains a dysfunctionality in both its structural and charismatic format.

- At Vatican II, the church was foundationally presented as the "mystery of the church." The title *Lumen Gentium* indicates that the mystery of the church is christological. Jesus, and Jesus alone, is the Light of the World. The church's mystery is to reflect the light of Jesus. Since the church has no light of its own, its mystery is to be the "mystery of the moon," reflecting the sunlight of Jesus, the Word of God.

- The people of God are those who hear this Word of God and try to live by the Word of God. The Word of God, the gospel or good news, is the first Word we hear, the first voice. This voice calls the church together. This voice calls the people of God into existence.

- The people of God hear the voice. They hear the Word of God. They hear the gospel or good news, and in their own words and their own actions they speak this Word of God. In this response to God's word, they reflect the Light of the World, Jesus. They become the mystery of the moon. As people of God they are not divided into cleric and lay. The people of God are the prior foundational depth in and through which the terms "cleric" and "lay" have meaning.

- "Cleric" and "lay" have meaning only on the basis of the church as mystery of the moon and on the basis of the church as people of God. In the primary Word of God, one hears the voice of God: God speaks. In the response of the gathered people of God, the people of God also speak. The people of God in word and action "re-speak" the Word of God and "re-flect" the Light of the World, Jesus. When we hear the phrase, "the church says," we must first of all hear God's Word; then we must hear the Word re-spoken in the entire people of God. Without this kind of hearing, we are apt to hear a word that is only clerical and not gospel, only lay and not gospel.

These are the positions that this section emphasizes. These positions are based on a sociological and anthropological analysis of all leadership, and the leadership of the Roman Catholic Church is no exception to this human conditionality. These positions are also based on the teachings of Vatican II, teachings that are foundational for an understanding of the church today.

This series of volumes is entitled Theology in Global Perspective. What I have written above owes much to the global perspective in today's theology. When Gustavo Gutiérrez first published *Theology of Liberation*, he used social analysis as a major grid through which he looked at the church in Peru in the late twentieth century. It was the use of social analysis that deeply disturbed his opponents. In the opponents' view, the question immediately arose: How can an institution established by God be judged by means of social analysis? Gutiérrez, however, remained firm in his approach. In other words, the application of social analysis to the church itself was part and parcel of liberation theology. Liberation theology was and remains one of the foundations for today's interest in global theology. We are indebted to liberation theologians for this global perspective. Their use of social analysis is absolutely necessary today, when we—a generation later—consider the Roman Catholic Church from a global perspective. By using social analysis, we come to the conclusions just listed. Since church leadership is not only clerical but both clerical and lay, then social analysis must play a role in today's evaluation of both the clerical and the lay aspects of Roman Catholic Church leadership. Since the end of Vatican II, the baptized people of God "officially" have an equal role in the fulfillment of the church's threefold ministry. In a post–Vatican II world and from a global perspective, the honoring of this basic Christian equality has become a must. Not to honor it can be seen as an instance of ecclesial dysfunctionality.

With these aspects of social analysis on leadership in general and their application to Roman Catholic leadership, and with a reminder of the basic meaning of church that the bishops at Vatican II bequeathed to us, let us move to the next subject of this chapter: namely, what is the "official" position on lay leadership and ministry in today's Roman Catholic Church?

OFFICIAL TEACHING ON LAY LEADERSHIP
IN THE POSTCONCILIAR CHURCH

In this section, I want to present as clearly as possible what we can call the official position on church leadership in the postconciliar Roman Catholic Church. The term "official" is ambiguous, since during Vatican II and throughout the postconciliar period there has not been a single official position on the issue of lay leadership and lay ministry. In fact, there have been subtle but clear differences and mixed signals in the description of lay ministry and leadership in various documents coming from Pope John Paul II and his curia. There appear to be several causes for this. A primary one stems from an apparent reticence about drawing the logical consequences from what we have been calling the common matrix of all believers. A comparison of the rather more expansive views of *Lumen Gentium* and the somewhat more restricted view of the *Catechism of the Catholic Church* brings this reticence into relief.

Lumen Gentium *on Laity and Leadership*

We discussed above in chapter 1 the fact that the Dogmatic Constitution on the Church, *Lumen Gentium*, placed material concerning the common matrix of all believers in the second chapter of the document. The council fathers did this over the objections of bishops who wanted chapter 2 to be on the church's hierarchy. By placing the material on the people of God prior to any discussion about cleric and lay, the bishops indicated that all baptized and confirmed Christians are basically equal. Faith and baptism are the common matrix from which all Christians come. We discussed further how three terms are applied to all baptized and confirmed Christians, namely, people of God, faithful of Christ, priesthood of all believers.

The bishops deliberately did not describe this equal status of all believers as "lay." That term is used for the issue of special lay ministries or apostolates that lay men and women perform in the church and in the world (LG 31). In *Lumen Gentium*, the term "lay" is discussed most thoroughly in chapter 4 (arts. 30-38), which is entitled "The Laity." The next chapter (arts. 39-42) on holiness is equally important because it drives home the fact that the common matrix gives the laity an equal opportunity to partake of the divine gift of holiness, which is the basis of every ministry and apostolate, both within the church and outside in the world.

By placing the material on the baptized and confirmed people of God in chapter 2, the bishops at Vatican II wanted to stress the common matrix of all believers. They also wanted to stress that this common matrix is the operative basis for all ministries in the church. This common matrix was further specified in *Lumen Gentium* in the following ways. It is God alone who *calls* individuals to become part of the people of God, the faithful of Christ, and the priesthood of all believers. In *Lumen Gentium*, institutional church leaders are not presented as the ones who foundationally call the individual Christians to share in the ministry and mission of Jesus. Moreover, it is God alone who *commissions* each of these baptized and confirmed persons to share in the threefold ministry of Jesus. Once again, *Lumen Gentium* does not present institutional church leaders as the ones who commission baptized and confirmed Christians for their threefold ministry. *Rather, all baptized and confirmed Christians are called and commissioned directly by God to share in the threefold ministry of Jesus the Christ.* Institutional church leadership, one must say, has a role in *discerning* whether God has truly called and commissioned someone for special ministries in the church. But this role is chiefly a kind of watchdog role that is necessary, for example, to protect the church from self-appointed people who may lack a realistic sense of their own capacities.

Bonaventure Kloppenburg, a Brazilian Franciscan, is especially insightful when he observes the following about the fundamental issues.

> Before someone is looked upon as either layman or deacon or priest or bishop or even pope, he should be considered first of all as a Christian or member of God's people. These terms express the basic condition, the primal state, the common element, the most important aspect, indeed the very reason why there exists a divine plan for the human creature. It is in this common foundation on which all else rests, that the greatness, dignity, and newness brought by Christ properly resided. Without it we would be nothing whether we happened to be pope, bishop, priest, deacon, or lay man.[3]

Kloppenburg's expressions, "basic condition," "primal state," "common element," and "common foundation," should be noted. One cannot speak about a clerical or hierarchical ministry unless one is first a Christian. The same can be said about the basis for specific lay ministries in the church. These, too, are based on the common foundation of being a Christian. Being a Christian means being called and being commissioned by God himself to share in the mission and ministry of Jesus.

The New Catechism on Laity and Leadership

The most detailed discussion of the church's ministry in the *Catechism of the Catholic Church* is found in the section entitled "The Church is Apostolic" (CCC 857-71), the final section of discussion of the four marks of the church: one, holy, catholic, and apostolic. From CCC 857 to 860, the *Catechism* speaks of the apostolic foundation of the entire church, and it is in this section that the *Catechism* addresses in a detailed way the issue of lay ministry. In CCC 857 the apostolic foundation of the church is described in three ways. (1) The church was built on and remains on the foundation of the apostles. (2) The church, in the power of the Holy Spirit, has retained and con-

---

3. Bonaventure Kloppenburg, *The Ecclesiology of Vatican II*, trans. Matthew O'Connell (Chicago: Franciscan Herald Press, 1974), 10.

tinues to hand on the teaching of Christ. (3) The church continues each day to be taught, sanctified, and guided by the apostles until Christ's return.

In this last section, the text informs us that the church continues to be "taught, sanctified and guided by the apostles until Christ's return, through their successors in pastoral office: the college of bishops assisted by priests, in union with the successor of Peter, the Church's supreme pastor" (CCC 857). There is no indication here that, through baptism and confirmation, all the people of God have been called and commissioned to share in either the teaching mission and ministry of Jesus or the other aspects of his work. Only the work of the pope, bishop, and priests is mentioned. By not addressing the common matrix of all believers, which is clearly in *Lumen Gentium*, this text contributes to what I call "the ambiguity" or the "mixed signal" regarding lay leadership in the church's official, postconciliar explanation of lay leadership. What the baptized-confirmed Christians do in their God-given and God-commissioned threefold ministry is clearly "apostolic." In their ministry, the church continues its foundational apostolicity. Not to refer to this aspect of the apostolic church, which is so emphasized in *Lumen Gentium*, is puzzling. While it may not be intended—and there is certainly in CCC 863 and 864 mention that both the ordained and the laity share in the vocation to the apostolate—the emphasis is on the hierarchy as the prime successors of the apostles. This impression is only deepened in arts. 871-73.

In the next section (arts. 858-60) the *Catechism* describes how Jesus chose the Twelve and sent them out to preach and heal. "In them," we read, "Christ continues his own mission." "Jesus unites them to the mission he received from the Father . . . from whom they received both the mandate for their mission and the power to carry it out." All of these are important statements; however, all the baptized-confirmed Christians have also received from God "both the mandate for their mission and the power to carry it out [the commission]." In fact, Christ's threefold mission and ministry is the basis for all mission and ministry in the church, clerical and lay. In art. 860, the text, which has so eloquently described the apostolic mission and ministry, ends with a citation from *Lumen Gentium*, but not from chapter 2 on the common matrix of all believers. Rather, it is a citation from chapter 3, "The Church Is Hierarchical." The citation ends with the following: "Therefore . . . the apostles took care to appoint successors" (LG 20). Who are these successors? Since this reference ends art. 860, one might legitimately raise such a question. However, in the *Catechism* the very next line presents the title for the following two articles, 861-62. The subtitle for these two paragraphs reads: "The bishops—successors of the apostles." It is clear that the editors of the *Catechism* understood the successors mentioned at the end of art. 860 to be the bishops. The *Catechism* has moved from apostolicity in general (art. 860) to the clerical or, better, the episcopal church (the subtitle for arts. 861-62). One asks: Why is the movement of thought in this context not a movement to the common matrix of all believers? Why is the movement abruptly to the bishops? Again, we are struck by the reluctance of the *Catechism* to make the common matrix of all believers as operative as this same matrix is operative in *Lumen Gentium*. The common matrix of all believers is continuously neglected. After a clear reference to the common matrix in art. 863, the *Catechism* begins a series of citations taken from the Vatican II Decree on the Apostolate of Laity, *Apostolicam Actuositatem*, in particular citing art. 2: "The Christian vocation is, of its nature, a vocation to the apostolate as well." Indeed, we call an apostolate "every activity of the Mystical body [that aims] to spread the Kingdom of Christ over the earth." Then, from art. 4, "Christ, sent by the Father, is the source of the Church's whole apostolate; thus the fruitfulness of apostolate for ordained ministers as well as for lay people clearly depends on their living union with Christ."

In the section entitled "Christ's Faithful: Hierarchy, Laity, Consecrated Life" (arts. 871-945) the laity is specifically treated in art. 897-913. The *Catechism* defines what is meant by laity in a clear way, in saying, "The term 'laity' is here understood to mean all the faithful except those in Holy Orders and those who belong to a religious state approved by the church" (art. 897).

To be accurate, while the *Catechism* does not dismiss the common matrix, neither does it use it as a foundation on which can be constructed a theological understanding of the unity of all church ministries. One cannot escape the judgment that the ministry of the hierarchy is considered more essential and important. The signals are not clear in the documents. Nevertheless, as we have seen above, the notion that baptism is a common matrix for the formation of all believers is foundational. Every baptized, confirmed, and eucharistic Christian shares equally in Christian life as a full-fledged and equal person in the people of God and the faithful of Christ, and also as a member of the one, foundational priesthood of all believers.

The bishops at Vatican II made this clear in *Lumen Gentium* 9-17. The expressions "people of God," "faithful of Christ," and "priesthood of all believers" were deliberately selected to indicate the richness of the baptismal-confirmed ministry of all Christians, whereby all Christians share equally in the ministry of Christ. To be faithful to the teaching of Vatican II, a presentation of church ministry today needs to begin with God sending Jesus (as found in LG 1-2), then continue with Jesus' own mission and ministry (as in LG 3), and only then move to describe the church as the body of Christ, the people of God, the faithful of Christ, and the priesthood of all believers (LG 9-14).

Once this basis is recognized, there is certainly a need for discussing theologically issues such as the division of labor between exercisers of the common priesthood (LG 10-11) and the ministerial priesthood of the ordained (LG 18-19). Is one wrong to make the judgment that subsequent practice and documents such as the *Catechism* do not bring these matters into relief with the same emphasis as is found in *Lumen Gentium*? Is the doctrine of the threefold task (*tria munera*), including the common priesthood that flows from the common baptismal matrix, properly emphasized? Or do subsequent actions and documents send the mixed signals we have discussed and detected above? We have been respectfully arguing that the *Catechism* is an example of the church's practical playing down of the foundational and operative role of the common matrix, thus not bringing into relief its importance, expressed in *Lumen Gentium*.

As a consequence of the mixed signals, an adequate post–Vatican II theological doctrine of lay ministry has not yet been clearly expressed, and therefore practical consequences have not been drawn. Mixed signals are sent. Perhaps it is too soon after the council to expect clarity. After every council, there has always been a long lag between the formulation of basic principles and widespread practical *understanding* of the issues involved. The central issue, though, is clear. While the foundation for understanding every ministry as flowing from baptism and confirmation is theoretically acknowledged, the church's central leadership appears more comfortable with stressing the hierarchical nature of the church and checking developments that play down or deemphasize the role of the hierarchy than in taking risks from listening carefully to the experience of the people of God.

This is not altogether surprising. Generally speaking, when one aspect of church life is altered, a host of other areas are affected. Any major change in the status of lay men and women within the church cannot help but reposition the role of priests and bishops. The Catholic Church is in the midst of a difficult process of repositioning and reclassifying.

To this is added the difficulty with which people adapt to change. For example, priests and bishops may find it hard to know what they should be doing. Busy laypeople may not grasp that this new understanding entails a radical personal conversion and deepening of their conscious relationship to Christ and the church. They are being asked to move from being passive members of the church to actively witnessing to Christ, the Spirit, and their gospel. In such a context, it is easy for members of one part of the church to point fingers at the other.

When one adds issues of the many cultural situations in which Catholicism finds itself, no one can imagine that solutions are going to be easy. Furthermore, there is the overarching problem of the hierarchy's practical acceptance of the notion that developments the church underwent in Europe in the last three centuries are normative everywhere. Add religious pluralism to the mix, and the situation becomes vastly complicated. Patterns in which leadership is exercised in one culture differ from those that work well in another. This leads to questions whether the structures of ordained leadership now mandated for the global church are appropriate everywhere. Then to questions like, Who decides? Should a church adapt traditional patterns of exercising leadership and authority or emerging patterns? Cultures do not remain stable, so how does one live in a house that is undergoing remodeling? Especially when people in the house disagree on what plans the remodeling should follow.

Add to such questions issues that arise when the church is a majority, a minority, or one of several relatively balanced religious groups in a given area. Leadership in a society that is 25 to 95 percent Catholic is different from that in a society that is only 1 to 2 percent Catholic. Facing such global issues changes the approach one takes to implementing theological principles on the tasks of order and ministry. What we are arguing in this book is that above all order and ministry cannot be understood if the fundamental, a priori nature of the principle of the common matrix of all baptized-confirmed Christians is not brought into relief. This principle of the common matrix is fundamentally important when one turns to the issue of a pluricultural church trying to face up to the needs of a globalizing world, especially when globalization itself is such a contentious issue.

Three conclusions seem important to list as we finish this section:

1. Church leadership enunciates at present no unified, official understanding of lay ministry vis-à-vis clerical leadership that seems convincing and resolves the tensions between what we have identified as the common matrix from the teaching of *Lumen Gentium* and the kind of doctrine and practice that one finds reflected in the *Catechism of the Catholic Church*. The result is mixed signals on lay leadership in the church today.

2. Following from the first conclusion, much effort is required on the part of both clergy and laity to understand and implement the implications of Vatican II. Drawing the practical consequences from this dialogue will be difficult for everyone.

3. Finally, given the varied conditions of the church, which is today paradoxically more globalized, and the fact that local conditions have become more important, the church faces issues of a magnitude never before experienced regarding creating an effective leadership. Both the attitude that we can return to the days when clerical life was an effec-

tive universal culture that could rely on common understandings among the clergy to guide the church and the notion that all attempts at maintaining strong vertical links deny local cultures the respect they deserve are equally romantic.

A HISTORICAL OVERVIEW OF LAY MINISTRY

From New Testament times to the present, the role of lay men and women in the church has varied considerably. At times, the layperson played a major role in official teaching, in liturgical life, and in the administrative oversight of the church. At times, the layperson was placed more at the edge of these three areas of church life. Just as important is the question of lay ministry or vocation *in the world*. In the era of Christendom in the West, when Roman Catholicism attained the structure it essentially still exhibits today, society was believed to be Christian. Although sin was self-evidently a factor, the order of society—insofar as it followed the teaching of the church—was believed to reflect the order of heaven. One of the key insights of Ernst Troeltsch, the great historian of the church's social history, is that Catholicism was (he wrote in 1910) still wedded to its medieval form and thus in tension with modernity as he saw modernity in his own day.[4] Troeltsch's observations seem little less valid today than when he made them. The difference, however, lies in the different evaluations that "modernity" today receives, in particular as globalization is seen to be one of its principal effects. At a theological level, today we are trying to absorb what it means that lay ministry should transform the world. In the age in which Catholicism adopted its present shape, the laity was expected only to follow the commandments of God and the church so as to attain salvation.

Modernity and modernizing in 1910, when Troeltsch wrote, were full of potential. Today, at the end of the bloodiest century in the history of humanity, modernity is judged to be far more ambiguous. Yet Catholicism has persevered in its present shape in a world where the first great revelations of globalization's reach were in World Wars I and II and the Cold War. In those bloody conflicts occurred the murder of millions upon millions by Nazis, Stalinists, and others. The United States entered into a war in Indo-China that cost the lives of two or more million to stop the march of Communism. In fact, the effects of its misjudgments radicalized a local liberation movement and pushed it deeper into a Marxism it might otherwise have aban-

---

4. See Ernst Troeltsch, *The Social Teaching of the Catholic Church*, trans. Olive Wyon (Chicago: University of Chicago, Midway Reprints, 1976), 1007-13.

doned if it did not have to appeal to Russian and Chinese "benefactors" who were equally intent on gaining advantage for their form of globalization.

In the matter of whether life can long endure the pollution caused by modernity, the verdict is still out. My point? We are today in a world far different from 1965 when *Gaudium et Spes* was basically optimistic about the potential for modernity to liberate humanity, especially if the church read the signs of the times.

The papacy of John Paul II was one in which a pope who was as suspicious of the globalizing West and its economic system as he was of Marxism became the leading religious leader in the world. His successor, Benedict XVI, is equally suspicious, and both are hard to classify as simple conservatives. The church has entered uncharted territory. As we do so, we look backwards to see if principles can be extracted that will help us discern the forms of order and ministry that will equip the church to minister better in a world that seems to have little to give it hope. It is impossible to present a complete picture of the layperson in church history. Still, one can offer a brief but fairly accurate overview of the ups and downs of lay involvement in the life of the Roman Catholic Church.

Four different historical periods can be delineated: (1) from New Testament times to the year 500; (2) from 500 to 1000; (3) from 1000 to the close of Vatican Council II; and (4) from Vatican II to the present. These divisions, however, are admittedly rough. No single event happened in 500 that marks it off from 501, nor in 1000 that marks an absolute watershed over against, say, 1200. Still, in about 500 and about 1000, certain factors emerged that brought about a change in the laypersons' role in church life. Obviously, both New Testament times and the times of Vatican II are more carefully measurable periods of history. Let us look at each of these periods in some detail.

From the New Testament and Earliest Christianity to 500

The New Testament does not use the terms "structural" and "charismatic" leadership. However, in the New Testament one does find examples of both structural or institutional and charismatic or personal leadership. In the New Testament data, the leadership role of Jesus himself is paramount. When Jesus began his public career, he was portrayed as a charismatic leader. He did not portray himself as a leader in any of the ordinary institutional positions. He was not a Jewish priest, nor did he belong to the group of rabbis. He was not a Pharisee, although much of his message was similar to the teachings of the Pharisees. He was neither a scribe nor a Sadducee. He was clearly not a

Zealot. How can we describe his activity and his leadership of disciples and followers?

Ekkehard Stegemann and Wolfgang Stegemann, in their book *The Jesus Movement: A Social History of Its First Century,* review the contemporary attempts by scholars to characterize the way in which Jesus himself developed a social group.[5] In the association of the early disciples with Jesus, all the various interpretations include structural elements as well as charismatic elements. In the New Testament writings, one finds a growth of organization among his disciples both before and after the death and resurrection of Jesus. A study of this organizational development is basic if one wants to understand the society that eventually came to be called the church and of which Jesus is the founding father.

Stegemann and Stegemann summarize their findings, first, in terms of the so-called sect model. The followers of Jesus, according to this interpretation, began as a sect within the many Judaisms of that time.[6] Jesus' followers constituted a sect similar to other Jewish movements at the time. A general description or semi-definition of sect is: a religious minority movement. This view became popular through the writings of Troeltsch, available through his epic *The Social Teaching of the Christian Churches,* published first in German before World War I, and available in English in the 1930s. Troeltsch was deeply influenced by Max Weber (1864-1920), who was a sociologist and an economist whose understanding of sect as a sociological phenomenon provided scholars with an analytical tool to understand the society of Jesus' times. The view that the Jesus movement was at first a Jewish sect remained popular until roughly 1970. Today the sect model is generally considered the most problematic interpretation, since the very word "sect" tends to be anachronistic. It is an early twentieth-century interpretation to describe a group, particularly a religious group, set apart from a central core. Although still used today by a few scholars, the sect model does not seem to be the most accurate way to describe the early Jesus communities.

The second model that was applied to the early community was the so-called millenarian model, which was promoted by J. G. Gager during the early 1970s. The millenarian model receives its name from the preaching of the imminent arrival of the parousia or end-time. Millenarian leaders have existed in almost every century of human life, and there were many millenarian preachers around the lifetime of Jesus. Jesus, in this view, is seen as one of

---

5. Ekkehard Stegemann and Wolfgang Stegemann, *The Jesus Movement: A Social History of Its First Century,* trans. O. C. Dean, Jr. (Minneapolis: Fortress, 1999), esp. 191-213.

6. For a good study of the variety of Judaism at the time of Jesus, see Jacob Neusner, "Varieties of Judaism in the Formative Age," in *Jewish Spirituality: From the Bible through the Middle Ages,* ed. Arthur Green (New York: Crossroad, 1987), 171-97.

the many Jewish preachers who stated that the final time was near. John the Baptist can certainly be described as a millenarian preacher, since he claimed that the end-time was near. Gager believed that Jesus arrived at the right moment.

> Only the initial spark of charismatic authority like that of Jesus was needed in order to ignite a millenarian movement in Palestine, which expected the imminent coming of the kingdom of God to bring about a reversal of social conditions.[7]

In other words, the times were ripe for a millenarian movement to take hold. The exact position of Jesus on the coming of the end of the world remains a moot issue. Raymond E. Brown presents the multiple interpretations that the New Testament offers on this matter.[8] In one way or another, Jesus himself seems to have preached an imminent end of the world. The exact time line cannot be determined from New Testament data alone. However, Jesus' call to repentance was based on the inexorable coming of God's judgment. This millenarian interpretation of the Jesus movement remains very persuasive among contemporary writers on Jesus.

The third model is called the "charismatic model," which is perhaps becoming the most generally accepted interpretation of the Jesus movement. Authors who have espoused this interpretation include Martin Hengel, Gerd Theissen, J. H. Schütz, and others. In this model, the charismatic leader is not simply a preacher; he must provide visible proof of an intimate relationship with the divine to be considered genuine.[9] The proof of the Spirit and of power is seen in the preacher's marvelous deeds and miracles. The Gospels present Jesus as such a charismatic-thaumaturgic (healer) figure. This charism draws a group of disciples and followers around a preacher, and this, too, finds expression in the Gospels. With a group of followers around Jesus, the Jesus movement itself began to take shape.

As time went on, the structure of the followers of Jesus was further delineated. One of the major moments in this regard was the formation of the "Twelve." We have already seen in chapter 1 how important this step was for the standard view of church authority in the Roman Catholic Church. The Twelve, in this standard view, have often been described as the first bishops, with Peter as the first pope. We have already discussed the general view that

---

7. J. G. Gager, *Kingdom and Community: The Social World of Early Christianity* (Englewood Cliffs, N.J.: Prentice Hall, 1975), quoted by Stegemann and Stegemann, *Jesus Movement*, 192.
8. Raymond E. Brown, *Jesus: God and Man; Modern Biblical Reflections* (Milwaukee: Bruce, 1977).
9. Stegemann and Stegemann, *Jesus Movement*, 193.

using these terms anachronistically reads later developments into earlier texts. It is more common today for biblical scholars to see the Twelve as a prototypical image of the twelve patriarchs and the twelve tribes of Israel. Jesus, in selecting the Twelve, dramatically indicates his intent to renew Israel. The Jesus movement was a revivalist movement, not the establishment of a new religion. It should be noted at this point that both the sect model and the millenarian model identify elements in the life and ministry of Jesus and the first generation of his followers that were really present. The question is which model is the most adequate overall.

Biblical scholars have noted that in the minds of the Jewish people at the time of Jesus, a revivalist interpretation would have been the first and proper way in which they viewed the Twelve: an image of renewal of Jewish religious life. In this view, the Twelve have had no "ecclesiastical" overtone at all. The people around Jesus would not have a clue as to what an "ecclesiastical" issue meant, nor did Jesus make any attempt to give the selection of the Twelve an ecclesiastical interpretation. The only overtone or interpretation possible for the meaning of the Twelve in the New Testament is a Jewish interpretation along the lines of a revival.

In the postresurrection continuance of the Jesus community, the Twelve remained in a major leadership role. They were certainly respected as charismatic individuals, reflecting the charism of Jesus himself. The movement from the Gospel of Luke into the Acts of the Apostles, for instance, sees the apostles continuing the ministry of Jesus in the power of the Spirit. Similarly, the Gospel portrays the Twelve as preaching the same message that Jesus preached and as men who worked miracles. The Twelve continued this message of a Jewish revival, which included a view that the end of the world would take place in the not too distant future.

Besides these elements of charismatic leadership, the Twelve exemplify a structural role as well. As the twelve tribes and their patriarchs are the bedrock of "Old Israel," the Twelve are the figurative bedrock of the "New Israel," and in a text such as Matthew 16:18, where Peter is given the title "rock," there is no question that the author of Matthew is making a reference to him as the first among the Twelve, who, in Matthew 28:16-20, are given the great missionary mandate to go forth to teach and baptize all nations. In all such texts, we are not in an either-or *doctrinal situation* but in a *first-order symbol world*, a both-and situation that sees the Twelve as having both charismatic and institutional leadership. There was, however, no apparent effort to institutionalize the office of the Twelve. In Acts 1:21-26, when Matthias is chosen to replace the traitor Judas, the motivation is to fill up the number of apostles as representatives of this dynamic. After this election, no continued institution of the Twelve took place. The Twelve fade from the New Testament vision, and with the death of the individual members of the Twelve, the institutional role of the Twelve ends.

To summarize elements we have discussed already above: (1) There is no single form of church in the New Testament and in earliest Christianity. Rather, several forms of church emerge, and present-day research shows that the forms of church differed widely. Several forms of leadership also emerged. (2) There is no structure in the New Testament that corresponds to what we call today cleric and lay. Indeed, such a reading is a *reading back* and a *reading into* the New Testament. (3) Among the several structures in the earliest Jesus communities, all have both organizational and charismatic elements. In the emergence of Paul as the "apostle to the Gentiles," we see a charismatic leader whose life, ministry, and teaching are extremely important for the growing realization that being apostolic is an essential mark of the church.

Each of the early Jesus communities struggled to determine its own organization, and in most cases we find the presence of major charismatic followers of Jesus, whose activity is highly visible. Mention must also be made of the brother of Jesus, James. In the postresurrection communities of Jesus followers, Peter, for a short time, remains an equally charismatic leader. To this list, one must add the Johannine leaders, who were also charismatic. This charismatic aspect of the Johannine leaders is evident in John's Gospel, in the Johannine Book of Revelation, and in the Johannine Letters. What we find in the New Testament are various combinations of both structure and charism.

In the New Testament, many people were seen as leaders. Mary, the mother of Jesus, was a leader. So, too, were Mary Magdalene and Martha. During early persecutions, martyred heroes and heroines, none of whom was ordained in the modern sense (including Peter, Paul, and many of the other "apostles"), were held up as models par excellence of following Jesus. The writers of the Gospels—Mark, Matthew, Luke, and John—were community leaders, even though we cannot identify them in any exact way. Other names can be added to this list of early leaders: Barnabas, Silas, Timothy, Titus, Prisca and Aquila (a married couple), Epaphroditus, Euodia, Syntyche, Clement, Philemon, Mark, Aristarchus, Demas, Epaphrus, Tychicus, Archippus, Andronicus, Junia, and Apaphras.

From New Testament times to roughly 500, laypeople enjoyed a variety of important roles within the church and its teaching, including leadership in liturgical and administrative structures. Again, there are a host of names. There were the major theologians of the second and third centuries: Clement of Alexandria, Origen (he was ordained only in 230 when he was forty-five years old), Tertullian, and Justin. The most honored Christians during this period were the martyrs, and they came from both what we would today call the ordained and the lay components of the church. Their martyrdom conferred on them an honor far superior to anyone else. A few names will suffice: the martyrs of Scilli, namely, Namphono, Madaura, Miggin, Sanam; the martyrs of Lyons, such as Blandina, Maturus, Alexander, Ponticus. In North Africa there were similar martyred heroes and heroines: Perpetua and Felicitas, as also Saturus, Satruninus, and Revocatus. Agathonika died at Pergamon around 161, and with her were Karpos and Papyus as well as a learned philosopher, Apollonius. In Rome, the *Acta* tell us of the martyrdom of Agnes, Cecilia, Felicitas and her seven sons, as also Sebastian, Cosmas, and Damian. All of these men and women could be called in today's language "laypeople." All of them were regarded highly as the ultimate disciples of Jesus and as men and women who fully incorporated the meaning of the Gospels. Some of these people, even today, are remembered in official eucharistic prayers.

Given contemporary critiques of the medieval "Christendom" model of church–state relations, it may seem incongruous to mention the lay status of Eastern and Western emperors of the Roman Empire from the fourth century on. Nevertheless, they were prominent laymen, which confirms that present day lay–clerical arrangements are not the only ones the church has known. Constantine, though only a catechumen, convoked the Council of Nicaea. He set the agenda for this council, presided over it, and made sure that the conciliar provisions were followed. A later emperor, Theodosius I, convoked the first Council of Constantinople, and still another emperor, Theodosius II, convoked the Council of Ephesus and maintained a tight control over it. The emperor Marcian convoked the Council of Chalcedon, which was the greatest of all the early church councils. Justinian I convoked the Second Council of Constantinople, and Constantine IV convoked the Third Council of Constantinople. These emperors were important institutional leaders of the church, and none was ordained.

Besides the major role of emperors in the life of the church, many laymen held senior positions both in the Roman curia itself and as the representatives of the bishop of Rome in the imperial offices in Constantinople, Alexandria, Antioch, and Milan-Ravenna. The pope's legate to the emperor's palace in Constantinople was in the majority of cases a layman. To say that laymen and to some degree laywomen were not highly placed in the church from New Testament times to 500 would be historically inexact.

To this group must be added the role of the empresses. Several of these women were very influential, particularly in the formation of the Byzantine laws concerning marriage and divorce. These women lobbied and obtained a better positioning of the wife in such legislation and even managed to provide legal protection for the children of divorced parents, as we see in the Code of Justinian.

Developments from 500 to about 1000

In the West, things changed between 500 and about 1000. During this period of time, however, there was no consistent and deliberate action on the part of Western church leadership to play down the role of the layperson in the ministry and mission of the church. One exception to this occurred when Pope Gregory the Great (540-604) removed from the Lateran curia not only all laypeople but also all presbyters.[10]

During this same period of time, there were major exceptions even to our lay versus clerical paradigm. Paramount among these exceptions was the role of Pepin and then of Charlemagne—indeed, in various ways all the early Western emperors after the collapse of classical Roman authority in the West in the fifth century. The Western emperors were not ordained clerics, but to call them "lay" would be anachronistic. Their position in the church was different from reign to reign, but it is clear that they exercised authority over the church that would make a modern canonist blush. Indeed, a consistent lay/ cleric distinction did not become dominant until the twelfth century, when the writings of Gratian (d. ca. 1159) made this either-or division popular. From 500 to 1000, emperors, monks, and nuns were not considered simply laypersons, nor were they considered clerics. Instead, it is historically more correct to say that from New Testament times down to Gratian in the twelfth century, there gradually developed four distinct classifications for the followers of Jesus: (1) the clerical or ordained Christian; (2) the emperor; (3) monks and nuns; and (4) laypeople.

When one gets into titles, interesting facts appear. The pope was referred to not as the Vicar of Christ but as the Vicar of Peter. As Vicar of Christ, the emperor was believed to have the God-given task of making sure that the bark of Peter was moving in a correct direction. Use of the title Vicar of Christ for the emperor was prevalent in Western Christian theology until the twelfth through the fourteenth centuries, when Pope Innocent III (1160-1216, pope from 1198) and Pope Boniface VIII (1234-1303, pope from 1294) claimed it. Did popes before this *approve* of such titles and of emper-

---

10. Kenan Osborne, *Ministry: Lay Ministry in the Roman Catholic Church, Its History and Theology* (Eugene, Ore.: Wipf & Stock, 2003), 164.

ors exercising such functions? Several didn't, but in an age where order was slowly being established in the chaos of the great migrations of the nations, strong hands were needed and the claims were not questioned.

The period from 500 to 1000 marked a low ebb in regard to educational possibilities for the ordinary layperson, for whom, in the West, education was minimal at best. Young people in the royal courts, of course, were often provided with excellent teachers, and some gained a strong educational background. In the monasteries, young men also had the opportunity for education, and after 800 the bright monks were strongly encouraged to become priests. Wealthy families provided a strong education for their children. The vast majority of people throughout Europe, however, were poor. For the most part, they were yoked to agriculture and the land in servitude to nobles. The decline in education is important to note, for without an education leadership is almost impossible. Catechesis was rudimentary. Gradually, the role of the layperson was to follow the basic commandments of God and the church, to confess sins and partake of the sacraments from time to time, and to receive salvation from an all-encompassing church. Accordingly, laypeople were more and more excluded from leadership roles.

From 1000 to Vatican Council II

From 1000 to Vatican II, there has been a steady pressure in the Roman Catholic Church to understand the laity as partaking in the *tria munera* of Christ and the church, which were gradually understood as teaching, celebrating the liturgy, and administering the church. To be noted is the fact that each of these roles was principally an *ad intra*, or internal, ministry. In the West, Christendom was the total organizing principle of society, and an *ad extra* ministry would make no sense, not least because (1) no major changes in society to alleviate poverty and free those in servitude were thought lawful; and (2) the notion that the ordained and religious were the paradigm of holiness gradually seems to have led to religious carrying on most public social ministries.

Nevertheless, at the beginning of the second millennium, education in the West moved beyond the monastic schools into the cathedral schools and then into the universities. With the rise of education and the development of quality schooling at the university level, many laymen and some laywomen moved into leadership roles, and since church and state were fairly united, a powerful lay influence on the church structures became noticeable. The papal approval of the Crusades gave crusaders a form of lay activity, even though history would judge it in mostly negative terms. The breakdown of imperial power and the rise of regions larger and smaller ruled by nobles whose allegiances were interlocked in webs of feudal fealty created a situation in which popes relied heavily on kings and princes who were more loyal to the papacy than to the emperor. In this situation, the loyal kings and princes received compensation by gaining control over church life in their own countries. As strange as it seems to modern sensibilities, the rise of kings and problems associated with rival claimants to the papal throne led to active and effective involvement by laity in the affairs of the church right down to the end of the Middle Ages. From 1500 onward, three major historical events took place that caused the clerical leadership of the Roman Catholic Church to oppose lay participation.

The first was the Protestant Reformation, which is conventionally dated to 1517. With the Reformers putting major emphasis on the common priesthood of all believers and rooting out church structures that could not be found in the New Testament, the clerical leadership of the Catholic Church took a dim view of lay participation in church leadership. Lay Catholic people, however, continued to be a strong presence in the life of the post-Reformation church, in spite of the anti-Protestant reaction by the clerical leadership of the church. Among the laypersons some remarkable women were highly regarded during their lifetime and were declared saints of the church after their death, for example, Teresa of Avila.

The second major event is the so-called Enlightenment, which spanned the eighteenth and nineteenth centuries, a period in which reason rather than faith was proposed as the prime criterion for all human life. The ordained leadership during this time took a dim view of a lay presence in church life, since those committed to Enlightenment principles seemed to want to weaken the structure of the church. To both clerics and laity who embraced Enlightenment positions, liberation from what Immanuel Kant (1724-1804) called "self-imposed tutelage" became a key goal.[11] The church's traditions were, of course, prime among the objects Kant thought needed to be cast off. Catholicism fought back, and for nearly two centuries, highly placed clerics sought to maintain a church on a plain above the Enlightenment's philosophical positions. One does not have to agree entirely with Kant to admit that that struggle left the intellectual life of the Roman Catholic Church in an isolated position.

The third event was the impact of the American and French Revolutions on peoples' understanding of divine rights of both kings and the ordained. These two revolutions took place at the end of the eighteenth century and

---

11. Immanuel Kant, *What Is Englightenment?* in *On History,* ed. Lewis White Beck (Indianapolis: Bobbs-Merrill, 1963; German orig., 1784), 3.

were related to currents of thought that were strongly anticlerical, especially in France. In the case of the American Revolution, British thought, especially ideas associated with the Bristol-born John Locke (1632-1704) and the Scottish Enlightenment led by figures such as David Hume (1711-1767), judged Roman Catholicism to be opposed to progress and to British interests. Very early in the formation of the United States, there were strong anti-Catholic movements that persisted into the nineteenth and twentieth centuries, made worse by the large numbers of Catholic immigrants pouring in from Ireland, Germany, Poland, and Italy. In Rome, the American Declaration of Independence and the Constitution were looked upon with grave misgivings, because they were founded on principles such as the equality of all human beings. The Declaration of Independence and the Constitution that enshrined its principles in legal language attacked the very foundations of the Roman idea that only the Catholic Church was legitimate and separation of church and state was unnatural.

As bishops and popes struggled to maintain their ancient privileges in France and Italy, anti-democratic positions grew stronger, and as a consequence of opposition to such movements, which most laypeople supported, a growth in the clericalization of the church grew. At another level, however, many laypeople played a major role in the charismatic leadership of the church in founding religious communities and lay fraternities dedicated to alleviating suffering, providing education, and spreading Christian values. The number of laymen and laywomen who were declared saints indicates a high degree of charismatic leadership. Many of these saints were lay Catholics who became very active in working to alleviate the social problems of the time: poverty, lack of education, destruction of family life, and slavery. As true as this remains, by the time of the Second Vatican Council, the church had turned its back on most modern currents.

At the risk of over-simplifying matters, when the archbishop of Venice, Giuseppe Roncalli (1881-1963), was elected pope and took the name John XXIII in 1958, many Catholic bishops, scholars, laity, and priests knew something had to be done to regain a position of critical engagement with the world. Many had long realized that untenably rigid doctrinal positions, which had poor support in scripture and tradition, needed to be abandoned. Pope John XXIII called for an ecumenical council and gave his reasons for it. The pope used a word that surprised many, when he called for *opportuni aggiornamenti* ("opportune updating") in his speech at the beginning of the council on October 11, 1962.[12] He had avoided the Italian word for "modernization,"

---

12. The text can be found in *Enchiridion Vaticanum, Documenti: Il Concilio Vaticano II*, 7th ed. (Bologna: Edizioni Dehoniane), [33-61] (the page numbers of the front matter, where various documents pertaining to the opening of the council can be found, are printed in brackets).

which would have plunged the council into debates on papal antimoderniza-
tion campaigns from 1848 through the mid-twentieth century. But he called
for updating so that "human beings, families, and peoples can turn their soul
to 'heavenly things.'" The pope's goal for the bishops at Vatican II was to
make the church credible as the messenger of the gospel in today's world. As
the council unfolded, five historical and contemporary issues hovered over
the proceedings. They continue to be present in Roman Catholic parishes,
dioceses, national conferences, and indeed in the universal church itself.

First, the bishops wanted to be true to the New Testament. On many occasions, the bishops deliberately shunned scholastic theological language in
favor of a more biblical language. On other occasions, the bishops realized
that major changes in understanding and interpreting the Bible had occurred
and needed to be reflected. At one level this process had been endorsed by
Pope Pius XII in his encyclical *Divino Afflante Spiritu* (1943), on the use of
historical-critical methods in studying the Scriptures. Pope John XXIII himself, prior to the council, encouraged the use of the historical-critical method
for the New Testament. Nonetheless, such approaches had not been taken,
and those who wrote about them found themselves under suspicion by
authorities who apparently disagreed with this agenda.

Second were the issues we have addressed in this book in terms of baptism
and confirmation as the common matrix of all believers.

Third, although it may not have been foreseen at the council, the principles of the council opened up studies in all the theological disciplines to lay
men and women. Today laity with graduate degrees in biblical studies, church
history, systematic theology, moral theology, and canon law may outnumber
the ordained. The principles of the common matrix would seem to say that
people with such expertise deserve to be put on an equal footing with the
ordained in such disciplines.

Fourth, at the council, what Karl Rahner would call the reality of the
"world church" began to emerge in the persons of dozens of African, Asian,
and Latin American bishops.[13] Rahner realized that the European *cultural*
domination of the church was, in principle, finished. Nevertheless, drawing
the practical conclusions from the emergence of a truly world church still has
not been dealt with adequately. While Africans and Asians can attain the
highest ranks of officeholders, only those who conform to the Roman notion
of what is culturally appropriate are selected to join such ranks. Latin Americans and North Americans, being mostly Caucasian, are less visible, but
again, only those who are willing to conform to the culture of the central

---

13. Karl Rahner, "Towards a Fundamental Theological Interpretation of Vatican II," *Theological Studies* 40 (December 1979): 716-27.

Roman administration are chosen. Under Pope John Paul II, the internation-alization of the curia progressed; however, inviting men and women who may have other views into the curia as officials or even as respected critics whose views are taken seriously seems not to enjoy favor.

Fifth, despite papal statements such as Pope John Paul's 1988 apostolic let-ter *Dignitatem Mulieris* (On the Dignity and Vocation of Women), many women still believe that they are second-class members. Admittedly, such feelings are more prevalent in places where women have received higher edu-cation and are respected members of professions once dominated by males; nevertheless, this presents the church with a great challenge. To such women, the church seems wedded to an outmoded culture. At a minimum, a more convincing case must be made why women are unfit to receive the charism for any and all leadership positions in the church.

The credibility of the Roman Catholic Church is at stake. The issues require the charism of discernment, but for the judgments of discernment to be accepted, under contemporary global standards, evidence and opinions need to be delivered publicly and responded to publicly. A global view is not an inward-looking view but one that convincingly is seen to move outward, beyond the culture of rectories and chancery and curial walls. There one finds a world populated by gifted women and men of great maturity and desire to help the church be the reflection of Jesus the Christ, the Light of the World. This is the missionary challenge of the whole church, and nowhere is it more important to find a way to engage the global church in real dialogue than in the family of questions that involve the role of the laity in ministries both within the church and in the larger world.

QUESTIONS FOR REFLECTION

1. What is the difference between structural (or institutional) leadership and charismatic and personal leadership? Give examples of each kind of leader-ship.

2. All human leadership is to some degree dysfunctional. Is the term applicable to church leadership? If so, how and when? If not, why not?

3. Do you think church leadership today is open to discussion with people who differ from present policies? Respond in terms of parish, diocesan, national, and international levels of church leadership.

4. Does the distinction between structural and institutional leadership and charismatic and personal leadership apply to cultures other than the Euro-American culture? Indicate some examples of these differences.

5. What challenges do baptism and confirmation—as the common matrix of all

believers—present in terms of how ordained and lay office and ministry should be understood? Review the content of *Lumen Gentium* chapter by chapter and discuss whether its insights seem to have been applied in churches you are acquainted with.

6. In what ways does our understanding of the multicultural nature of the world and the evaluation that all nations are fundamentally equal have an impact on the church today? Discuss the values at play when international and local church leaders are discussing whether to insist on unity or cultural diversity in shaping leadership ministries.

7. From a reading of relevant texts in *Lumen Gentium* and the Vatican II Decree on the Apostolate of the Laity, *Apostolicam Actuositatem*, what are most important aspects of the lay vocation? Are they being presented adequately in the church you are acquainted with?

8. What does the history of lay–clerical relations contribute to understanding lay vocation and ministry today?

9. Is what you read in *Lumen Gentium* and *Apostolicam Actuositatem* likely to be helpful in the formation of lay leadership today? Do these documents themselves seem realistic about life as a layperson today?

10. List your ideas on how the laity could be better consulted about issues you judge to be crucial at the parish, diocesan, national, and international levels of Catholicism today.

SUGGESTIONS FOR FURTHER READING AND STUDY

Congar, Yves M. J. *Lay People in the Church: A Study for a Theology of Laity*. Translated by Donald Attwater. Westminster, Md.: Newman Press, 1965. The classic study of the laity, one of the most important books by the great French theologian, whose ideas were among the most important behind the teaching of the Second Vatican Council on the nature and mission of the church.

Cueto, Elnora, and Dean Dicen, eds. *Stories of the Heart: Treasures of the Soul*. Manila: Philippine Catholic Lay Mission, 2002.

John Paul II, Pope. *Christifideles Laici*, Apostolic Exhortation, The Vocation and Mission of the Lay Faithful in the Church and in the World (December 30, 1988).

Osborne, Kenan. *Ministry: Lay Ministry in the Roman Catholic Church: Its History and Theology*. Eugene, Ore.: Wipf & Stock, 2003.

5

Dreams for the Future

EVERY FUTURE BECOMES REALITY in part because of dreams. People dream about who and what they can be and do. Dreams may seem idealized and unreachable, but they beckon us to move beyond our present boundaries. Without dreams, vital living comes to an end. Imagination is one of God's greatest gifts to human beings. Through imagination, artists have painted and sculpted breathtaking works. Through imagination, musicians have gathered together an audio universe of wondrous beauty. Through imagination, ordinary men and women have raised loving children and developed compassionate, caring, and supportive families. Through imagination, men and women look beyond the aches and pains of their manual labor and feel in their hearts the loving smile of spouses and children.

The church in a globalized world must be an imagining and a dreaming church.[1] Outward looking not inward gazing is, today, not simply a *good* thing for the church. Rather, it is the *only* thing that the church can do, if it wishes to play a vital role at all in the contemporary globalized world. Not to imagine and not to dream will doom the church to sit on the sideline of history. Imagination has a point of departure: the now. Imagination also has a point of arrival: the future. Imagination and dreaming, therefore, require a two-directional vision. For a theology of order and ministry from a global perspective, we must study the now and imagine the future.

A GLOBAL PERSPECTIVE REQUIRES TWO-WAY CONVERSATION

Today people are much more conscious of the integrity of all cultures. However, cultures are neither realities that change easily, nor are they realities that must be changed when outsiders want them to. Much has changed in the last fifty years. In a bygone day, most people held normative views of cultures and

---

1. On the relationship of imagination to the issue of environment and colonialism, see Ilya Prigogine and Isabelle Stengers, *Order out of Chaos: Man's New Dialogue with Nature* (New York: Bantam, 1984).

tended to think other people's cultures were odd or inferior to their own. Christianity arrived in Asia, the Americas, Oceania, and Africa on ships captained by men who had little doubt about the superiority of Western culture. Missionaries from the West, Protestant and Catholic, were heirs to a view that European civilization and culture were superior to all others. It took a long time for the West to learn how wrong that view was.

We live today in a world where it is impossible any longer to speak of a "Christian culture." We also live in a world in which not only every culture but Christianity itself is known be the product of its history and, in principle, changeable. It easy to accept the principles of cultural and historical relativity. It is much more difficult to accept the consequences, yet today's global situation increasingly demands a two-way conversation. This two-way conversation will be a major part of realizing dreams for a future when God will be known, praised, and served in churches that are vitally rooted in their own cultures, while having wings that allow them to soar around the world and rejoice in all the variety the Creator has brought forth.

In official statements of the Roman Catholic Church, acceptance of this two-directional dynamic is affirmed as ideal, but in practice it is not always what we hear. Actually, we hear mixed signals, and they come to us from high-level official church documents. The mixed signals refer in differing ways to the relationship between culture and Christianity. The Vatican II Pastoral Constitution on the Church in the Modern World (*Gaudium et Spes*) has presented one signal. We read:

> There are many links between the message of salvation and culture . . . Nevertheless, the Church has been sent to all ages and nations and, therefore, is not tied exclusively and indissolubly to any race or nation, to any one particular way of life, or to any customary practices ancient or modern. (GS 58)

In this text, the bishops are making it quite clear that the church is not tied to any single culture, but has a latitude of choices and a plethora of options. *Gaudium et Spes* continues in this line of thinking:

> The church is faithful to its traditions and is at the same time conscious of its universal mission; it can, then, enter into communion with different forms of culture, *thereby enriching both itself and the cultures themselves.* (58; emphasis added)

Gaudium et Spes clearly indicates a two-way street: culture enriches the church and the church enriches the culture. In the modern history of the church, however, the record of Catholics has been ambiguous, but the emphasis has often fallen on how Christianity discerns negative elements in other cultures and, at least implicitly, has wanted to replace them with what are called "Christian" elements. In retrospect, many of those elements were really Western cultural values that had become the cultural form through which the church came to understand its essential identity. The record, though, is complex. The work of scholars such as Lamin Sanneh, Ogbu Kalu, Andrew Walls, John Baur, and Kwame Bediako on African Christian history; that of Gustavo Gutiérrez, Paulo Suess, Alex García Rodríguez, Paulo Deiros, and Stuart McIntyre on Latin America; that of Andrew Ross, Peter Phan, Samuel Hugh Moffett, and Mathias Mundadan on Asia; and the two-volume *History of the World Christian Movement* by Dale Irvin and Scott Sunquist need to be read. This very incomplete list of authors is meant only to convey the idea that a new body of literature is growing up in postcolonial and mission studies that show that the history of Christian mission was far more complicated than the criticism of anthropologists and historians of even twenty years ago would lead one to suspect.

In China, for instance, Matteo Ricci (1552-1610) was not an exception. His superior, Alessandro Vallignano, and fellow Jesuits Roberto di Nobili and Alexandre de Rhodes were part of an attempt by Jesuits to adapt Catholic missions to Asian realities. Less flatteringly, it is also a fact that Catholic missions in places like West Africa went nowhere for three hundred years because Catholic priests and missionaries were associated with the slave trade and a royal form of native African governance that was rooted in slaveholding.[2] Christianity in Africa began to progress only when, in the early nineteenth century, slaves freed by the British for fighting against the Americans first fanned the fires of a smoldering anti-slavery movement and then led and inspired a Protestant missionary movement.[3] The first edition of Louis J. Luzbetak's book *The Church and Culture* became a milestone in the Catholic understanding of cultural plurality and the need to adapt. Luzbetak (1918-2005) was a theologically conservative Catholic, but as a student of Wilhelm Schmidt and a careful reader of papal encyclicals on mission from the early 1900s on, Luzbetak crystallized insights that Johannes Schuette introduced into the Vatican Council decree on mission, *Ad Gentes*. *Ad Gentes* and *Gaudium et spes* sent immensely positive signals of a willingness of the church to have a two-directional relationship and conversation with non-European cultures.

---

2. See John Baur, *2000 Years of Christianity in Africa: An African History, 62–1992* (Nairobi: Paulines, 1994), 55-152.

3. See Baur, *2000 Years*, 105-25; Lamin O. Sanneh, *Abolitionists Abroad: American Blacks and the Making of Modern West Africa* (Cambridge, Mass.: Harvard University Press, 1999), 238-49.

By 1975, however, Pope Paul VI detected a kind of uncritical romanticism about cultures that seemed to deny the need for the dialogue between Catholicism and cultures to be not just friendly but also critical. He signals this in the apostolic exhortation on evangelization, *Evangelii Nuntiandi,* where we read the following:

> The gospel and evangelization cannot be put in the same category with any culture. They are above all cultures . . . They [the gospel and evange-lization] can penetrate any culture while being subservient to none. (EN 19-20)

Many see in these words of Paul VI a mixed signal, since they emphasize a view somewhat different in tone from *Gaudium et Spes.* In the exhortation of Paul VI, the implication is that the church is *transcultural,* perhaps even _supracultural._ There seems to be little recognition that the church itself has a culture formed in the history of the West. The danger of forgetting or deny-ing this Western cultural particularity is that church leaders, thinking that the church is transcultural or supracultural, do not feel obliged to engage in a two-way critical dialogue. Not doing so is equally perilous whether the cross-cultural dialogue fails to occur between the church leaders and modern Europe, which has moved far from medieval culture, or between the curia and Chinese and Congolese cultures. The great temptation is for a church with a transcultural complex to think it can penetrate all cultures and transform any culture without letting its own cultural values be brought into question.

Today's global perspective must move toward critical mutuality. Moving into different cultures will change the church. Contemporary postmodern philosophy, which is primarily a Euro-American philosophy, is right in see-ing that everything human is historical, relational, finite, limited, and cultural. There is nothing finite that can be truly transcultural. In the history of the Roman Catholic Church, the Franciscan intellectual tradition, perhaps best typified by St. Bonaventure and John Duns Scotus, has continually taught that only God is above contingency. In this perspective, all created reality is contingent and unnecessary, and therefore all created reality can be subject to change.[4] Asian philosophy, by and large, presents a worldview in which there is interrelational mutuality, not isolated and individualized identity.[5]

A two-directional approach rather than a unilateral approach is an integral

---

4. Kenan B. Osborne, *The Franciscan Intellectual Tradition* (St. Bonaventure, N.Y.: Franciscan Institute, 2003).

5. See Wing-tsit Chan, *A Source Book in Chinese Philosophy* (Princeton, N.J.: Princeton University Press, 1963), 14-48.

part of today's global perspective. A globalized theology must be capable of two-directional dialogue. The same is true of how one understands order and ministry. Ecclesiology, the theological study of the nature and structure of the church, needs to envisage a much more vibrant two-directional conversation.

Two contemporary documents illustrate the divided state of mind of the Roman magisterium in this entire area. In the instruction *Inculturation and the Roman Liturgy*, the authors state that inculturation does designate a two-directional movement.[6] The document states that this two-way direction mirrors the description of the double movement found in John Paul II's encyclical *Redemptoris Missio* (art. 52). In both of these documents, the church espouses taking the path of assimilating particularized cultural values, when they are compatible with the gospel. At one important level, this is helpful, but at another, the adoption of a reality from a new culture can only be done if it helps to express effectively the message of Jesus. Such an approach is utilitarian, meaning that cultural realities are valued if they have a practical effectiveness for conveying the good news. Cultural exchange, however, when it is truly a two-directional exchange, goes far deeper than utilitarianism. One culture offers to another a new way to envision the world. In evangelization the evangelizer serves as an agent of the Holy Spirit to offer a follower of another culture or religious way an entrée into the world as known through the eyes of Jesus. But the "receptor" culture is not simply a useful vehicle to help, say, a Korean accept Christ. Rather, a Korean sees different things in Christ and the gospel as a result of being formed by different literature, oral traditions, arts, language, and history. As a result, Koreans—both those who become Christian and those who do not—have something to offer the world Christian community. In their response to the Gospel message, their own forms of music and dance offer new vehicles to sing God's praises from new points of view. Those who do not become Christian understand their traditional religions differently from the dialogue, and Christians understand better the seriousness, depth, and ability to inspire that Korean religious traditions had and have. All these are insights that could not come to maturity if Koreans had not entered into dialogue with the gospel.

Other cultures ask us a burning question: *Do you see what we see?* It is precisely the dialogue that results from this kind of question that makes today's interfacing of global cultures and religion a two-directional process, not simply a utilitarian exchange of concepts. Cross-cultural interfacing helps us see our world differently and therefore opens up new vistas, new dreams, and new ways of imagining.

---

6. Congregation of Divine Worship and the Discipline of the Sacraments, *Inculturation and the Roman Liturgy* (Vatican City, 1994), no. 4.

Since structures of order and ministry are core dimensions of church life and are integral to how churches are structured, the shape of church leadership itself must be the result of two-directional dialogue. A different culture may point to different ways of structuring leadership. Church leadership needs to let itself be enriched by the depths of cultures other than the standard Euro-American culture. Adaptation for utilitarian purposes is inadequate. This leads to a second characteristic of a theology of order and ministry from a global perspective.

CULTURAL STYLES OF LEADERSHIP AS POTENTIAL MODELS FOR CHRISTIAN LEADERSHIP

Every culture has its ways of structuring leadership.[7] These forms of leadership involve a certain sacred quality, since a healthy culture is not just arranged functionally. Instead, cultures reflect a people's experience of the divine and the holy. From the studies of historians of religions, anthropologists, and political scientists, we know that structures of leadership reflect the way a people sees the very order of the cosmos. Since the French and American revolutions, to be sure, democracies have generally been wary of acknowledging this deeper dimension of political life, but it is a reality even in highly secularized societies.

We could spend a number of pages going deeper into this matter and offer insights from sociologists such as Emile Durkheim and historians of religion such as Mircea Eliade. In the interests of brevity, it may be sufficient to say that when Christianity encounters a new cultural milieu, the process of setting up the local church must involve a two-way dialogue to ensure:

1. that local people are able to share with representatives of the central leadership of the church the major elements of the worldview that local patterns of leadership incarnate

---

7. Today we are blessed with a large number of books and articles on church and culture. It would be out of place here to offer a detailed bibliography. I offer the following only as a sampling of the richness of today's literature on the subject. *Asian Christian Theologies: A Research Guide to Authors, Movements, and Sources,* ed. John England et al., 3 vols. (Maryknoll, N.Y.: Orbis Books, 2002, 2003, 2004). These volumes give an expansive and detailed study of Asian theologies. *The East Asian Pastoral Review* continues to be an up-to-date source on Asian theological endeavors. Of note for our purposes is vol. 39, *The Mission of God: Its Challenges and Demands in Today's World,* by Peter C. Phan. See also *The Future of the Asian Churches: The Asian Synod and Ecclesia in Asia,* by James H. Kroeger and Peter C. Phan (Quezon City, Philippines: Claretian Publications, 2002). For the issues of non-Christian religions, see Paul F. Knitter, *Theologies of Religions* (Maryknoll, N.Y.: Orbis Books, 2002). For the Latino culture in the United States, see Timothy Matovina and Gerald E. Poyo, eds., *¡Presente! U.S. Latino Catholics from Colonial Origins to the Present* (Maryknoll, N.Y.: Orbis Books, 2000).

2. that there be no hasty decisions that a local church must resemble the sending church
3. that all churches, especially in this day of rapid, confusing cultural change, be given the chance for this kind of dialogue
4. that the marks of a true church of Christ—being one, holy, catholic, and apostolic—be given careful attention so that what evolves truly signifies the universality of the church as it confesses Christ and lives the Christian life

The goal of inculturating the church is to allow the Spirit of Christ and the gospel to come to fruition. Tradition is important in handing on the experience of the church in trying to embody all these values. Part of that experience involves negative experiences with cultures, because every culture is also ambiguous. In the European experience, for example, Catholicism had to adapt to Germanic warrior culture and the structures of pledging one's loyalty to higher lords in a feudal system. The results were not altogether a blessing.[8] Should we expect that the case will be different today? The point that must be made, of course, is that no culture is immaculately conceived, and so discernment is necessary to be sure that the cultural elements that are taken into the church be as purified from elements incompatible with the gospel as possible.

Forms of leadership that have developed over centuries in China or Indonesia, for example, may reflect a deep interaction of these peoples with the divine. But there are two other elements to be considered. First, the temptation of unrealistic romanticism. All cultures are continually changing. That process appears to be proceeding faster and more radically today than at any time in history. One could adapt forms of leadership that fit well in the villages of the Indonesian islands. But in an age of rapid urbanization, will those patterns work well in Djakarta? Discernment and realism have never been more important than today.

Second, *agapē*, self-giving love that knows no boundaries, is the hallmark of the Christian ethos. It has profound resonances in, for example, Buddhist cultures, where compassion for all living beings is the supreme sign of the genuineness of one's experience of Enlightenment. Are the ways in which Buddhist monks bring novices closer and closer to Enlightenment the best way to help neophyte Christians understand what following Christ in the Spirit means? At a minimum, even when the values of two religious systems seem to be very close, dialogue is necessary to be sure that the cultural forms

---

8. See Richard Fletcher, *The Barbarian Conversion: From Paganism to Christianity* (New York: Henry Holt, 1997), 228-84.

one embraces are truly going to work. The Anglican bishop of Kuala Lumpur, Hwa Yung, has written a very challenging book on the issues at stake in the quest for forms of understanding and practicing the contextualization of Christianity in Asia.[9]

How one names leaders is not the important issue. The reality *is* important. Every culture has its own sacred forms of leadership, and the sacredness of these forms cannot be summarily set to one side, nor can new forms of sacred leadership be summarily imposed. Paradoxically, one of the greatest challenges to the church today is finding forms of leadership and community that will speak to the 75 or more percent of Europeans who fall into the categories of "believing and not belonging," "belonging but not believing," and "not believing but belonging" today.[10] What glimpses of the sacred do such Europeans have? What kind of evangelizing agent can overcome their indifference and hostility to the church? Is the church able to enter into the kind of serious dialogue necessary to speak to such people?

Leadership, then, deserves serious study. A generation ago it was possible for Westerners to think of themselves as the gatekeepers and guardians. They could have felt quite progressive if they read a book such as John S. Mbiti's *Introduction to African Religion*. He points out that certain names have a religious meaning and have a leadership meaning.[11] For example, in Uganda, the name *Muwanga* means "the one who puts things in order." A Ugandan sees order in a person who has the leadership name *Muwanga*. Even more, the *Muwanga* who puts things in order does so because God has sent this particular *Muwanga* to the people, which of course reminds Christians that, in the Christian view, God acts in a similar way. Ordination is a call and commission from God.[12] Mbiti offers an entire chapter on religious leaders in Africa,[13] in which he discusses medicine men, diviners, mediums, and seers and describes ritual elders, rainmakers, and priests. There are as well traditional central leaders with a variety of names. Again, Mbiti, like many other African theologians, is calling us to see what various African people see in their leadership. Do we see what they see as order and ministry, even as holy

---

9. Hwa Yung, *Mangoes or Bananas: The Quest for an Authentic Asian Christian Theology* (Oxford/Irvine, Calif.: Oxford Regnum Books, 1997); see esp. the postscript, 240-41.

10. These are among the categories that Grace Davie suggests in her books on Christianity in contemporary Europe. They include *Religion in Britain since 1945: Believing without Belonging* (Oxford: Blackwell, 1994) and *Religion in Modern Europe: A Memory Mutates* (Oxford: Oxford University Press, 2000).

11. John S. Mbiti, *Introduction to African Religion* (Oxford: Heinemann Educational Publishers, 1991).

12. Mbiti, *Introduction to African Religion*, 28.

13. Mbiti, *Introduction to African Religion*, 153-64. See also Elizabeth Isichei's *A History of Christianity in Africa* (Grand Rapids: Eerdmans, 1995).

order and holy ministry, in their own special leaders? What we are asked to envision is something more than a utilitarian adaptation.

Today it is not as if such questions are not important, but the pace of urbanization, the toll taken on the morale of peoples by genocides, HIV/AIDS, the pollution of traditional culture by violent and sexually explicit forms of entertainment, and the disappearance of traditional village structures makes the question far more difficult than it was only a generation ago. Progressive-minded missionaries and African church leaders were sure then that African cultural patterns were capable of being utilized and that Roman intransigence was the enemy. After twenty years it is harder to say that, and so we are at a point in time when the need for two-way dialogue is even more necessary.

It is important, then, to realize that when a decision is made not to follow traditional cultural leadership patterns, it does not automatically mean that traditional cultural and religious leaders are no longer honored and respected. In Spanish-speaking regions one finds even today a great deal of respect for the *curandero*. Even though the *curandero* is not an order or ministry accepted by the church, many people continue to acknowledge the holiness of the *curandero*. In Korea today, there are shamans. Protestant and Catholic Korean churches do not openly acknowledge the role of shamans, but many Christians do. If we have a two-way street, are these Christian people who accept other cultural leaders telling us something that, as *Gaudium et Spes* says, might enrich the church? Are they not telling us that we need to see order and ministry in a more global perspective? They also point to something that every Westerner needs to emblazon in his or her consciousness. We consider that next.

THE LINGERING EFFECTS OF COLONIAL-ERA DISREGARD OF LOCAL SOVEREIGNTY

In many colonial activities on the part of the Euro-American people from 1500 to 1960, local sovereignty was frequently disregarded. This attitude by agents of colonialism often included a disregard of local leadership by missionaries, government agents, and businessmen. The effects of this disregard of local leadership can hardly be overemphasized. The aftermath of colonialism remains a major issue in today's third world. Jeroom Heyndrickx refers to this lingering scar of colonialized and trashed sovereignty as the foreign stigma.[14] Whether justified or not, almost all writers on church activity from

---

14. Jeroom Heyndrickx, "From 'Mission in China' to 'Inter-church Exchange,'" *SEDOS Bulletin* 28, no. 5 (1996): 138-45.

the fifteenth century to the twentieth make the churches a partner of the colonialists. It matters little that a brilliant study like that of Paul Kollman on the work of the Catholic Spiritan order in eastern Africa shows such charges to be so general as almost to be meaningless.[15] It is the belief of almost all intellectuals in the third world that this is the case, and one of the most serious burdens that church members bear is the accusation that Christianity is a colonization of the mind—non-African, non-Indian, non-Chinese, non-Quechua, and so forth. This accusation is common currency regarding colonialism in North and South America, in Africa, and in both East and South Asia.

Overcoming that legacy will depend in large measure on the willingness of the church's central administration both to listen intently and to be seen as listening intently. A key area in which such dialogue needs to take place is the liturgy. That, of course, opens the question of order and ministries. Once again, however, the Catholic community seems to give mixed signals. Dysfunctionality is not too strong a word to characterize the situation.

For clarity's sake, order needs to be brought into questions raised by three key texts from the Vatican II conciliar magisterium and official Roman documents. The first document that the bishops at Vatican II approved, on December 4, 1963, was the Constitution on the Sacred Liturgy, entitled *Sacrosanctum Concilium.* In art. 37, the document says:

> Even in the liturgy the Church does not wish to impose a rigid uniformity in matters which do not involve the faith or the good of the whole community. Rather does she respect and foster the qualities and talents of the various races and nations. Anything in these people's way of life which is not indissolubly bound up with superstition and error she studies with sympathy, and, if possible, preserves intact. She sometimes even admits such things into the liturgy itself, provided they harmonize with its true and authentic spirit.

These opening lines set a definite tone: rigid uniformity is clearly not the starting point. The text encourages cultivation and fostering "the qualities and talents of various races and nations." This same openness continues in arts. 38 and 39. This last article deserves to be cited directly:

> Within the limits set by the standard editions of the liturgical books it shall be for the competent territorial ecclesiastical authority mentioned in

---

15. See Paul V. Kollman, *The Evangelization of Slaves and Catholic Origins in Eastern Africa* (Maryknoll, N.Y.: Orbis Books, 2005).

article 22:2 to specify adaptations, especially as regards the administration of the sacraments, sacramentals, processions, liturgical language, sacred music and the arts—in keeping, however, with the fundamental norms laid down in this Constitution.

What we see in this conciliar document is openness and positive encouragement for cultural, liturgical adaptation and change and, if need be, even radical adaptation and change. This is one signal, and it is positive. After the publication of the Constitution on the Sacred Liturgy and associated norms implementation, a number of committees were formed to reconstruct all the sacramental liturgies of the Roman Catholic Church. All the liturgically reconstructed sacramental rites were translated into a plurality of languages. Music was written to enhance these new rites. Commentaries were written, explaining the new rites. Para-sacramental liturgies were also developed in a plurality of languages, and a book of blessings was officially published under Vatican auspices. There is no doubt at all that the sacramental life of the Roman Catholic Church has been changed, adapted, and developed in a spectacular way. The hopes of the bishops at Vatican II have been in large measure realized. In all of the sacramental reformulations, the criteria and norms set down in the constitution on the sacred liturgy were carefully studied, and these same criteria and norms were applied to all of the various sacramental and para-sacramental renewals.

Thirty years later, in 1994, the Congregation for Divine Worship and the Discipline of the Sacraments issued an instruction on these same matters. The authors of this instruction acknowledge that major changes in liturgy took place after Vatican II and that the issue of culture and liturgy had been a strong motivating force for many of these liturgical changes (nos. 1-8). The norms established by *Sacrosanctum Concilium* are accepted, but certain words that this instruction uses in the introductory section are meant to clarify the reasons for drawing up a new instruction on liturgy and culture. We read that the norms found in the conciliar document are "here defined." Certain principles in the conciliar statement "are explained more precisely," and "the directives are set out in a more appropriate way" (no. 3). There is no doubt that the norms established by Vatican II were general in tone. The instruction states that the norms of *Sacrosanctum Concilium* are the basis for further developments. *Sacrosanctum Concilium* is, then, the lens through which the 1994 "Instruction on Inculturation and the Roman Liturgy" is to be read.

The authors move on to contextualize the processes of inculturation that have occurred in the church over the past two thousand years. These paragraphs are similar to the historical contextualization that is found in the present volume. In nos. 9-15, the early history of the gospel within a Semitic culture is described. The authors maintain the standard approach to the church's explanation of its institution. The contemporary issues from biblical scholars, church historians, and patrologists are not even hinted at. The impression one gets from this rendition is that Jesus established the church in substantial detail, and, as a consequence, this detailed institution sets up an immediate roadblock to change. If Jesus instituted liturgical rituals, they are beyond change. Although this detailed institution is precisely the focus of the current biblical scholars, church historians, and patrologists, the authors pass over these issues in silence, indicating, so it seems, that the contemporary issues do not deserve any preferential treatment.

In nos. 16 to 20, the instruction considers the interfacing of cultures and the church from the second century to the present. In this brief historical survey, church leaders are portrayed as discerning—and always correctly—which cultural realities can be assimilated and which ones cannot. The portrait in the instruction lacks the dramatic picture of the church leaders not knowing what to do; in the instruction, the struggles are ironed out, and only an irenic historical development is envisioned. This kind of portrait goes against historical data, since the liturgy over the centuries has been changed and challenged into its new forms. The instruction's presentation of the historical drama of cultural and liturgical mutual interfacing is so mechanistically and therefore positively described—using the word discernment—that the actual liturgical history appears idealized and non-real. Such a portrait excludes changes that did not occur in such a smooth and well-discerned way. Discernment, we hear, is the continual work of the Holy Spirit within the church. The human side of liturgical change is ignored, and therefore changes have always had happy endings because of divine discernment. All of the above sets the stage for the main part of the instruction, which deals precisely with cultural change. The instruction moves forward not with an openness but with a major *caveat*: liturgical change cannot be disruptive since the Holy Spirit is always present.

From nn. 21 to 32, the instruction presents its main themes on liturgical inculturation today. Some words and phrases provide us with the mentality of the authors: "Because it is Catholic, the church overcomes the barriers which divide humanity" (n. 22). The "church is called to gather all people, to speak the languages, to penetrate all cultures" (n. 22). In this view, the church, apparently, glides through space-time in a serene and unifying way and the central bodies of the church serenely make decisions affecting everyone.

We read, "The church has the duty to transmit them [the sacraments] carefully and faithfully to every generation" (no. 25). But who is meant by "the church." Nowhere in the instruction is the church, portrayed as the people of God, seen as the agent of transmission. Time and again, what is unspoken is the notion that <u>clerical church leaders make the decisions.</u> In cultural adaptation, however, the people have an important role to play. It is the people, not the clerical leaders, who experience and understand a given culture in its widespread and profound dimensions. Nonclerical individuals and groups can be used, but only in a secondary and auxiliary way. Some are experts on a given culture, and they can offer advice; some are local leaders, and they too can provide insight. The clerical leaders of the local and regional church, however, are the only ones who have the final say.

Cultures themselves ordinarily do not change because a certain level or ranking of leadership quarterbacks the process. Cultural change is a process that moves in and through a people at an everyday level and in an everyday pace. The leadership "accepts" the changes and blesses the changes, thus giving some official endorsement. But this blessing and endorsement occur at the end of a process of cultural change; it is generally not the impetus for the process of cultural change.

In 2004, the Congregation for Divine Worship and the Discipline of the Sacraments issued another instruction, this one entitled *Redemptionis Sacramentum* (Sacrament of Redemption) with a subtitle reading: "On certain matters to be observed or to be avoided regarding the Most Holy Eucharist."[16] The tone of this instruction differs from that of both documents considered above.

The Vatican II Constitution on the Sacred Liturgy is given a place of honor, but *Redemptionis Sacramentum* is not the most operative document throughout this lengthy instruction. Rather, the authors have put together a detailed restatement of regulations found in canon law, in the introductory statements of the Roman Missal, and in various statements issued by several sacred congregations. The tone is legalistic and juridical throughout. Paragraph after paragraph is simply a reminder of what these legislative documents have advocated. One finds very little in this instruction for a theology of order and ministry from a global perspective. The perspective is not one in which global realities require local decision. Instead, <u>the perspective is that of maintaining clerical leadership</u>. It repeats recent regulations. The tone is also didactic: these are the regulations and those involved in the eucharistic liturgy at any level should abide by these regulations. The details are minute, and no effort is made to indicate whether a certain liturgical requirement is of greater

---

16. Congregation for Divine Worship and the Discipline of the Sacraments, Instruction: *Redemptionis Sacramentum* (Vatican City, 2004).

or lesser value than another. The regulations go beyond the eucharist to other sacraments and then to matters of devotion. The reality of cultural diversity is touched upon, but the document offers little help for the pastoral needs of churches moving through cultural change. Of the three documents we have considered this is the least global.

CONCLUDING THOUGHTS ON GLOBAL CATHOLICISM AND CULTURE

There is no doubt that the churning aftermath of Vatican II has proved confusing, and that sincere voices have called both for a more conservative approaches and for updating, progressive approaches. All of this has played a role in the way in which order and ministry have been interpreted within a global theological perspective. We find this back-and-forth movement fairly dominant in official documents on liturgy. Nevertheless, the tendency to make liturgical celebration more uniform makes it hard to avoid concluding that the scope for different theologies and practical adaptations of order and ministry in a globalized perspective is reduced.

The point I wish to make is that the furor over culture, liturgy, worship styles, and rules is not the fundamental issue. We are instead back to the question, What difference do *perspectives* make in a globalized world? Recall that saying "globalized" does not mean that uniform solutions need to be found for every problem, because one of the paradoxes of globalization is that global trends produce different results in different cultures. Therefore the questions are: What forms of worship, order, and ministry are necessary to make manifest a universal faith? And what forms can be adapted to suit local conditions?

Since liturgical celebration is the celebration of people, and since the peoples of this earth are culturally diverse, some level of cultural adaptation for church order, ministry, and liturgical celebrations is a must. The bishops at the Vatican Council said in several places that the eucharist is central, even the highpoint, of Christian life (see SC 2, 5-6; LG 7, 17; PO 5; GS 38). Both the council and the four popes who have served since the council have emphasized that the eucharist makes the church and the church makes the eucharist. If, then, the eucharist is so central, the celebration of the eucharist needs to touch individuals on more than an occasional basis. It is the center of life, the point to which laity returns from their attempts to embody Christ and his Spirit "in the world" to renew themselves and touch sacramentally the One to whom they have given themselves in faith. The way a Melanesian mother, a Chinese chemistry teacher, a Pakistani policeman, an inner-city Chicago nurse, or a Peruvian subsistence farmer in the Altiplano will do this, as one might expect, will be different. If the form of eucharistic celebrations is legislated with a one-size-fits-all mind-set, then for many of the people of God the eucharist will not reveal and create a vital church, nor will a vital community celebrate the eucharist.

The local church is the only existential and actual reality in which a eucharist is celebrated. There is no church "in general." There are only con-crete assemblies gathered around word and sacrament. Theologians quite properly argue about the ways in which local congregations and larger dioce-san units are most properly called "the local church." From such discussions, important as they are, we prescind. Still, it is clear that the needs of local con-gregations differ, and thus liturgy cannot be legislated as if the eucharist were a cloned reality. Liturgy, in its actual celebration, exists only as a celebration by a concrete local assembly meeting at specific spatial and temporal coordi-nates. Because this is the nature of all liturgy, the characteristics of a local sit-uation must be taken into account at every celebration of every liturgical expression. Yet local communities and dioceses are not islands; they exist in the middle of larger cultural, linguistic, political, and geographical units, and they are instantiations of the church universal. Because Catholicism includes a hierarchical dimension in which bishops are central figures in communion with other bishops and the bishop of Rome, liturgical forms and both church order and the sacrament of order are not simply matters for a given local community to decide on its own. The church is fundamentally a reality of communion, and communion entails give-and-take in dialogue.

This view implies the need to consider even major structural changes, not only in liturgy but also in the shape of leadership roles in the church at large and in its liturgy. Traditionally these leadership roles have included the responsibility for liturgical leadership and the maintenance church order and giving some form of guidance to the local church's ministry in the broader world. On the issue of how to make actual liturgy alive in culturally different people we need to dream and to imagine. We need to look forward more than backward. We need to let cultures nourish the Euro-American church, just as the Euro-American church needs to nourish a different culture. We need, in all of this, not simply to be multicultural, but equicultural. A global perspec-tive of order and ministry is the only possible way in which the church's pres-ent order and ministry will, today, survive. This is the dream for the future.

We conclude this volume on the theology of church order and church ministry from a global perspective with the following words of Pope John Paul II from in his encyclical *Fides et Ratio* (Faith and Reason):

Cultures share the dynamics of human life.
Like human beings they change and advance,
assimilating new experiences;
> open to mystery and the desire for knowledge,
> they have the capacity to receive divine revelation.

Cultures pervade the living of Christian faith,
which in turn gradually shapes them.
> Again and again the Pentecost event is repeated;
> hearing the good news they say:
>> "We hear them telling in our own tongues
>> the mighty works of God" (Acts 2:7-11).

The Gospel allows people to preserve their cultural identity.
The community of the baptized is marked by a universality
that can embrace every culture,
bringing what is impilict in them to the full light of truth.
> No culture can become the criterion of truth.
> The Gospel is not opposed to any culture;
> it delivers cultures from the disorder caused by sin,
>> and at the same time calls them to the fullness of truth.[17]

---

17. We have taken this citation of *Fides et Ratio* 71 from the abridged, sense-line edition of the encyclicals of John Paul II, edited by Joseph G. Donders, *John Paul II: The Encyclicals in Everyday Language*, definitive edition of all fourteen encyclicals, 3rd ed. (Maryknoll, N.Y.: Orbis Books, 2005), 348.

Bibliography of Texts Related to Order and Ministry

OFFICIAL ROMAN CATHOLIC DOCUMENTS

The Documents of Vatican Council II

Flannery, Austin, ed. *Vatican Council II*. Vol. 1, *The Conciliar and Post Conciliar Documents*, new rev. ed. Vol. 2, *More Post Conciliar Documents*, new rev. ed. Northport, N.Y.: Costello, 1996, 1998.

Sacrosanctum Oecumenicum Concilium Vaticanum II: Constitutiones, Decreta, Declarationes. Vatican City: Libreria Editrice Vaticana, 1966. Original Latin text.

Encyclicals and Apostolic Exhortations of Pope John Paul II

Redemptor Hominis, Encyclical, The Redeemer of Humankind, 1979.
Dives in Misericordia, Encyclical, The Mercy of God, 1980.
Laborem Exercens, Encyclical, On Human Work, 1981.
Slavorum Apostoli, Encyclical, The Apostles of the Slavs, 1985.
Dominum et Vivificantem, Encyclical, Lord and Giver of Life, 1986.
Redemptoris Mater, Encyclical, The Mother of the Redeemer, 1987.
Sollicitudo Rei Socialis, Encyclical, On Social Concern, 1987.
Dignitatem Mulieris, Apostolic Letter, On the Dignity and Vocation of Women, 1988.
Redemptoris Missio, Encyclical, The Mission of the Redeemer, 1990.
Centesimus Annus, Encyclical, The Hundredth Year: "New Things, One Hundred Years Later," 1991.
Veritatis Splendor, Encyclical, The Splendor of Truth, 1993.
Ordinatio Sacerdotalis, Apostolic Letter, On Reserving Priestly Ordination to Men Alone, 1994.
Evangelium Vitae, Encyclical, The Gospel of Life, 1995.
Ut Unum Sint, Encyclical, That They May Be One, 1995.
Fides et Ratio, Encyclical, Faith and Reason, 1998.
Ecclesia de Eucharistia, Encyclical, On the Eucharist in Relationship to the Church, 2003.

Encyclicals and Other Documents of Pope Paul VI

Mysterium Fidei, The Mystery of Faith, 1965.
Sacerdotalis Caelibatus, On the Celibacy of the Priest, 1967.

Ministeria Quaedam, On the Renewal of Regulation of First Tonsure, Minor Orders and the Subdiaconate in the Latin Church, 1972.
Evangelii Nuntiandi, Announcing the Gospel, 1975.

The New Catechism

Catechism of the Catholic Church. Vatican City: Libreria Editrice Vaticana, 1st ed., 1993; 2nd ed., 1997; U.S. 2nd ed., South Bend, Ind.: Our Sunday Visitor, 1997.

Compilation of Classic Catholic Dogmatic Texts

Denzinger, Henricus, and Adolfus Schönmetzer, eds., *Enchiridion Symbolorum Definitionum et Declarationum de Rebus Fidei et Morum,* 36th ed. (Freiburg im Breisgau: Herder, 1976).
Dupuis, Jacques, and Josef Neuner, *The Christian Faith: In the Doctrinal Documents of the Catholic Faith,* 7th ed. (Staten Island, N.Y.: Alba House, 2001).

Documents of Roman Congregations

Official texts of most documents are available at Web sites of the issuing congregation; begin at www.vatican.va.
Congregation for Divine Worship and the Discipline of the Sacraments, Directory for Sunday Celebrations in the Absence of a Priest (1988). Many dioceses and bishops' conferences have issued implementation guidelines for this Directory.
_____. Instruction on Inculturation and the Roman Liturgy, 1994.
_____. *Instructio, Varietates legitimae,* 1995.
_____. Fifth Instruction for the Right Implementation of the Constitution on the Sacred Liturgy of the Second Vatican Council (*Liturgiam Authenticam*), 2001.
_____. Instruction, *Redemptionis Sacramentum* on certain matters to be observed or to be avoided regarding the Most Holy Eucharist, 2004.
Congregation for the Clergy and seven other congregations. *Instructio, Ecclesiae de mysterio,* 1997.
Congregation for the Doctrine of the Faith. *Declaration on the Question of the Admission of Women to the Ministerial Priesthood.* Edition with commentary prepared by the United States Catholic Conference, Washington, D.C., 1977.

Code of Canon Law

Codex Iuris Canonici (Code of Canon Law [of the Roman Catholic Church]), promulgated by Pope John Paul II, January 25, 1983. English translation under the auspices of the Canon Law Society of America, *Code of Canon Law: Latin-English Edition.* Washington, D.C.: Canon Law Society of America, 1983.

Coriden, James, Thomas Greek, and Donald Heintschel, eds. *The Code of Canon Law: A Text and Commentary.* New York: Paulist Press, 1985.

Documents of the Federation of Asian Bishops' Conferences

Rosales, Gaudencio, C. G. Arévalo, et al., eds. *For All the People of Asia.* Vol. 1, *Documents from 1970 to 1991.* Maryknoll, N.Y.: Orbis Books, 1992.

Eilers, Franz-Joseph, ed. *For All the Peoples of Asia: Federation of Asian Bishops' Conferences.* Vol. 2, *Documents from 1997 to 2002.* Quezon City: Claretian Publications, 2002.

———, ed. *For All the Peoples of Asia: Federation of Asian Bishops' Conferences.* Vol. 3, *Documents from 1997 to 2002.* Quezon City: Claretian Publications, 2003.

GENERAL BIBLIOGRAPHY

Alberigo, Giuseppe, Jean-Pierre Jossua, and Joseph A. Komonchak, eds. *The Reception of Vatican II.* Washington, D.C.: Catholic University of America Press, 1987.

Alberigo, Giuseppe, general ed., and Joseph A. Komonchak, ed. *Vatican Council II.* 5 vols. English edition. Maryknoll, N.Y.: Orbis Books, 1995-2000.

Amaladoss, Michael. *Life in Freedom: Liberation Theologies from Asia.* Maryknoll, N.Y.: Orbis Books, 1997.

Antón, Angel. "Postconciliar Ecclesiology: Expectations, Results, and Prospects for the Future." In *Vatican II: Assessment and Perspectives*, vol. 1. New York: Paulist Press, 1988.

Armstrong, Regis, Wayne Hellmann, and William Short, eds. *Francis of Assisi: Early Documents.* New York: New City Press, 1999.

Bevans, Stephen B. *Models of Contextual Theology.* Revised and expanded edition. Maryknoll, N.Y.: Orbis Books, 2002.

Bevans, Stephen B., and Roger P. Schroeder. *Constants in Context: A Theology of Mission for Today.* American Society of Missiology 30. Maryknoll, N.Y.: Orbis Books, 2004.

Boff, Leonardo. *Jesus Christ the Liberator.* Translated by Patrick Hughes. Maryknoll, N.Y.: Orbis Books, 1978. Orig. Portuguese ed., 1972.

Bornkamm, Günther. "πρεσβυς – πρεσβυτερος" [*presbys – presbyteros*]. *Theological Dictionary of the New Testament,* edited by Gerhard Friedrich, 6:651-83. Grand Rapids: Eerdmans, 1968.

Bowe, Barbara. *A Church in Crisis: Ecclesiology and Paraenesis in Clement of Rome.* Harvard Dissertations in Religion 23. Minneapolis: Fortress, 1988.

Brown, Raymond. *The Churches the Apostles Left Behind.* New York: Paulist Press, 1984.

———. *The Gospel According to John: Introduction, Translation, and Notes,* vol. 2. Garden City, N.Y.: Doubleday, 1970.

————. *Jesus: God and Man; Modern Biblical Reflections.* Milwaukee, Wis.: Bruce, 1967.

Brown, Raymond E., Karl Paul Donfried, and John Reumann. *Peter in the New Testament.* New York: Paulist Press, 1973.

Browne, Maura. *The African Synod: Documents, Reflections, Perspectives.* Maryknoll, N.Y.: Orbis Books, 1996.

Bradshaw, Paul. "Eucharist: Early Christianity." In *The New Westminster Dictionary of Liturgy and Worship,* ed. Paul Bradshaw. Louisville: Westminster John Knox Press, 2002.

————. "Ordination." In *The New Westminster Dictionary of Liturgy and Worship,* ed. Paul Bradshaw. Louisville: Westminster John Knox Press, 2002.

————. *Ordination Rites of the Ancient Churches of East and West.* New York: Pueblo, 1990.

Bradshaw, Paul, ed. *The New Westminster Dictionary of Liturgy and Worship.* Westminster, Md.: John Knox Press, 2002.

Burrows, William R. *New Ministries: The Global Context.* Maryknoll, N.Y.: Orbis Books, 1980.

Campenhausen, Hans von. *Ecclesiastical Authority and Spiritual Power in the Church of the First Three Centuries.* Translated by J. A. Baker. Stanford, Calif.: Stanford Universtiy Press, 1969. Orig. German ed., 1953.

Cavanaugh, William T. *Theopolitical Imagination.* London: T&T Clark, 2002.

Chan, Wing-tsit. *A Source Book in Chinese Philosophy.* Princeton, N.J.: Princeton University Press, 1963.

Cheah, Joseph. "Negotiating Race and Religion in American Buddhism: Burmese Buddhism in California." Doctoral diss., Graduate Theological Union, Berkeley, Calif., 2004.

Chia, Edmund. *Thirty Years of FABC: History, Foundation, Context and Theology.* Hong Kong: FABC, 2003.

Claesson, Gösta. *Index Tertullianeus A–E.* Paris: Études augustiniennes, 1974.

Congar, Yves M.-J. "The People of God." In *Vatican II: An Interfaith Appraisal.* Notre Dame, Ind.: University of Notre Dame Press, 1966.

Connolly, R. Hugh. *Didascalia Apostolorum.* Oxford: Clarendon Press, 1929.

Cooke, Bernard. *Ministry to Word and Sacraments: History and Theology.* Philadelphia: Fortress, 1992.

Davie, Grace. *Religion in Britain since 1945: Believing without Belonging.* Oxford: Blackwell, 1994.

————. *Religion in Modern Europe: A Memory Mutates.* Oxford: Oxford University Press, 2000.

Donders, Joseph G., ed. *John Paul II: The Encyclicals in Everyday Language.* Definitive edition of all fourteen encyclicals. 3rd ed. Maryknoll, N.Y.: Orbis Books, 2005.

Duffy, Eamon. *Saints and Sinners: A History of the Popes.* New Haven: Yale University Press, 1997.

Dupuis, Jacques. *Toward a Christian Theology of Religious Pluralism.* Maryknoll, N.Y.: Orbis Books, 1998.

Dupuy, D. "Theologie der kirchlichen Ämpter." In *Mysterium Salutis* IV/2. Einsiedeln: Benziger, 1973.

England, John, et al., eds. *Asian Christian Theologies.* 3 vols. Maryknoll, N.Y.: Orbis Books, 2002, 2003, 2004.

Fabella, Virginia, P. Lee, and D. Kwant-sun Suh, eds. *Asian Christian Spirituality: Reclaiming Traditions.* Maryknoll, N.Y.: Orbis Books, 1992.

Featherstone, Michael, ed. *Global Culture: Nationalism, Globalization and Modernity.* London: Sage, 1990.

Fitzmyer, Joseph A. *The Gospel According to Luke: Introduction, Translation, and Notes.* 2 vols. Anchor Bible 28, 28A. Garden City, N.Y.: Doubleday, 1981.

Fletcher, Richard. *The Barbarian Conversion: From Paganism to Christianity.* New York: Henry Holt, 1997.

Florez, Generoso. *Appeal to the Church: The Mission of the Church in Asia.* Gujarat Sahita Prakash, India: Anand Press, 1986.

Fredricks, James. *Faith among Faiths: Christian Theology and Non-Christian Religions.* New York: Paulist Press, 1999.

_____. *Buddhists and Christians: Through Comparative Theology to Solidarity.* Maryknoll, N.Y.: Orbis Books, 2004.

Friedman, Jonathan. *Cultural Identity and Global Process.* London: Sage, 1994.

Gager, J. G. *Kingdom and Community: The Social World of Early Christianity.* Englewood Cliffs, N.J.: Prentice Hall, 1975.

Galot, Jean. "Christ: Revealer, Founder of the Church, and Source of Ecclesial Life." In *Vatican II: Assessment and Perspectives,* vol. 1. New York: Paulist Press, 1988.

Gibaut, John St. H. *The Cursus Honorum: A Study of the Origins and Evolution of Sequential Ordinations.* New York: Peter Lang, 2000.

Görres, Albert. "Pathologie des katholischen Christentums." In *Handbuch der Pastoraltheologie,* Bd. II/1. Edited by Franz Xavier Arnold, Karl Rahner, Victor Schurr, and Leonhard Weber. Freiburg im Br.: Herder, 1996.

Grant, Robert, and Graham Holt. *The Apostolic Fathers: First and Second Clement.* New York: Thomas Nelson & Sons, 1965.

Grillmeier, A. "Dogmatic Constitution on the Church" (Chapter II). In *Commentary on the Documents of Vatican II,* vol. 1. Translated by Kevin Smyth. New York: Herder & Herder, 1967.

Gutiérrez, Gustavo. *A Theology of Liberation: History, Politics and Salvation.* Translated by Caridad Inda and John Eagleson. Maryknoll, N.Y.: Orbis Books, 1973.

Hennesey, John. *American Catholics.* New York: Oxford University Press, 1981.

Herberg, Will. *Protestant, Catholic, Jew: An Essay in American Religious Sociology.* Garden City, N.Y.: Doubleday, 1960.

Heyndricks, Jeroom. "From 'Mission in China' to 'Inter-church Exchange.'" *SEDOS Bulletin* 28, no. 5 (1996).

Irvin, Dale T., and Scott W. Sunquist. *A History of the World Christian Movement.* Vol. 1, *Earliest Christianity to 1453.* Maryknoll, N.Y.: Orbis Books, 2001.

Isichei, Elizabeth. *A History of Christianity in Africa.* Grand Rapids: Eerdmans, 1995.

Kalilombe, Patrick A. *Doing Theology at the Grassroots: Theological Essays from Malawi.* Gueru, Zimbabwe: Mambo Press, 1999.

Kim Yong-Bock. "An Asian Proposal for Future Directions of Theological Curricula in the Context of Globalization." *East Asian Pastoral Review* 20, no. 3 (2003).

Klentos, John. "Eucharist: Easter Churches." In *The New Westminster Dictionary of Liturgy and Worship.* Westminster, Md.: John Knox Press, 2002.

Kloppenburg, Bonaventure. *The Ecclesiology of Vatican II.* Chicago: Franciscan Herald Press, 1974.

Knitter, Paul F. *Theologies of Religions.* Maryknoll, N.Y.: Orbis Books, 2002.

Kollman, Paul V. *The Evangelization of Slaves and Catholic Origins in Eastern Africa.* Maryknoll, N.Y.: Orbis Books, 2005.

Komonchak, Joseph A., Mary Collins, and Dermot Lane. *The New Dictionary of Theology.* Wilmington, Del.: Michael Glazier, 1987.

Kraft, Robert A. *The Apostolic Fathers: Barnabas and the Didache.* New York: Thomas Nelson & Sons, 1965.

Kroeger, James, and Peter Phan. *The Future of the Asian Churches: The Asian Synod and Ecclesia in Asia.* Quezon City: Claretian Publications, 2002.

Küng, Hans. *The Church.* New York: Sheed & Ward, 1967.

Lakeland, Paul. *The Liberation of the Laity: In Search of an Accountable Church.* New York: Continuum, 2003.

Latourelle, René, ed. *Vatican II: Assessment and Perspectives.* 2 vols. New York: Paulist Press, 1988.

Lea, H. C. *A History of Auricular Confession and Indulgences in the Latin Church.* Philadelphia: Lea Bros., 1896.

Lee, Jung Young. *Marginality: The Key to Multicultural Theology.* Minneapolis: Fortress, 1995.

Legrand, Hervé-M. "The Presidency of the Eucharist according to the Ancient Tradition." In *Living Bread Saving Cup.* Collegeville, Minn.: Liturgical Press, 1982.

———. "Traditio perpetuo servata? The Non-ordination of Women: Tradition or Simply an Historical Fact?" *Worship* 65 (1991).

LeSaint, William P. *Tertullian.* Westminster, Md.: Newman Press, 1951.

Lonergan, Bernard J. F. "The Transition from a Classicist World-View to Historical Consciousness." In his *A Second Collection,* edited by William F. J. Ryan and Bernard J. Tyrell. Philadelphia: Westminster, 1974.

Luzbetak, Louis J. *The Church and Cultures.* Maryknoll, N.Y.: Orbis Books, 1988.

Matovina, Timothy, and Gerald E. Poyo, eds. *¡Presente! U.S. Latino Catholic from Colonial Origins to the Present.* Maryknoll, N.Y.: Orbis Books, 2000.

Matsuoka, Fumitaka, and Eleazar Fernandez. *Realizing the America of Our Hearts.* St. Louis: Chalice Press, 2003.

Mbiti, John S. *Introduction to African Religion.* Oxford: Heinemann Educational Publishers, 1991.

McBrian, Richard. *Encyclopedia of Catholicism.* San Francisco: HarperSanFrancisco, 1995.

McNeill, William. *The Rise of the West: A History of the Human Community.* Chicago: University of Chicago Press, 1963.

Moeller, Charles. "History of *Lumen gentium*'s Structure and Ideas." In *Vatican II: An Interfaith Appraisal.* Notre Dame, Ind.: University of Notre Dame Press, 1966.

Neusner, Jacob. "Varieties of Judaism in the Formative Age." In *Jewish Spirituality: From the Bible through the Middle Ages,* edited by Arthur Green. New York: Crossroad, 1987.

Omi, Michael, and Howard Winant. *Racial Formation in the United States: From the 1960s to the 1980s.* New York: Routledge, 1986.

Osborne, Kenan. "Envisioning a Theology of Ordained and Lay Ministry." In *Ordering the Baptismal Priesthood,* ed. Susan K. Wood. Collegeville, Minn.: Liturgical Press, 2003.

———. *The Diaconate in the Christian Church: Its History and Theology.* Chicago: National Association of Diaconate Directors, 1996.

———. *Ministry: Lay Ministry in the Roman Catholic Church; Its History and Theology.* Eugene, Ore.: Wipf & Stock, 2003.

———. *Priesthood: A History of the Ordained Ministry in the Roman Catholic Church.* Eugene, Ore.: Wipf & Stock, 2002.

———. *The Franciscan Intellectual Tradition.* St. Bonaventure, N.Y.: Franciscan Institute, 2003.

———. *Reconciliation and Justification.* Eugene, Ore.: Wipf & Stock, 2000.

Park, Andrew Sung. *The Wounded Heart of God: The Asian Concept of Han and the Christian Doctrine of Sin.* Nashville, Tenn.: Abingdon Press, 1993.

Phan, Peter C. *Being Religious Interreligiously: Asian Perspectives on Interfaith Dialogue.* Maryknoll, N.Y.: Orbis Books, 2004.

———. "The Mission of God: Its Challenges and Demands in Today's World." *East Asian Pastoral Review* 39 (2002): nos. 3/3.

———. *The Asian Synod: Texts and Commentaries.* Maryknoll, N.Y.: Orbis Books, 2003.

———. *Christianity with an Asian Face: Asian American Theology in the Making.* Maryknoll, N.Y.: Orbis Books, 2003.

Philips, Gérard. *La Chiesa e il suo Mistero.* Milan: Editoriale Jaca Book, 1975.

Pieris, Aloysius. *An Asian Theology of Liberation.* Maryknoll, N.Y.: Orbis Books, 1988.

Prigogine, Ilya, and Isabelle Stengers. *Order out of Chaos.* New York: Bantam, 1984.

Puglisi, James F. *The Process of Admission to Ordained Ministry: A Comparataive Study.* 3 vols. Collegeville, Minn.: Liturgical Press, 1996-2001.

Quasten, Johannes. *Patrology: The Apostolic Tradition.* Vol. 1. Westminster, Md.: Newman Press, 1953.

Rahner, Karl. "Towards a Fundamental Theological Interpretation of Vatican II." *Theological Studies* 40 (December 1979): 716-27.

Robertson, Roland. *Globalization: Social Theory and Global Culture.* London and Thousand Oaks, Calif.: Sage, 1992.

Ruether, Rosemary Radford. *Sexism and God-Talk: Toward a Feminist Theology.* Boston: Beacon Press, 1993.

Russell, James C. *The Germanization of Early Medieval Christianity: A Sociohistorical Approach to Religious Transformation.* New York: Oxford University Press, 1992.

Sacchi, Paolo. *Jewish Apocalyptic and Its History.* Sheffield: Sheffield Academic Press, 1990.

Sanneh, Lamin. *Translating the Message: The Missionary Impact on Culture.* Maryknoll, N.Y.: Orbis Books, 1989.

———. *Whose Religion Is Christianity? The Gospel beyond the West.* Grand Rapids: Eerdmans, 2003.

Schillebeeckx, Edward. "The Catholic Understanding of Office in the Church." *Theological Studies* 30 (1969): 569-71.

Schölligen, G. *Ecclesia Sordida? Zur Frage der socialen Schichtung frühchristilicher Gemeinden am Beispiel Karthagos zur Zeit Tertullians.* Münster: Aschendorf, 1984.

Schreiter, Robert J. *The New Catholicity: Theology between the Global and the Local.* Maryknoll, N.Y.: Orbis Books, 1997.

———, ed. *Mission in the New Millennium.* Maryknoll, N.Y.: Orbis Books, 2001.

Segundo, Juan Luis. *A Theology for Artisans of a New Humanity.* Translated by John Drury. 5 vols. Maryknoll, N.Y.: Orbis Books, 1973-75.

Shorter, Aylward. *Toward a Theology of Inculturation.* Maryknoll, N.Y.: Orbis Books, 1994.

Sobrino, Jon. *Christology at the Crossroads: A Latin American Approach.* Translated by John Drury. Maryknoll, N.Y.: Orbis Books, 1978.

———. *Jesus the Liberator.* Translated by Paul Burns and Francis McDonagh. Maryknoll, N.Y.: Orbis Books, 1993.

Sobrino, Jon, and Felix Wilfrid, eds. *Globalization and Its Victims.* London: SCM Press, 2001.

Spence, Jonathan D. *The Search for Modern China.* New York: W. W. Norton, 1990.

Stackhouse, Max L., et al., eds. *God and Globalization.* Harrisburg, Pa.: Trinity Press International, 2000, 2001, 2002, 2004.

———. *Globalization, Public Theology, and New Means of Grace.* Santa Clara, Calif.: Santa Clara University, 2003.

Stegemann, Ekkehard, and Wolfgang Stegemann. *The Jesus Movement: A Social History of Its First Century.* Minneapolis: Fortress, 1999.

Stiglitz, Joseph E. *Globalization and Its Discontents.* New York: Norton, 2003.

Stuhlmueller, Carroll, ed. *Women and the Priesthood.* Collegeville, Minn.: Liturgical Press, 1978.

Sullivan, Francis A. *From Apostles to Bishops: The Development of the Episcopacy in the Early Church.* New York: Newman Press, 2001.

Tanquerey, Adolphe. *A Manual of Dogmatic Theology.* New York: Desclee, 1959.

Tertullian. "De Exhortatione castitatis." In *Tertulliani Opera.* Vol. 1, *Opera Monatanistica.* Turnholt: Brepols, 1954.

Van der Meer, F. *Augustine the Bishop: Church and Society at the Dawn of the Middle Ages.* New York: Harper Torchbook, 1965.

Wang Ling-Chi. "The Structure of Dual Domination: Toward a Paradigm for the Study of the Chinese Diaspora in the U.S." *Amerasia Journal* 21 (1955).

Waters, Malcolm. *Globalization*. New York: Routledge, 1995.

Yung, Hwa. *Mangoes or Bananas: The Quest for an Authentic Asian Christian Theology*. Oxford/Irvine, Calif.: Oxford Regnum Books, 1997.

Index